JOURNALISM IN THE AGE OF VIRTUAL REALITY

Journalism in the Age of Virtual Reality

How Experiential Media Are Transforming News

John V. Pavlik

Columbia University Press   New York

Columbia University Press
Publishers Since 1893
New York   Chichester, West Sussex
cup.columbia.edu
Copyright © 2019 Columbia University Press

Library of Congress Cataloging-in-Publication Data
Names: Pavlik, John V. (John Vernon), author.
Title: Journalism in the age of virtual reality : how experiential media are
    transforming news / John V. Pavlik.
Description: New York : Columbia University Press, [2019] | Includes bibliographical
    references and index.
Identifiers: LCCN 2019006034 | ISBN 9780231184489 (cloth : alk. paper) |
    ISBN 9780231184496 (pbk. : alk. paper) | ISBN 9780231545518 (ebook)
Subjects: LCSH: Journalism—Technological innovations. | Online journalism. |
    Virtual reality—Social aspects.
Classification: LCC PN4784.T34 P38 2019 | DDC 070.4/3—dc23
LC record available at https://lccn.loc.gov/2019006034

Columbia University Press books are printed on permanent and durable acid-free paper.
Printed in the United States of America

Cover design: Martin N. Hinze

Contents

Acknowledgments

I offer my thanks to all those who helped make this book more than a virtual reality. I am especially grateful to Philip Leventhal, editor at Columbia University Press, for his insight and guidance in the development of this undertaking. Thanks as well to Eli Noam, founder of the Columbia Institute for Tele-Information (CITI), for inviting me to speak on a panel titled "Future Content" in October 2015; it inspired many of the ideas contained herein. I give special thanks to Michael Guillorn of IBM for his observations about emerging technologies and the implications for journalism. My deepest thanks and love to Jackie, my wife, for her love, support, and collaboration, and to our daughters, Tristan and Orianna, for their love and many digital insights.

JOURNALISM IN THE AGE OF VIRTUAL REALITY

Introduction

This book examines the nature, parameters, and consequences of virtual reality, augmented reality, and other experiential media on journalism, especially the content of news. Enabled by advances in technology platforms, experiential news presents an opportunity to engage an increasingly fragmented public. In addition, I will discuss the practical, ethical, and political implications for those who create the news as well as those who consume or interact with that content. The book outlines a conceptual framework for critically understanding this evolving news form. Central to this analysis is an examination of the evolving user experience, which is increasingly interactive, multisensory, and immersive.

The shifting nature of journalism and media content reflects the notions of scholars such as Harold Innis, Marshall McLuhan, and James Carey, who have suggested that the parameters of a communication medium can shape media content, form, and meaning.[1] I do not contend that this changing landscape is technologically determined. Rather, a confluence of forces including economic, legal, and cultural factors will shape this shift in media and journalism.

This book also does not suggest that experiential news will replace more traditional forms of journalism and media content. Throughout the history of journalism, as earlier developments have transformed or fueled changes, traditional forms have continued, although their roles have generally shifted to positions of less dominance especially among younger segments of the population. Evidence suggests that such is likely to be the case in an era of experiential journalism and media content. Data from a Pew Research Center report, for example, indicates that in the United States, newspapers continue to have a high overall level of reach, although it is declining. Total U.S. daily newspaper circulation (print and digital combined) in 2017 was thirty-one million for weekdays and thirty-four million for Sundays.[2] Yet, those numbers are down significantly from previous years, by about 10 percent from the previous year and by roughly 50 percent since 1990. Moreover, audiences, particularly younger segments, are substantially more likely to access newspaper content in digital forms.[3] Two-thirds (66 percent) of digital newspaper consumption is among those aged eighteen to forty-nine. Meanwhile, more than half (54 percent) of printed newspaper consumption is by those aged fifty or older. Notably, the development of the "phablet" (that is, a generation of large-screen smartphones with screens between five and seven inches) has fueled digital news consumption. Among persons aged twenty-five to thirty-four, phablet users are the heaviest consumers of news.

Today's public is engaging in wide-sweeping new media behaviors and news habits, which are increasingly mobile and social and occur via experiential media. These shifts portend profound implications for a transformed journalism in the twenty-first century. For journalism to be successful in this transformation, it will be essential to both understand the nature of experiential media and grapple with their effective use in journalistic content. Much as journalism pioneers in the late 1940s and early 1950s grappled with how to best use the emerging medium of television to create quality news content, journalists today need to assert new methods and techniques to produce journalistic excellence in an increasingly virtual media world.

In the pages that follow, this book offers eight chapters that provide a guide to achieving that journalistic excellence in experiential news.

Chapter 1 situates the shifting nature of contemporary journalism in a historical context, arguing that we are entering a third age of news content or journalistic stories.

Chapter 2 discusses the nature of design and a set of six principles and practices that journalists can employ in creating quality experiential news content, which can better engage the evolving news public.

Chapter 3 focuses on the news user's experience. The multisensory, interactive, and immersive nature of this experience is most evident in augmented reality and virtual reality. It is increasingly a part of other emerging media forms, including interactive audio devices, ultra-high-definition video, and artificial-intelligence and data-driven media platforms.

Chapter 4 examines the encoded nature of experiential news. Geolocation, data, and algorithms signal a fundamental shift in the ways news content is not only delivered but also accessed and engaged by the public.

Chapter 5 reviews the interactive documentary, a new news format that has emerged as an increasing international standard in journalism over the past two decades. This interactive news format represents a core dimension of experiential news, and the award-winning news content I discuss in this genre provides a roadmap to creating excellence in journalism content in the coming decades.

Chapter 6 outlines the emergence of drones to provide an essential reporting tool for creating innovative experiential news. Drones have been in development for more than a century but have emerged since 2010 as a mobile platform that can provide unique, geo-located, mobile news coverage and enable compelling news experiences for a public whose media expectations are a far cry from those of a generation ago.

Chapter 7 articulates several of the key factors that will shape the development and potential adoption of experiential news, including economic, technological, and regulatory considerations both domestically and internationally.

Finally, chapter 8 provides an experiential media parable to overlay a moral framework on the development of experiential news. The fake-new crisis that emerged in the 2016 U.S. presidential election may pale in comparison to the potential artificial realities of the decade ahead. Journalists will need to embrace a strong set of ethical practices to ensure that experiential news leads to a fuller and more robust explication of truth, understanding, and trust on matters of public interest and importance.

CHAPTER ONE

Experiential Stories

Situating the Transformation of Journalism in Historical Context

Journalism content, or news, is evolving through three basic stages of development. For most of history, the content of journalism has emphasized the telling of the story.[1] Town criers notwithstanding, early media forms were largely limited to textual formats, whether carved as hieroglyphics on stone tablets in the time of the ancient Egyptians or printed in bound books in the time of Johannes Gutenberg. With the advent of large-circulation printed newspapers and mass communication in the nineteenth century, text-based narratives continued as the dominant form of mediated communication, and the presentation of news was largely limited to these formats.

The invention of photographic technologies, motion pictures, and wireless and wired communication laid the foundation for a shift in the narrative form of media and news. Radio communication continued the linear story-telling narrative form in a spoken audio environment that was based heavily on the written word. More visually oriented media soon became increasingly dominant. The twentieth century ushered in sweeping changes to the most popular narrative media forms, putting increasing emphasis on the sight and sound dimensions of story telling with the growth of motion pictures, television, radio, and sophisticated publishing platforms for printed media such as magazines and newspapers.

The advance of high-speed internet, mobile and wearable technology, and a spectrum of other digital developments has set the stage for the emergence of experiential media (EM) and experiential news.[2] Whether in handheld or wearable media systems that deliver to the user 360-degree video, virtual reality (VR), and augmented reality (AR); advanced digital video platforms such as ultra-high-definition (UHD) and three-dimensional television; or other networked environments such as interactive speakers, media are poised to deliver not just stories but news experiences. In these experiential media forms, the individual engages content as a participant in multisensory, interactive narratives including news. Immersive environments are those that envelop individuals (or groups) or allow them to enter into a virtual space. Immersion helps to transform the individual from audience member into user and even to participate in media content or news stories. Kinetic (motional) and haptic (tactile) forms of media, including many handheld and wearable technologies, are looming on the near-term horizon to further drive this shift toward experiential media and news. A sense of presence in the story is an increasing quality of the user's experience with media content.[3]

Though they seem quite new, experiential media have been in development for centuries, especially in the underlying arena of wearable technologies. Wearables date to at least seventeenth-century China, where inventors in the Qing dynasty developed an abacus ring to serve as a miniature counting device.[4] In Europe in the late eighteenth century (1780) the pedometer was developed to measure walking. A century later (1965) the first exoskeleton was developed (though prototypes date to the 1800s) to enhance human action via a wearable platform.

Recent years have seen a rapid acceleration in the development of underlying experiential technologies. In 1989 computer scientist and mathematician Steve Mann designed the first wearable computer capable of image and sound capture, processing, and wireless transmission.[5] In 2000 the Ericsson company introduced the mobile-phone-enabled Bluetooth wearable earpiece, advancing miniaturized, hands-free, mobile phone operation.[6] The first lightweight, commercial wearable camera, the GoPro Hero, emerged in 2004, although the device used thirty-five-millimeter film. A digital version of the wearable camera with a ten-second video capacity was launched in 2006. In 2013 Google Glass was the first high-profile wearable device offering augmented reality to the consumer. Glass failed in the general consumer marketplace, largely because of an adverse social reaction, with many in the public viewing the use of Glass by others as a potential invasion of privacy. Initially, public reactions to encounters with people wearing Glass were curiosity and a sense of novelty, but within a few weeks or months, many people who saw someone wearing Glass realized they were not only being watched but were likely being recorded in video and that the video was being uploaded to the internet, and they did not like that. In one notorious case, a technology writer wearing Glass in a San Francisco bar was apparently assaulted by other bar patrons who were upset over the fact that videos of their drinking and other bar activities were being uploaded online. The Glass wearer's video went viral as a first-person eyewitness account of how things could go wrong with head-worn AR.[7]

Yet Google's early foray into the consumer-wearable AR marketplace helped to set the stage for more successful contemporary AR eyewear that emerged in 2018, including a public that was apparently more willing to accept wearable technology (in that it has not generated a public backlash). Google also continued its entry into experiential media, debuting the better-received Google Cardboard, a low-cost virtual-reality headset that operates via a smartphone, such as an iPhone or Android device. Recent years have witnessed an onslaught of numerous other wearable digital devices in the experiential media realm, including a spectrum of head-mounted VR displays and handheld virtual-touch systems. These wearable technologies have not only transformed the user interface but also laid a foundation for the emergence of experiential media on a global scale and for the advance of experiential news.

ELEMENTS OF A JOURNALISM STORY

Before examining the ways in which experiential media are allowing journalists to tell stories in new ways, it is helpful to describe the more traditional and foundational elements of the news story. Journalism has long played a vital role in reporting news and information and providing opinion guidance for the public. These roles have been seen as particularly crucial for preserving and protecting the health of democratic societies, especially in helping the electorate make informed choices.

As digitization has transformed the media and communication environment, traditional news media have faced an increasing crisis with regard to their presence and influence in the arena of public communication and discourse. This crisis includes a loss of audience—consumers of news—as well as a loss of advertising sponsorship, which is a primary financial foundation for much of the journalism industry, especially in the United States. The public has migrated to digital communication platforms including social media such as Facebook, Instagram, Snapchat, and Twitter and online search engines such as Google (now part of corporate behemoth Alphabet Inc., which also owns YouTube). Not surprisingly, marketers have increasingly invested their resources in these digital platforms to employ highly efficient, algorithm-driven media to engage consumers with their advertising messages. Traditional news and entertainment media organizations have seen their revenues drop, and in response they have sought new business models, often increasingly based on digital subscriptions or other data-driven advertising models. News leadership has also encouraged innovation in story-telling forms, such as interactive documentaries, which utilize the digital media that are increasingly favored by both the public and marketers. These new story-telling forms require changes in journalistic practices and work methods as journalists must learn to use new tools such as virtual reality to tell their stories. Achieving this adaptation has challenged many news organizations around the world.

In journalism, a news story consists of three main elements: the facts, the sources of information that the reporter relies upon, and the presentation of the story. Fake news aside, a journalistic story does not mean a fable. It is a story that represents the real world as observed and reported by journalists. The story in journalism is not imagined or subject to embellishment; it is based on facts, which are the identifiable bits of information that the reporter has verified as truthful or accurate, such as who or what is part of the event or issue. The 2016 U.S. presidential campaign and the advent of the Trump presidency propelled journalism, and society more broadly, into a somewhat unexpected debate over just what are facts and what is truth. Former press secretary Sean Spicer and President Trump's counselor Kellyanne Conway even propounded the notion of "alternative facts," a notion that many journalists and journalism scholars decry.[8]

Journalism is always a representation of the past or an edited or selective presentation of the present or the anticipated future. Though some philosophers suggest that humans can never have a perfect understanding of the truth, it is nonetheless something that journalists and news consumers can and should strive for as the foundation for informed decision-making. Reporters should seek to provide the most accurate, reliable, complete, and contextualized presentation of the facts or of the bits of information they can collect from diverse and reliable sources. Experiential media, I would argue, offer perhaps the most powerful reporting and story-telling tools yet invented to pursue a fuller understanding of our world. Using experiential media, stories can be more nuanced and complete and can be experienced from multiple angles or perspectives. Ultimately, however, truthfulness still depends on the quality of the reporting and the reporter's integrity to assemble facts honestly and fairly.

Journalists generate stories by conducting original investigations and reporting, which take a wide range of forms. Journalists employ direct observation, which can be translated into written accounts, photographs, video, or experiential news. Reporters interview eyewitnesses to events and expert sources; interrogate documents and records, especially those from the public or governmental arena; and sort and analyze vast troves of data in increasingly digital form. They cull the facts or data from extensive reporting and assemble them into a narrative form called the news story.

In journalism, quality also means thorough fact-checking, which typically involves confirming an alleged fact from a second, ostensibly reliable source. Reporters and editors supplement this with news judgment about what is important and fair, what is in the public interest, and what adheres to ethical principles and practices. News reporting is evolving rapidly as new technologies emerge and as data- and algorithm-driven methods are on the ascent, even as traditional methods are still central.

Stories in journalism deal with real people and places, actual processes and events. Journalists tell these stories in an attempt to answer questions called the five W's: who (or whom), what, when, where, why, and sometimes how. Historically speaking, these stories (especially when written) often follow a structure that begins with a lead (or lede) sentence containing the most important elements of the story, followed by a nut graph expanding on key elements and providing the main thesis of the story, and then the body of the story with least important elements toward the end. Breaking or hard news often uses this story structure, which is known as the inverted pyramid, as it puts the most important, essential information at the start (forming the wide base of the pyramid at the top), followed by nonessential background information or facts of lesser importance (forming the narrow tip of the pyramid at the bottom), which can be deleted or edited out to make a story more concise.

Journalism stories, especially hard news, of the twentieth century tended to feature a narrative structure that revolved around two dimensions: (1) the most important facts tended to come first, and (2) stories used a structure that implied or assumed a beginning (how the story started), middle (where it went), and end (how it concluded or its consequences).

An example of a standard hard news lede from events of 2015 might be "Freddie Gray died in police custody in Baltimore yesterday." This lede contains who (Freddie Gray), what (died, stated in the active voice), when (yesterday), where (in Baltimore), and even touches on the how (in police custody).

A typical breaking-news item might report on a robbery, revealing the most important facts of the case and implying what happened first (the robbery and the extent to which anyone was harmed), involving whom (victims or suspects), how the case proceeded (whether the police caught the suspect), and eventually how it turned out (whether the suspect was convicted). This information probably would not be reported all in one version of the story, at least not initially, but would be delivered in a series of reports over time, perhaps days, weeks, months, or even years. Illustrative of this is the 1979 Etan Patz child-kidnapping case in New York City. First reported as an unsolved case, it developed new aspects and frames in 2015 with the arrest and trial of a suspect resulting in a hung jury and finally a retrial and conviction in 2017.[9] Various factors affect the relative importance of the different facts and people in a story. For instance, the involvement of a celebrity in a crime greatly heightens the "who" element of a story. Stories generally identify the sources the reporter has relied upon in gathering the facts and attributes those facts to the appropriate, respective sources.

Hard news tends to be serious and timely (e.g., a mass shooting), while soft news deals with less important, serious, or timely matters (e.g., a cute dog story). Historians of journalism suggest the inverted pyramid is partly a result of the introduction of an earlier technology, the telegraph, in the middle of the nineteenth century.[10] Before the advent of the telegraph, journalism often featured a more leisurely, literary writing style with the most newsworthy elements placed at the end of a story. However, use of the telegraph was expensive (about a penny per character in the currency of the day) and sometimes unreliable, so editors wanted to be sure the most important facts were transmitted and thus put an emphasis on the five W's at the beginning of a story.

Quality journalism stories continue to rely on great writing and editing. They also increasingly require superior multimedia production to effectively, clearly, and compellingly present the news and capture attention, especially in a highly saturated media environment. Of course, one must be careful in not letting the demand to capture attention violate the standards of journalistic story telling. Note that I have been referring to journalistic story telling (two words), not storytelling (a single word), to differentiate the story methods of journalism from the techniques used in oral and other forms of dramatic stories or plays where embellishment and imagination often are preeminent. Contemporary journalists and journalistic organizations have struggled to adapt to the changing demands of the digital age, and sometimes the lines between story telling and storytelling have blurred.

Original reporting and fact-checking have suffered as staff sizes have shrunk and pressure to increase audiences and revenues has grown. For instance, in 2014 a highly regarded news organization, *Rolling Stone* magazine, broke an important story about an alleged gang rape at the University of Virginia.[11] The largely first-person narrative featured many of the elements of dramatic story telling and captured the attention of much of the American public. Eventually, however, in 2015 a Columbia Graduate School of Journalism investigation discredited the story and documented the many key mistakes that *Rolling Stone*, its editors, and the reporter made in producing the story.[12] The Columbia investigation revealed fundamental lapses in reporting, editing, and fact-checking and an overall failure in basic standards and practices of journalism. As a result, *Rolling Stone* lost a defamation lawsuit in 2016 involving the investigation and its assertion that an associate dean at the University of Virginia had been the "chief villain" in the case.[13]

ANALOG MEDIA STORY MODEL

Figure 1.1 summarizes a general model of the story in traditional analog media. This model widely characterized mainstream news media in the United States and internationally in the twentieth century.

The elements in figure 1.1 align around three main dimensions. First are the fundamentals necessary as a foundation for excellence in story telling in journalism. These include the research or reporting, writing, and editing needed to achieve accuracy and authenticity as well as the structural elements, such as narrative format and voice. The story approach and structure are usually linear and feature a third-person perspective.

Second are the features and capabilities of the medium of communication (newspaper, TV, or radio), including the design and production

❖ Fundamentals
  ➢ Extensive research or reporting (including sources)
  ➢ Story approach (straight news, feature story)
  ➢ Structural elements
    ■ Static/fixed time/place
    ■ Episodic
    ■ Linear
    ■ Perspective (third-person narrative)
❖ Features of the Medium
  ➢ Quality presentation in words, pictures, video, and sound
  ➢ Passive audience
  ➢ Single/dual modality
❖ Message Substance
  ➢ Social meaning or public significance
  ➢ Authenticity
  ➢ Surprise, nuance
  ➢ Vividness, clarity, and distinctiveness
  ➢ Accuracy and other qualities

FIGURE 1.1 Traditional Model of Journalism Stories

needed for the corresponding modalities of communication (audio or video).

The content form—or modality of communication such as text, audio, or video—is generally based on the parameters of the medium of delivery. Print media generally emphasize the written word, which can be supplemented by images (photographs and graphics). Electronic media emphasize a greater breadth of modalities, including audio, video, graphics, and text. In television, images and video are presented within a frame that is horizontally oriented and takes in about thirty degrees of a human viewer's field of view (humans have a field of view of about 180 degrees horizontally and 135 degrees vertically).[14] Media objects are usually centered in the typical person's field of view, with her or his peripheral vision generally falling outside the media frame. This is in contrast to virtual reality and omnidirectional or spherical photography, which can fill the field of view.

Producers of media content aim for a consistently high level of quality in these content elements. Quality has several dimensions, including production excellence (high resolution, good framing, and lighting), but in journalism, quality also intersects with aspects of message substance, including accuracy and other dimensions.

Third are the substantive characteristics of a story, which are highly relevant to the story's presentation. Substantive characteristics include the social meaning and public significance or resonance of a story, the unexpectedness or surprising nature of the story (what is new or novel), and the vividness of the presentation through words, sounds, or images. A story about a terrorist attack, for instance, demands photos or video of any destruction or loss of human life. A story about an unexpected recipient of a Noble Peace Prize calls for photos or video of the surprising winner. A story about a U.S. presidential candidate's new economic policy proposal merits detailed textual interpretation and data-driven analysis presented in graphical format.

In this model, the story structure is linear with an implied beginning, middle, and end. The story is published or broadcast in a fixed form, place, or time, and any necessary corrections are made subsequently. Context is generally limited as editors focus on a single spine or frame for each story arc, which is typically organized around a discrete event or issue.

The public consumes the story as it is delivered by mainstream media on a scheduled publication or broadcast schedule. People read, watch, or listen to the content as presented, with little opportunity to provide feedback or to interact with the story other than face-to-face with friends or family or in the form of a letter, email, or phone call to an editor.

Stories feature one or two modes of human communication, such as text, image, sound, or moving image. Journalists typically conceptualize the story in the form of an episode or event (or occasionally a process). The narrative voice or perspective is typically in the third person with writing in the past tense (e.g., she said). This perspective tends to imply neutrality, or at least impartiality, on the part of the journalist. The story approach is almost always a nonparticipatory narrative, with the journalist attempting to present the facts and sources in a value-free or value-neutral fashion. In news stories, the journalists try to report only the facts and not their opinions or evaluations. Research has suggested that this style of "objectivity" in the narrative may be flawed, problematic, or somewhat illusory in that any reporter or news organization brings a bias, whether personal, cultural, or commercial.[15] Bias can enter into the journalistic process at various levels, critics contend, such as in the selection of what stories to report, how to frame or structure a story, what sources to rely upon, and even what words are used. Some suggest that photographs, even more than words, can introduce bias. This can occur not just in the digital manipulation of images but in the selection of subject matter or how the image is framed or even lit. "The apparent impartiality of photographs can conceal as much as it reveals—especially when the subject is violence or prejudice," notes one observer.[16]

Attempts at objectivity may drain some of the emotion that is innate in stories that might otherwise encourage audiences to care about or become more involved in the news. Such critiques of the notion of objectivity in journalism rest at least in part on the work of Michel Foucault, who argued that the pursuit of neutral, objective knowledge that culminates in "truth" is flawed without an independent and critical examination of how power shapes the dominant system of cultural beliefs.[17]

In the digital age, many journalists still adhere to the goal of objectivity despite these critiques. Nicholas Lemann, former dean of the Columbia University Graduate School of Journalism, explains, "I think objectivity is really important and is a goal to strive for. And the fact that people can't achieve it doesn't mean it should be thrown out as a goal."[18]

Yet the objectivity model is also evolving to incorporate related approaches that place greater emphasis on the goals of balance, fairness, impartiality, and independence of the journalist or news organization. In a sociological analysis of the *New York Times'* newsroom procedures, Nikki Usher has found that the *Times* remains fully committed to reporting the news under a model of objectivity, but it is adapting to the "tension and change" resulting from the growing pressures of "immediacy, interactivity, and participation" in the digital age.[19] Usher explains, "Objectivity is still a strategic ritual and a vaunted professional aspiration." But, she adds, journalists are "adjusting the ways they incorporate their workflow and professional aspirations in an entirely different working environment from the past."

In the wider news environment, an increasingly frequent blurring of notions of fact (measurable or observable information) and opinion (a point of view with regard to the facts, situation, issue, or participants) is also contributing to or exacerbating the problem of objectivity in journalism. It is worth noting that while the human journalist may not be objective, the methods of news-gathering or presentation may be objective (or at least value free or value neutral); free of judgment, opinion, or evaluation; and replicable and transparent. They are somewhat akin to elements of the scientific method, which are meant to be neutral and replicable by others in order to verify results, findings, or facts (although some would say even those methods can contain bias).

In *Journalism as Activism: Recoding Media Power,* Adrienne Russell contends that journalists should be advocates for facts, not for an artificial balance of viewpoints.[20] For instance, in reporting about climate change, she argues, news media should not offer stories in which climate change deniers are quoted alongside climate scientists, as if the two perspectives are equally legitimate. Through experiential media, journalists can present stories that incorporate conflicting views but should do so with enough nuance to articulate a dubious perspective and thereby reveal the flawed reasoning or inaccurate factual assertions that underlie the beliefs of a climate change denier (or of a flat-earther). Experiential media can help engage audiences in empathetic narratives that facilitate an understanding of the truth in controversial and complex stories. By incorporating multiple perspectives, experiential media may help break through the filter bubble or internet echo chamber in which social media users surround themselves exclusively with like-minded viewpoints.[21] Although any content, including experiential news, is potentially subject to manipulation, a quality news organization can build a reputation of trust by adhering to the facts while presenting them in the nuanced capacity enabled by experiential media.

DIGITAL TRANSFORMATION: THE ADVENT OF COMPUTERS IN JOURNALISM

When journalism pioneer Fred Friendly introduced the UNIVAC computer into the CBS Television newsroom for election-night coverage in 1952, it signaled the beginning of a new computational era in journalism.[22] Since that night, advances in computing and related technologies have continued to shape journalism.

Far from deterministic, these technological changes have given innovative journalists new tools with which to improve the quality of news coverage, gain efficiencies in production, and enable new techniques for reporting and story telling. These changes have also raised a variety of ethical concerns, threatened privacy, and opened newsrooms to the dangers of computer hackers. Some might also contend that they portend the end of human journalists, who would be replaced by algorithm-driven digital reporters or bots.

Unquestionably, the rise of digital media and the internet have ushered in sweeping changes to the media landscape and have transformed the story-telling palette for the journalist of the twenty-first century. Breaking news is almost as likely to flow from an amateur citizen reporter equipped with a smartphone as from a professionally trained and paid journalist.[23] The qualities and characteristics of such news reporting may vary widely from the traditional assumptions and tenets of professional journalism. The changes can even influence the substance of what is reported in a digital news story. In professional journalism, one of the basic reporting techniques has been to rely on humans as primary sources of news. As such, most news media professionals, at least in the United States, have long had an aversion to relying on anonymous sources, with some famous exceptions. For instance, *Washington Post* reporters Bob

Woodward and Carl Bernstein relied on the anonymous source going by the name Deep Throat during the early-1970s Watergate investigation that led to the resignation of President Richard M. Nixon. Journalists have held that the use of anonymous sources can undermine the credibility of the news and perhaps jeopardize accuracy or truthfulness by exposing reporters to biased sources of news or information. Only in rare circumstances should journalists rely on anonymous sources, such as when revealing sources' identities might threaten their safety (e.g., whistle-blowers might suffer retribution) or otherwise harm them in some fashion (e.g., revealing the identity of rape victims might cause further emotional or psychological injury).

A digital story, especially an experiential one, has important implications for a reporter's use of anonymous sources. In particular, in the digital age the breadth of sources has widened greatly, and the nature of those sources has shifted. Although there have long been leaks and other anonymous sources in journalism, in the digital age the potential for massive big data sets, such as those delivered anonymously via WikiLeaks to news media worldwide, has grown. In an experiential media context, 360-degree video cameras and other data sources such as security cameras make visual news more widely available, and that video may often include images of children or other people who are unaware that they are being recorded. How and when reporters should utilize such material presents ethical challenges. The importance of the story, the question of whether the information could be gotten any other way, and the potential harm in not reporting the story all factor in to the decision.

Susan Sarandon's 360-degree video diary "The Crossing" provides a contemporary experiential example. Produced in collaboration with RYOT and its owner, HuffPost (formerly the Huffington Post), the 2016 series provides an immersive exploration of the global refugee crisis and what it is like to be on the Greek isle of Lesbos, where many refugees have landed. Most of the migrants' faces are seen, but their names are kept confidential.[24] Although what Sarandon is doing is common to television reports that obscure faces, with 360-degree video cameras, there is a subtle difference. With traditional, directional cameras, subjects typically know or realize they are being photographed or video recorded. With 360-degree cameras, many people in the camera's omnidirectional field of view may be unaware that a camera is recording them. Reporters who might consider using such video may have an ethical imperative to reveal to people that they have been recorded even if their identities will be obscured in postproduction.

Through the layering and linking of content, digital journalism stories (such as interactive data visualizations or maps with embedded content) have the potential to provide rich contextualization to the episodes or events that may have been their original impetus. For instance, a digital story about the 2015 riots in Baltimore, Maryland, might include online links that extend far beyond the specifics of the circumstances that resulted in one young black man's death. They could provide historical context based on data regarding housing, community segregation, and income inequality along racial lines that have long affected Baltimore.[25]

Digital journalism stories increasingly utilize the qualities or characteristics of the networked, digital, and mobile media environment, including interactivity and immersion. Stories often feature a wide spectrum of content formats and modalities, including text, audio, video, and emergent forms, such as animation, haptic or tactile presentations (e.g., 3-D printed objects), data visualizations, and locative media.[26] Digital stories also increasingly deliver dynamic narrative or nonlinear story structures to provide a more vivid and distinctive approach to news.

Much of the impetus for the development of new digital story-telling forms arises from the struggles of journalism leadership and news organizations to adapt and innovate in a changing media landscape. Northwestern University journalism professor Pablo Boczkowski notes that beginning in the analog age and continuing into the digital, mainstream journalism was increasingly characterized by homogenous, commoditized content that undermined audience engagement.[27]

As I have written elsewhere, the digital age demands a three-stage model for the development of journalistic content.[28] The first stage is content that is created for analog media but is repurposed (put in digital format, sometimes adding links to websites) for the internet. The notion of repurposed or derivative work has long been common to much media story telling, fictional or factual. Derivative work here refers to news (or other media content) that is based upon and draws from other published content. This is a common practice in many areas of journalism, including in satire such as in editorial cartoons, op-eds or editorials, and news reporting.

Whether in old-time radio, where many plays were based on previously written or produced stories, or in contemporary news media, much media content is based at least in part on previously created works or expression. Radio and television news and documentaries often draw upon newspaper reports that introduce or break original news stories. A classic example are reports based on stories that the *New York Times* and the *Washington Post* broke in 1971 about the failures of decades of U.S. military strategy in Vietnam based on the so-called Pentagon Papers, documents leaked to those newspapers by Daniel Ellsberg.[29] Television, radio, and even newspapers across the country subsequently published stories based on the original reporting of the *Times* and the *Post*. One illustration of derivative journalism that was decades in development is a 2010 *POV* video report reflecting on the long-term impact of the publication of the Pentagon Papers.[30]

Even newspaper (or online) journalists who conduct extensive original reporting also often draw upon other published materials, citing that work as contextual information or sometimes not even acknowledging the specific source of other background facts or figures. The nature of such derivative work in story telling is poised for potentially substantial change in the coming years with the growth of media mobility, networking, and code. A news story, for example, may develop as a network of linked news content that connects through hyperlinks to previously published materials. Moreover, news aggregators can utilize this capacity to link to original source materials as a means to establish the veracity of a story. For instance, scripts for in-depth television reports often feature dozens of footnotes to original source material, but these footnotes are typically not made available to the audience, though they could be in a digital environment as a form of greater transparency and public engagement. Experiential news can advance this capacity even further by utilizing augmented reality or other forms of interactivity to annotate facts, sources, and foundational materials that news consumers can examine in detail and on demand.

Algorithms may play a key role in the evolving nature and impact of derivative work in digital news story telling. As the internet and digital media have grown, derivative works have expanded greatly, and how such derivative work shapes news stories and meaning is an increasingly significant arena.

This intersects as well with important legal decisions regarding fair use of copyrighted materials. While expressions in the public domain have long been drawn upon for media stories, digital mash-ups have become a major part of the online landscape. In one such case in 2015, *Lenz v. Universal Music Group*, a three-judge panel on the U.S. Court of Appeals ruled in a favor of Stephanie Lenz, a mother from Gallitzin, Pennsylvania, who "went on YouTube and uploaded a 29-second video of her toddler dancing while Prince's 'Let's Go Crazy' played in the background."[31] The panel of judges ruled that Lenz's video was not an infringement on the copyrighted song. The fair use clause of the Digital Millennium Copyright Act (DMCA) allows it since Lenz did not create the video for commercial purposes and because her clip was shorter than thirty seconds.[32] Moreover, she used the song in a manner for which it was originally intended, as background for dancing. Her baby's dancing was, in essence, a commentary on the song, much like a news report or review about Beyoncé's 2018 Coachella performance that features twenty-nine seconds of her singing.[33] How the court's decision affects digital story tellers who wish to create narratives based on derivative works is an important consideration in the development of experiential journalism. As news in the online and mobile arenas grows, journalists may explore compelling experiential formats that incorporate user experience based on a variety of immersive content that is copyright protected by others but is subject to the fair use clause of the DMCA.

Identifying derivative work such as Lenz's once required a human investigator searching YouTube for use of materials for which Universal held the copyright. Today, this search process is almost entirely driven by algorithms. Programming code searches YouTube and elsewhere online, scanning audio, video, and other files for the use of any copyrighted material. Whether used in stories or not, such content is automatically flagged, and companies such as Universal send cease and desist letters to whoever is deemed legally liable for the online content. As algorithms continue to evolve and expand, story tellers also may utilize them to identify potentially valuable content to incorporate in an experiential news story for a particularly sought-after emotional or intellectual impact. In journalism this might take the form of a story based on social media data; an algorithm might track posts and identify patterns, outliers, and potential local sources and generally help a reporter to provide the broad context to a specific story. In an experiential context this might involve how users are sharing their augmented reality or virtual reality news-related experiences.

The second stage in the digital journalism model is content that is created originally for online and mobile distribution but with little design for the digital environment. Such content is still commonly found in many news stories and across media platforms, and much of this content is of high quality, at least in terms of the fundamentals of good story telling. To illustrate, HuffPost published a story on May 21, 2018, about a U.S. Supreme Court ruling in a case involving employers' use of class-action waivers in arbitration agreements.[34] The article incorporates text, photos, and a half dozen links to related online content such as earlier related coverage on HuffPost. But beyond links, the story does not feature any other interactive, immersive, multisensory, or data-based content that would allow users to delve more deeply or experientially into the story about what the implications might be for them specifically.

Third in the model is a nascent form of journalism with news content created for the digital, online environment and designed to utilize or exploit that environment's unique capabilities. This form of digital story telling in journalism has advanced substantially, although it is still a relatively small portion of the total volume of digital journalism. Experiential news is a prime example of this developing form of journalism.

The main digital innovations to date tend to be in terms of production methods and workflow, where tools such as digital cameras and digital editing software are used in creating multimedia news content and sharing it for public comment via social media.

PUBLIC RELEVANCE

Quality journalistic stories require more than excellent fundamentals and effective utilization of the digital media environment. They need messages of substance, delivering social or public relevance, surprise, or authenticity. An interesting case study comes in the form of the *Chicago Defender*, historically an important print voice—and now also digital— for the African American community. In the mid-twentieth century *Defender* editor Richard Durham created an innovative, historically inspired program called "Destination Freedom," which was produced in collaboration with the *Defender* for broadcast on radio, that era's new media form. In its early days, the *Defender* urged African Americans in the Great Migration from the South to cast off Jim Crow by seeking opportunity in the North.[35] In that spirit, in 2015 Kai El' Zabar, executive editor of the *Defender*, developed stories that likewise reflected an empowering narrative.[36] One banner headline, both in the newspaper and online, illustrates the twenty-first-century theme of empowerment: "Wake Up: There's No Justice for Black Men."[37] Among the techniques used in the story, El' Zabar has developed a stylebook for the paper that includes a reintroduction of the phrase "the Race," which the paper's founder, Robert Sengstacke Abbott, favored decades ago. El' Zabar is also returning the focus of the paper to local stories framed within a larger narrative, an approach especially amenable to experiential news because of its immersive and interactive nature.

Through their potential to build empathy, experiential stories might engage users actively in empowering narratives. Experiential news can enable agency by allowing users to experience a story from a source's point of view and, through interactive design, take action and see its consequences. An interesting case in point can be found in an NPR (National Public Radio) story that aired on June 14, 2018, about Flag Day. It featured commentary from Rutgers journalism and media studies faculty member Chenjerai Kumanyika, whose podcast *Uncivil* in 2018 won a Peabody Award for excellence in its reporting of the untold stories of the U.S. Civil War.[38] Kumanyika, an authority on diversity, offers his perspective on what it is like to be a black American journeying down a residential block where home after home displays the U.S. flag. In today's politically divisive times, display of the U.S. flag can carry more than simply a message of patriotism and can evoke a spirit of nationalism. An experiential news story that allows the news consumer to virtually walk down such a street seeing things from the point of view of a person of color could be especially effective in advancing understanding.

CHAPTER TWO

Digital Design in Experiential News

The content of journalism and media is in the midst of a sea change. Content is migrating away from a traditional environment based on linear, single- or dual-modality media forms such as text on a printed page, moving pictures on a TV screen, or sound from a radio receiver. In the digital arena, content is shifting toward more interactive, on-demand, networked, multisensory, and mobile communication platforms such as handheld and wearable devices.

As such, journalism and media content on digital platforms rest especially on a foundation of design. Design refers to the development of a plan or conceptualization for the creation of an object or system, such as a media interface.[1] This interface—the software or technology that allows the user to access media content or interact with a digital device—represents a fundamental transformation of the news user's experience. Across a variety of media environments, news content places an increasing emphasis on engaging users in an experiential environment where they are interactive participants in a narrative that is navigated through an increasingly natural user interface such as voice command, gesture, or touch.

Within a content context, design refers to the aesthetic and functional dimensions of how a narrative is presented, experienced, or interacted with in a media environment or on a digital platform. Design has long been an important consideration in news media and story telling.[2] But in the digital age design becomes an even more fundamental, pervasive, and paramount consideration as computational systems increasingly combine with content and as form and function merge. Design, as a field, is attracting increasing amounts of research, analysis, and theory, and this has significant implications for experiential journalism.

Design in digital content incorporates a number of key principles, including a realistic (authentic) and even hyperrealistic visual style (as adapted from art, meaning ultra-high-resolution imagery and video that goes beyond photo-realistic); simplicity, composition, and customizability of the user interface within a single frame (e.g., a screen); systems of interaction to control the user experience (increasingly natural and intuitive systems such as those that are audio or voice based); and ambient sound, which is increasingly present throughout a story and includes music and environmental acoustics. Research suggests that the user interface can play a central role in immersive media experiences, including journalism.[3] The design elements of an immersive user experience can give news consumers a sense that they are actually experiencing a story as if present at, participating in, or witnessing a news event. Although traditional news media can give readers or viewers a limited form of experience, it is not one that envelops or surrounds the reader. Combined, these elements can not only better engage news users but also help them understand and remember the story.

Design is especially vital in the case of experiential news content, which rests upon a model of active user engagement or experience. In particular, six principles of design are particularly relevant to the production of quality experiential journalism or news.

(1) Interaction: users' active engagement in experiential news
(2) Immersion: news content that envelops the user
(3) Multisensory presentation: sight, sound, and haptic user engagement in a three-dimensional user environment
(4) First-person perspective: users' experience of virtual presence as a participant in or witness to news
(5) Nonlinear narrative: users' control of their content experience unbounded by a temporal sequence or pathway
(6) Natural user interface: intuitive user control, navigation, and customization of the content experience enabled by touch, gesture, gaze, and voice

INTERACTION

In today's media environment, stories and content of almost all types, including news, are increasingly interactive. Interactivity refers to active user engagement in the story, and it takes two main forms. First is interaction between or among users and media story tellers, including journalists. Often this interaction comes via public participation in social media, especially via mobile platforms. The second form of interaction is between the consumer or user of a digital story and the content itself. The content is designed in a fashion that enables and invites the user to somehow manipulate or contribute to it, not to distort meaning but rather to allow exploration, participation, and deep dives into the data upon which the story rests.

Understanding of interactivity, both its nature and its consequences, is rapidly growing. Researchers are increasingly investigating interactivity and its role in the human-media experience.[4] Based on this research literature, interactivity can be defined as a form of dialogue (or exchange) between humans and what are increasingly digital media or between and among humans via digital media. Moreover, research suggests that interactivity facilitates engagement with the news narrative and helps bring the individual more deeply into the public sphere to distribute, discuss, debate, and digest news content and issues.[5]

To illustrate the first form of human-to-human media interaction, one might consider the evolving form of story telling on the social media platform Snapchat (whose parent organization rebranded itself as simply Snap in 2016). Snapchat—which is popular as a social media platform for creating and sharing personal stories (including AR-enhanced selfies) from and on mobile devices—includes content and stories from media and news organizations such as the *Daily Mail*, *National Geographic*, and the *Washington Post*. Snapchat reflects the shifting habits of news users away from traditional news content platforms and toward news and entertainment delivered via social networks.

It is worth noting that international data from 2018 shows a shift in this pattern that is largely due to the spate of fake news and other recent problems (such as privacy breaches) that have plagued social media giant Facebook. The Reuters Institute for Journalism's digital news report states, "The use of social media for news has started to fall in a number of key markets—after years of continuous growth. Usage is down six percentage points in the United States, and is also down in the UK and France. Almost all of this is due to a specific decline in the discovery, posting, and sharing of news in Facebook."[6] Facebook aside, social media, including Snapchat, is still an important platform for how the public, especially youths, get their news.

In the realm of user-generated content (UGC), Snapchat users employ their mobile phones or tablets to create stories quickly and easily. These stories are typically nonfictional narratives, but not necessarily journalistic in nature. In other words, Snapchat UGC stories usually are not of great interest or relevance to the general public, although they may be and sometimes are. People use Snapchat to tell friends, families, and sometimes even the general public about their recent experiences or personal activities, often humorously. Via their mobile devices, Snapchat users collect images and video clips called "snaps" and assemble them into stories. Snapchat says, "Stories string Snaps together to create a narrative that lasts for 24 hours. To create a Story, a user choose [*sic*] to add their Snaps to their Story. Depending on their privacy settings, the photos and videos added to a Story can be viewed by either all Snapchatters, just the user's friends, or a customized group."[7] These stories offer a glimpse into the current experiences of users' Snapchat friends. Such stories are somewhat akin to human-interest features in journalism.

Although text can be used exclusively, many Snapchat stories feature an edited compilation of the users' photos, videos, and audio as supplemented by graphics or location filters to tell short narratives. Most stories run less than a minute but can be several minutes or even longer. Most are shared with family or friends, but on special occasions they can be publicly shared. In contrast to mainstream journalism, Snapchat user-created stories are not typically vetted for accuracy or subject to fact-checking before distribution. There are some requirements of stories, however, that help to authenticate them. These requirements include the geo-tagging of photos for college campus stories.[8]

Snapchat periodically hosts stories based on a theme, such as special events, holidays, unusual weather, or locations, and users can submit their theme-based stories for possible wide-scale distribution. Whereas most Snapchat stories are seen shortly after posting and by only a few people, theme-based stories can be seen over time and by thousands or millions of Snapchat's estimated 191 million daily users spread across diverse regions and populations. In this case, Snapchat's human editors first review submissions to assess their suitability for widespread distribution. Popular Snapchat-themed stories have included city-based narratives organized around places ranging from New York to Paris to Istanbul. For instance, in 2014 twenty-three million people viewed a Snapchat story on Oktoberfest in London,[9] and in 2015 some twenty-five million people viewed a Snapchat story on New York City's "Snowmageddon" blizzard under the "Our Story" filter.[10]

In 2016 Snap introduced a wearable device called Spectacles. The sunglasses-style device features a high-resolution video camera and internet connection to capture and share short video snippets of no more than ten seconds. This form of first-person video generated public interest and some enthusiasm but struggled in the marketplace. Snap subsequently introduced Spectacles 2.0, adding a second camera and a higher price tag. Snap is reportedly working on a version 3.0 that may add the capability for augmented reality.[11]

In 2018 Snapchat introduced AR into its social content in the form of fifteen-second animations called 3-D Bitmojis.[12] Users access the camera app on their mobile devices to view short cartoons that look as though they are happening in front of them on a street, the sidewalk, or a table. In one case, a barefoot man or woman walks across red-hot coals seemingly unscathed until, at the end, the feet suddenly and humorously start to smoke and then burst into flame. Journalism might use such 3-D Bitmoji AR to transform editorial cartoons—the longtime staple of newspapers that often offer political-satire drawings—which could be reimagined as 3-D AR animations.

Design considerations increasingly play a central role in story development and presentation across all digital media forms including participatory news story telling. Among the key factors are the user interface and how it facilitates a user's engagement with the story's content and the ability to share it via social network. Though they are known for their brevity, social networking media have even become a platform for the design of long-form story telling. One example is Steller,[13] which allows users to design long-form stories that combine photographs, video, and text. These stories might include dozens of photos and might take five minutes or more to explore. One user's story, for instance, offers a

photographic essay about her visit to the Greek island of Santorini, featuring thirty-four photos of the island that was famously devastated by
a massive volcanic eruption in the sixteenth century BC.[14] The Steller
community is still growing, and stories typically have audiences in the
hundreds or thousands. The author of the Santorini story, for example,
has sixty-one followers, but her story has 290 likes as of this writing.

Further reflecting the growing demand for long-form content, in
2018 Instagram enabled its one billion users to upload one-hour videos,
which had previously been limited to one minute, comparable to the
ephemeral video stories featured on Snapchat.[15] Instagram hopes to rival
Google's YouTube, which has always allowed long-form video uploads
and now has 1.9 billion users.

In addition to human-to-human interaction, interactivity in story
telling also occurs through engagement between the story's consumer
and the content itself. For instance, a citizen might click on an object in
a news story presentation to access additional embedded content or to
customize the information in the story. Interactivity can take the form
of a clickable menu for navigation through documentary content. This
navigation is increasingly intuitive and natural for the user and may be
based largely on small physical movements. Navigation may even employ
the human gaze, as has been tested in the AR-enabled situated documentary.[16] In this form of immersive journalism, users, wearing see-through
AR headsets, see and hear the physical environment surrounding them
and also see (and hear) digital objects that the journalist has layered into
the scene and geo-tagged to relevant objects as part of a story. Situated
documentaries on the Columbia University Morningside Heights campus in Manhattan, New York, include the 1968 student protest, the pre-
history of the campus when it was the home of the Bloomingdale Asylum for the Insane in the 1800s, and the tunnels that honeycomb beneath
the campus that were initially built to connect buildings that were part
of the Bloomingdale Asylum.[17] Users navigate through the immersive
narrative by looking at digital objects in their field of view, such as a
virtual flag that represents a digital point of entry into a story, and holding their gaze a half second.

Interactivity can involve humans and artificial intelligence (AI)
embedded in a story or digital media form. In a case pointing to an experiential future in which users are unencumbered by a physical device,

pedestrians near London's Canary Wharf in 2015 encountered a digital billboard featuring artificial intelligence. The billboard delivered an interactive public service message about domestic abuse. A camera embedded in the billboard scanned the faces of those who walked by, and the interactive system used an AI algorithm (intelligent machine vision) to recognize when each person looked at the billboard.[18] The sign displayed a battered female victim of domestic abuse, and as each person looked at the billboard, the woman's bruised face began to heal. The sign's textual message invited the public to not turn a blind eye to domestic violence. The interactive billboard represents a potentially compelling form of experiential story telling in which users engage in a two-way digital narrative in a public setting. Such technology could offer journalism a pathway to create AI-enabled, publicly engaged experiential news. For instance, a local story about a proposed new development could be experienced on location.

Such public engagement with media narratives has deep roots. Radio programs during the medium's earliest years in the 1920s and '30s often featured performances before live audiences, whose real-time feedback could inspire or otherwise engage performers. Fans' letters or published critiques provided a less timely type of response, and early audience ratings or measurement research techniques added another form of limited interaction.

However, the networked, digital age has transformed the notion of audience interaction. Audiences themselves are becoming more akin to participants in programs and stories, with real-time engagement via social media being the increasing norm. Moreover, this participation can occur on a national and even worldwide scale and can take place on an almost instantaneous basis. With important roots in newspaper reporting, the #MeToo movement that emerged in late 2017 quickly became a national and international phenomenon, largely due to the capabilities of social networks such as Twitter. "On October 15, 2017," Pardis Mahdavi reports, "American actress Alyssa Milano posted a tweet urging women to speak up and out about their experiences with sexual assault or harassment using the phrase 'me too.' Overnight, social media erupted, as #MeToo took hold in every corner of the world."[19]

Nearly ubiquitous wired and wireless broadband connectivity enables high-speed, on-demand uploading and downloading of content, fostering not only citizen participation and sharing of media content but also on-demand media consumption. This is evident in the commercial popularity and success of mobile apps and online services that feature original audio programming such as *Serial* or *The Moth Radio Hour* or repackaged audio content from the past such as old-time radio plays on RadioSpirits.com. Although these digital audio examples illustrate the advances in media distribution, they also reflect the changing media habits and expectations of an increasingly mobile news-consuming public. These changes are essential for the development of experiential journalism, which depends on digitally connected and immersed news consumers.

IMMERSION

Immersive media content, or content that increasingly envelops the user, is developing rapidly. As augmented-reality and virtual-reality media forms enter the marketplace, immersive content, including news, is becoming ubiquitous in the physical environment. For instance, AR augments can be tagged or anchored to objects and locations in the physical world, and users can access this immersive content anywhere via a mobile, networked device such as a smartphone. Although game developers are in the forefront of immersive AR and VR content production (such as *Pokémon Go*), cinematic, documentary, and mainstream journalism production are also in rapid development.

A wide range of media and technology companies are developing AR and VR content across a variety of genres. Among the developers are leading news media organizations, including Gannett (especially its flagship *USA Today*), the *New York Times*, the *Wall Street Journal*, and the *Washington Post* (which Jeffrey P. Bezos, founder of retail giant Amazon, bought for about $250 million in 2013); a host of entertainment companies such as Comcast, Disney, Legendary Entertainment, Netflix, 20th Century Fox, Time Warner, and Sony; and major technology firms, including Google, Facebook, and Microsoft.

Lorne Manly reports there is an explosion of VR content production occurring.[20] "Virtual reality—once the stuff of science fiction—is still in its infancy," he notes. "But there's already a gold rush around the technology, which plunges viewers into a simulated 3-D environment and lets them explore their surroundings as if they were really there."

Cinematic VR (or VR motion pictures) is an immersive content arena in which quality is already in evidence: the 2017 Academy Awards saw the first-ever Oscar-nominated VR film, *Pearl*.[21] This has important implications for journalism. Both the narrative grammar of cinematic VR and the priming of the audience base can help advance the growth of experiential news, especially in the form of documentary VR production.

Although it is reported to be refocusing on AR content, Jaunt is among the companies that has produced cinematic VR. Dozens of Jaunt's cinematic VR experiences are available for free download.[22] These cinematic VR experiences, most of which are five to ten minutes long, allow users to enter into a 360-degree video narrative as if present in the story.[23] Although the VR content can be displayed on a mobile or desktop device, for fully immersive 3-D experiences users wear VR headsets such as Google Cardboard, Samsung Gear VR, HTC Vive, or Oculus Rift or Go. Jaunt's VR productions include such narratives as "The Mission," an adventure where users join a World War II Special Operations team "dropped into a raging battle on the Eastern Front," and "Black Mass" (not to be confused with the 2015 movie about gangster Whitey Bulger), in which users find themselves held captive, and their "nightmare has just begun. Mature viewers only."[24] Jaunt has also produced nonfiction VR experiences. "The North Face VR" employs 360-degree video to enable users to virtually join climbers Cedar Wright and Sam Elias as they scale cliff faces in Yosemite National Park and Moab, Utah. An immersive musical Jaunt VR experience enables users to join former Beatle Paul McCartney as he performs "Live and Let Die," providing users with a sense of presence as if onstage during the performance. Journalists might use such an approach to transform music reviews into more immersive news experiences.

Beatles fans may also be interested in the "Abbey Road Studio" VR experience created in 2015 in partnership with Google. The interactive experience allows users to go online to visit the legendary recording studio where the Beatles created their *Abbey Road* album. With 360-degree images and video, visitors can virtually enter the studio and experience recordings as if present with the Beatles in 1967. The VR experience lets users remix Beatles music and also explore the musical stories of other artists who have recorded at the studio such as Amy Winehouse.[25]

Documentarians might utilize such an approach to innovate more engaging forms of biographical or cultural profiles.

Jaunt has also coproduced VR news content.[26] An example is the Jaunt–ABC News VR coproduction "Inside Syria," which invites users to explore parts of Damascus in the company of reporter Alexander Marquart. As Marquart narrates the threat that ISIS poses to some of Syria's most important archeological sites, the user can look around the inside of a mosque or a *souq* (old market), with stereoscopic (omnidirectional and 3-D) video providing a virtual tour.

Alchemy VR has created multiple immersive cinematic experiences. Its first such VR experience is a time-traveling journey narrated by Sir David Attenborough. Using immersion and interactivity to enliven science education, the experience enables users to journey back in time to the theoretical origins of life on Earth. This approach could be useful for science journalism in a variety of subject areas.

To help build VR content, Facebook launched Oculus Story Studio, which operated with Pixar veteran Saschka Unseld as creative director.[27] Oculus Studio developed VR story telling and created several cinematic VR experiences, including "Dear Angelica," "Lost," and "Henry."[28]

These developments indicate the potential for a dramatic increase in both the volume and quality of experiential content including in news. Production of experiential content is apparent in a wide swath of media industries and content domains.

Yet a number of challenges exist. Although there are interesting examples of experiential content, including in journalism, few if any productions have achieved widespread public attention and engagement. Production costs are still very high, and this is a particular problem for journalism organizations, whose budgets are often constrained. Public access is limited as well, although, as we will see in later chapters, the installed base of technology on which users experience VR content is growing rapidly as costs have fallen for both consumers and producers.

Sports is a nonfiction arena gaining VR traction. In 2015 NextVR broadcast an NBA Golden State Warriors' game live in VR,[29] marking the first time a professional sporting event was broadcast live to a national audience in VR. It was "no accident that the Warriors were playing. The team's co-owner, the longtime entertainment executive Peter Guber, is also a major investor in NextVR, the virtual reality company that filmed the home opener."[30] Through VR, broadcasts offer new types of graphics, editing, and announcing via multiple stereoscopic cameras. Fans experience the game from multiple perspectives such as from under the hoop. It is anticipated that the VR platform will create a feeling of being on the court with the players. Next-generation VR broadcasts are expected to integrate social media, enabling texting and commenting within the VR environment. Other sports and leagues are increasingly offering fans VR game experiences. College basketball's March Madness, for example, has offered fans live VR game coverage of the NCAA Final Four Semifinals and National Championship in partnership with CBS.[31] Or football fans can use VR to experience an actual practice session with the New England Patriots football team.[32]

VR narratives are poised to evolve even further as the boundary between game and story experience blurs. When Ralph Baer invented the video game in the 1960s, his vision was "interactive television."[33] In the decades since, story (or narrative) has become increasingly central to the interactive and immersive game experience. Samsung, for instance, has designed games that integrate story experiences into VR. Among the first offerings in this regard is *Gone*, a VR experience that enables the user to enter into a thriller narrative.[34] In 2015 Sony likewise introduced a VR approach to game play on its popular PlayStation VR. In many video games, experiential formats have enabled designers to create virtual worlds where narratives follow the unique rules and characteristics of those invented environments. Virtual worlds such as the Animus in *Assassin's Creed* or Pyramid in *Enslaved* are key elements in user experience, where the laws of our actual human universe may not apply. Journalistic applications might include creating a simulated statehouse or courtroom where users can experience the process of drafting legislation or a judicial proceeding based on actual events or cases as reported by journalists. Or a virtual world could be an effective platform to let users experience a hypothetical future environment where rising seas have transformed America's coastal cities. Journalists might base this virtual world on actual projections of the scientific study of climate change.

Filmmaker Chris Milk has worked with the *New York Times* on various VR projects. He explains that quality content will be a key requirement for the successful development of the VR experience. Moreover, the quality of VR content is apt to utterly transform user engagement in a narrative. The challenge, as he sees it, is to find the appropriate stories and topics that lend themselves to being told in VR or other experiential media. He writes, "An experience that's not great in a movie theater is just a boring movie; an experience that's not great in virtual reality can ruin the rest of your afternoon."[35]

Nonny de la Peña, a pioneering journalist, has created immersive narratives on subjects such as human rights abuses, human trafficking, and hunger in America's cities.[36] Dubbed the "godmother of Virtual Reality," de la Peña is convinced of the power of such immersive experiences.[37] "You really engage on scene in a way that gives you this incredible connection to where you are," de la Peña told the *New York Times*.[38] "And that's why, early on, I was calling it an empathy generator, an empathy machine." The *Times* reports that many journalists and journalism educators believe "that the visceral nature of the experience makes a viewer a new kind of witness."

Immersive forms of journalism are poised to accelerate internationally. For instance, in November 2015 the France-based Global Editors Network (GEN) announced a program to aid its international news membership to design immersive reporting capabilities. Jean Yves Chainon, director of AR, VR, and 360-degree video at GEN, proclaims, "It's become increasingly clear for editors and news executives that immersive journalism will be an integral component of the media landscape in the near future."[39] Chainon describes some of the key issues in developing immersive stories and the evolving nature of the news production process: "Besides new ways to frame the shot and tell the story, the bulk of the added workflow comes from postproduction 'stitching': the typical 360-degree video camera mount consists of at least six individual GoPros, whose video feeds must then be stitched together into a seamless frame."

Chainon further explains that the process of creating immersive stories increasingly relies on both computer code and new skill sets for the human journalist, although, as he notes, "the process is now largely automated through algorithms and software such as Kolor or Videostitch."[40] He continues, "The resulting image typically requires a number of tweaks which, at this point in time, still need to be performed manually. Another challenge comes from 'ghosting,' in reference to objects disappearing as they get too close to the cameras."

Journalists using wearable devices such as head-worn cameras and displays and other technologies will be able to capture and deliver immersive video and other media reports in real time and on demand for users who are similarly equipped for an immersive experience. This may signal a type of nonscripted, interactive, and immersive video journalism that could be used in breaking news such as reporting on political protests, journeys through exotic locations (e.g., a favela or shantytown in Rio de Janeiro), refugee migration patterns, or environmental disaster zones. Diverse users could be engaged across cultures through intuitive interfaces that perform voice translation in real time. For instance, an interview with a non-English speaker could be translated in real time to the local news consumer's preferred language.

MULTISENSORY PRESENTATION

The tools that journalists have available play a central role in what news they report and how they do it. In the nineteenth century, still photography and, later, motion picture cameras enabled new types of newsgathering and new kinds of stories that could be told. As a frame of reference, early experiments that Eadweard Muybridge conducted with film in 1886, commissioned by industrialist Leland Stanford, used motion film capturing twenty-four frames per second to enable humans to see how a horse actually runs for the first time.[41]

History also provides a twentieth-century precedent in the reporting of award-winning journalist Lowell Thomas. Covering an Arab conflict in the early 1900s, Thomas introduced the world to Britain's T. E. Lawrence, known as Lawrence of Arabia.[42] In the 1950s Thomas reported via Cinerama, an early form of immersive media that was shot with multiple cameras and displayed via three projectors onto a massive curved screen.[43] It enveloped the viewer both visually and in surround sound, but high cost and technical demands limited the potential use of the novel platform.

In the twenty-first century, the content of digital stories derives from an increasingly wide array of sources and types of data, ranging from familiar media forms such as cameras and microphones to the varied types of sensors in the world's billions of digital devices such as smartphones, wearables, and aerial drones. These new devices benefit not only professional journalists but also the growing number of citizen reporters who are now able to capture and distribute news stories as never before. Professional news reporters in the field equipped with smartphones still serve a primary news-gathering role in journalism, experiential or not. But even more ubiquitous is citizen reporting now that an estimated four billion or more people worldwide use camera-equipped smartphones. Citizen reporting usually involves video, photos, and audio captured via mobile devices and often serves as a source of breaking news, such as police-citizen confrontations or protests.

Sree Sreenivasan, the former chief digital officer for the Metropolitan Museum of Art in New York and a former journalism professor at Columbia University, notes that an estimated one trillion photographs were taken in 2015, even more in the years since then.[44] Ordinary citizens took many if not most of these photos, and the vast majority were for private use and have no relationship to journalism. Yet when news breaks, these photos (and videos) can serve as an important news resource. For instance, many of the videos and photos of the civil war in Syria have come from citizen reporters. Moreover, citizen reporting is typically highly engaged in social networking, and the photos and videos that are shared rapidly and widely online can feed directly into systems for experiential news production and distribution.

To date, the role of citizen reporting in experiential news is still very limited. But as the number of consumers equipped with 360-degree, 3-D, and ultra-high-resolution cameras and other experiential data sources grows, the potential is significant. Examples of citizen-produced nonfiction, experiential content include 360-degree videos produced by Sam Earl, whose 360-degree videos feature a panoramic tour of the Baa Atoll in the Maldives and an immersive skydiving experience.[45]

As more citizens are equipped with 360-degree cameras, and as the production process grows easier, it is increasingly likely that such experiential content will become at least an occasional resource for breaking news reporting, much as drone footage has become an increasingly common source for aerial views of news events.

The Internet of Things (IoT) is poised to exponentially increase the number of online data points that can serve as multisensory resources for experiential news stories. Increasing volumes of research suggest that the IoT is likely to progress toward the Internet of Everything, and that may open up new entrepreneurial opportunities including for people seeking to develop experiential content. Robert Pepper, formerly of the telecommunications company Cisco, has presented data on the global growth of the IoT, and it reinforces this scenario. Data suggests that by 2019, 43 percent of worldwide internet traffic will be machine to machine (M2M).[46] This will include a wide spectrum of devices, including cars, wearable devices such as Fitbits, connected homes, and a great deal of cameras and other sensors. M2M communication may involve robots sharing news and information, real or fake, signaling a future in which much of the world's flow of news does not even involve humans as reporters or receivers. Consequently, M2M communication is apt to become a significant source of data for experiential journalism, but not necessarily involving humans.

Pepper and other industry analysts report that there were 4.9 billion connected devices in 2015.[47] They forecast that the number of connected devices will reach nineteen billion by 2019 and fifty billion by 2020. Cisco data indicates that the United States will be among the countries with the highest rate of IoT. By 2019, 58 percent of internet connections in the United States will be to devices.[48] But the country with the highest percentage of M2M internet connections will be South Korea at 72 percent. Pepper suggests that a new form of digital divide is likely to emerge by 2019, with less M2M connectivity in developing nations such as India, which has just 13 percent. These less-connected countries will likely be at an economic disadvantage since much commerce will flow via the IoT, and they will lag in access to news, especially the experiential, which will increasingly involve IoT connectivity.

In concert with the ascendance of cognitive computing (e.g., decision-making or problem-solving algorithms applied to data collected from an increasing array of sensors) and increasing globalization (e.g., diversity or language translation built on machine learning), the potential to utilize expanding IoT sources for journalism content will grow. Journalists, for example, will be able to create experiential stories that tap into IoT data streams to offer interactive experiences driven by algorithms. For example, air quality data could be collected and automatically synthesized into a real-time news visualization customized to each user's exact location.

Chip maker Intel is putting sensors on a wide spectrum of devices in an effort to advance the IoT. Putting sensors into sporting goods can transform fans' sports experiences. One observer reports, "For live sports fans, Intel has joined forces with Replay Technologies, and [Intel CEO Brian] Krzanich proclaimed that the company's freeD technology will 'set a new standard for fans everywhere.' It turns video into full 360-degree 3D video—so that you can view a Kevin Durant dunk from literally any perspective."[49] Beyond sports, the possibilities are similarly dramatic. Drones with sensors, for example, can "shine their LED lights in harmony with a symphony," as a video by Intel shows. Multisensory news content generated from these IoT feeds is poised to grow substantially.

For journalism, IoT could play a substantial role in news content. Among the possibilities envisioned by journalists at the Associated Press is a wide range of reporting capabilities.[50] These include using small, networked digital sensors, called Raspberry Pis, to "monitor vibration and noise from entertainment and political venues to identify the most popular songs at a concert, or the biggest plays of a game, or even the quotes that resonate the most at campaign rallies." They could similarly measure water quality in Rio de Janeiro, air quality in Beijing, the impact of construction sites in any city, or foot traffic at public transportation stops in any community to determine usage. Experiential stories could enable users to virtually visit the venues that are reported on and enable them to observe things for themselves, all based on precise, data-driven narratives.

As the IoT continues to expand, it is likely that there will be increasing linkages between media content and real-world objects. This intersection of media and physical computing is the subject of research on tangible media at the MIT Media Lab. Under the direction of Hiroshi Ishii, this research focuses on giving dynamic physical form to digital information. One project called Andante involves representing music as digitally animated characters.[51] Another project called Pneumatic Shape-Changing Interfaces "involves fabricating 'shape-changing interfaces through pneumatically driven, soft-composite materials.' The applications include designing a multi-shape mobile device, table-top shape-changing tangibles, dynamically programmable textures for gaming, and a shape-shifting lighting apparatus."[52] Media content might engage such technology to extend narratives from the digital environment into the real world, potentially giving news users a novel means to explore a remote location in a story or a data-driven visualization.

Such capabilities evoke images of a popular computer programming trick circulated online in the early 1990s. A friend once sent me an email asking whether I was thirsty and wanted a soda. If so, the message indicated, I should click on the soda icon pictured in the email. I clicked as directed, and the CD-ROM drive promptly opened, suggesting a tray for a beverage. As an early example of experiential content, it was a clever, effective, and entertaining surprise, at least in 1990. It also foreshadowed the potential to manipulate various real-world objects from cyberspace in the twenty-first century.

Because of its networked, digital nature, the IoT also raises the crucial specter of threats to cybersecurity for journalism generally and for experiential news in particular. The FireEye Cyber Threat Map illustrates the potential vulnerability of any system connected to the internet, providing real-time data on the continuous stream of cyberattacks happening around the world.[53] To anyone viewing the map, it is apparent that cyberattacks are clearly an international phenomenon and a critical threat to countries all over the world. Media companies, including news media and social media, have frequently been the targets of these attacks. A report released in 2015 shows that more than half (52 percent) of media companies around the world have been victims of cyberattacks.[54] The BBC was the victim of a significant attack in late 2015 and was forced to go offline for about three hours.[55] In 2016 international hackers used the vulnerability of the IoT, including internet-connected smart TVs, to launch a cyberattack that disrupted internet service for hours, including that of Twitter, Spotify, Netflix, Amazon, and Reddit.[56]

For news media, it is essential that content be protected against attack and potential manipulation. This is an especially acute need in an era marked by widespread fake news. Protecting experiential news from manipulation is particularly important for several reasons. First, because of its heightened multisensory realism, experiential news that has been hacked and manipulated can lead to great potential influence on public opinion. Second, the relative newness of experiential news makes the public less likely to have well-developed critical abilities or digital literacy that would enable users to recognize when that news has been manipulated. Third, users who might engage with altered experiential news might actually suffer direct harm from the manipulation. For instance, content might be modified to send an electric shock or a more tangible impact on the user. The rise of fake news online in the 2016 U.S. presidential campaign illustrates how such techniques can be used to capture public attention during a time of increasingly fast-paced and fragmented news distribution, especially via social networking media.[57]

Security concerns aside, journalists have at their disposal many new tools and techniques to tell stories in multisensory form. Stories can engage not just sight and sound but also touch and other modalities, potentially all five human senses. Experiential stories can utilize content with increasingly high production quality, including high-resolution and immersive audio and video material. While many current platforms provide a mix of sight, sound, and tactile engagement, some more experimental VR systems deliver even more comprehensive multisensory content or experiences. For instance, the VR Sense Arcade Cabinet combines wind, scent, rain, and more to heighten the user's sense of complete immersion in the narrative.[58] Journalism has yet to test such a platform as a story-telling environment, but the likelihood is growing as more news organizations enter the experiential media arena. Perhaps more importantly, the rise of a quality multisensory media system may transform how the public engages with the news.

The research of Colorado State University's Pete Seel suggests that as digital media develop increasing capabilities to generate and deliver high-resolution content (both sight and sound), viewers will gain a growing sense of presence because the imagery and audio will be increasingly lifelike and enveloping, displayed on curved, large-screen TV displays or presented on stereophonic sound systems or wearable devices. Presence—meaning the emotional, cognitive, and even physical (haptic) state or sense of being within or in proximity to a mediated environment—in immersive media has significant implications for stories and related research. "As television and video displays grow in screen size and sharpness with improved 4K and 8K resolution, future research needs to be conducted on the effects of telepresence," Seel contends.[59]

Telepresence has been studied since at least the 1990s as a key element of immersive media experiences, though only recently in a journalism context.[60] Taeyong Kim and Frank Biocca state, "The term telepresence has been used to describe the compelling sense of being present in a mediated virtual environment."[61] They add, "The concept of telepresence is becoming an important component in our understanding of how people experience television, virtual reality, and other mediated environments."[62] Research might explore how journalists could use the qualities of telepresence to tell stories that fully surround individuals and engage their entire field of view or sensory experience. Telepresence can shape users' perception of events by making them appear real and multisensory in the physical world. Research suggests that when users are immersed in a story, they are more apt to believe it. Telepresence has a more powerful impact on users' emotions as well. Consequently, users are especially likely to believe a news story presented immersively, and the heightened emotional impact associated with telepresence is also a factor that journalists need to consider when designing experiential news. Users may respond strongly to events, and if those events involve violence, tragedy, or other dramatic elements, there is potential for users to experience posttraumatic stress.[63] Users may also overestimate the importance of events, circumstances, or facts in a story as a result of their heightened emotional state.

In many ways, the technical quality of contemporary multisensory media displays can facilitate the user's engagement in an immersive experience. When users see an image or video, hear an acoustical presentation, or otherwise experience (for instance, via haptics) content that appears to their senses as reality, they are more apt to believe it is real, or at least a truthful representation of reality.

Ultra-high-definition (UHD) video illustrates the capacity for experiential media to appear real without requiring the user to don a wearable display. As implied by its name, ultra-high-definition video contains substantially more pixels (dots of light) than in previous TV systems. A 4K display contains roughly four-thousand pixels of horizontal resolution, and 8K has double that. As such, 4K UHD video displays four times the number of pixels as high-definition TV (HDTV), and twenty-one times that of standard-definition TV. This means that images on UHD displays can be substantially sharper than on even the best HDTV displays. UHD displays use a form of technology called organic light-emitting diodes (OLED), which enables not only the thin structure of the display but also a wide spectrum of improved visual capacities at a significantly lower level of power usage. Equipped with high-fidelity sound systems, these UHD displays can give users a sense of reality in viewing and hearing content that appears completely lifelike despite the fact it is a mediated representation.

LG has introduced a new OLED display that is "two and a half millimeters thick—about the thickness of four stacked credit cards. The result is a TV set that is either 65 inches or 77 inches wide diagonally, but that practically disappears when viewed from the side, as it's about one-tenth of an inch thick." The display features high dynamic range, or HDR, technology, which delivers "inkier blacks and more vibrant colors" via Dolby Vision technology.[64] "LG also introduced in 2016 a TV that can be rolled up like a scroll."[65]

UHD gives journalists at least three additional visual capacities. First, UHD delivers a substantially greater color gamut. This means that UHD offers the ability to display almost the entire color spectrum of light visible to the human eye. This is at a level far greater than HDTV systems. Second, UHD offers much greater dynamic range, HDR, which means that UHD gives substantially greater contrast in each frame of video. It allows the viewer to see objects in the video that might otherwise be in the dark, meaning that UHD video could enable viewers to see into a darkened window or an open door bathed in sunlight. Imaging systems called computational cameras present similar possibilities. Computational cameras that are currently in development may advance visual capabilities even further, allowing the display of light in portions of the spectrum that are not visible to the unaided human eye.[66] Finally, UHD provides a much higher frame rate, about 120 frames per second (FPS), four times that of HDTV; the next generation will capture 240 FPS. The rapid sequential display of multiple, slightly altered images during each second of a video is what creates the apparent motion in a moving picture; therefore, more frames, or images, per second will generate smoother motion. For this reason, UHD captures and displays high-speed motion much better than HDTV.

UHD enables journalists to explore previously impossible immersive capabilities and aesthetic possibilities in designing visual narratives. For example, ultra-close-up shots or depictions of ultra-fast-moving objects (e.g., the flight of a hummingbird, which can beat its wings up to eighty times per second; a honeybee's wing, which vibrates two hundred times per second) become available to visual story tellers. Among the earliest examples of the compelling use of 8K video was in media coverage of the 2018 Olympics in PyeongChang, South Korea.[67] The use of 8K video allowed viewers to see the games in sharper, more lifelike images with more vibrant colors and on larger displays without pixelation. As 8K video becomes more standard in terms of production and user experience, applications to journalism in a wide spectrum of domains will emerge, for instance, in medical and science reporting. Of course, just because we can do something does not necessarily mean we should. Choosing when to utilize new tools to create experiential news is both a production issue and an ethical one.

Videographers can use UHD cameras to shoot without the need for substantial artificial lighting because UHD cameras capture high-quality imagery in natural lighting. This can substantially reduce cost, increase production flexibility, and minimize the impact on subjects being recorded. These capacities are on display in *Planet Earth II*, an award-winning PBS documentary series that premiered in 2017. The production employed UHD cameras, natural lighting, and drones to produce extraordinary footage, such as extreme-close-up video of a three-toed sloth swimming in the waters off the coast of Escudo de Veraguas, Panama, and a "baby iguana running for its life through a pit of hungry snakes."[68] BBC One has also released a series of 360-degree nature videos, including immersive journeys in the slot canyons of Arizona, in the Kashmir Mountains in search of snow leopards, and in the Costa Rican jungle.[69]

Currently, UHD requires internet protocol television (IPTV) for delivery and display, including via IP-connected devices such as Amazon Fire TV, Android TV, Apple TV, and Roku. These platforms support the high-efficiency video-coding (HEVC) chip. Digital television systems, such as over-the-air broadcasting, satellite, or cable networks, cannot deliver the UHD signal because they lack compatibility with the HEVC chip. IPTV also enables interactivity. In contrast to IPTV, cable and broadcast TV use a different compression and transmission technology, MPEG-2 (motion picture experts group), to deliver digital video. UHD must be degraded for delivery to and display on these platforms. MPEG-2 video is limited to linear HDTV and not interactive, ultra forms including UHD. With rising numbers of people opting to cut the cords to their TVs and turning to IPTV, the so-called over-the-top (OTT referring to devices such as Apple TV and Roku) TV industry is beginning to generate a significant base of users connected for UHD. This TV viewership trend is creating a generation of consumers who will be able to access interactive TV and will expect new content experiences.

Eli M. Noam, Columbia University professor of economics and finance, suggests what this new content experience may be. Noam, who studies media in an increasingly interactive global environment, notes that ultrafast broadband networks will deliver more than simply greater volumes of content; they will deliver "ultra content."[70] Ultra content means stories that are much richer (e.g., multiple modalities, interactivity, depth) and that offer much more intensive information. Noam adds that this ultra content will feature at least two forms of content interactivity: horizontal and vertical. Horizontal interactivity offers capabilities that link between narratives or content packages, and vertical enables engagement deeply into data and the narrative or content itself.

As the interactive environment develops, traditional linear TV service, or video delivered linearly to the consumer, will decline. Complementary services such as on-demand TV will also see the potential to increase in the OTT environment. Viewing the full resolution available in UHD video also requires a UHD TV set. Data on consumer adoption of UHD TV suggests rapid growth in the coming decade. According to Chris Forrester, "Information Handling Services (IHS Markit Ltd.) says that it expects the global number of households with a 4K/UHD TV to grow from a mere 28m in 2015 to 335m during 2020."[71] The largest number of homes with UHD TVs, 25.9 million, will be in North America, primarily the United States. The rate of adoption of UHD sets is dramatic. From 2016 to 2017, the number of UHD-set-equipped homes doubled to sixty-six million.

Industry leaders such as Lachlan Murdoch, executive cochairman of 21st Century Fox, forecast that IPTV is likely to grow increasingly dominant in the overall television marketplace. Such forecasts anticipate that IPTV will deliver improved program quality, diversity, and functionality in the viewing experience. For instance, Apple TV can support viewing 4K, 360-degree images and video.[72] Such content is being produced for home viewers from a number of companies, including Disney, Showtime, and Discovery, and Netflix has produced extensive 4K content for on-demand viewing, including popular original series such as *House of Cards*, *Marco Polo*, and the *Moving Art* documentary series.[73]

For journalism, it is essential to develop experiential news designed for IPTV, or consumers will look toward other forms of ultra content. Once established, consumer media and news habits are often slow to change.[74] If journalism is not a major force as IPTV grows, it will find the audience and associated factors (e.g., engagement on matters of public importance, revenues derived from IPTV) difficult to reengage.

Animation is also an increasingly visible format for interactive, experiential ultra content in journalism.[75] One early example is the often delightful and sometimes even poignant Google Doodle. Google Doodles are interactive animations that typically tell a story, often from the past and sometimes with a strong social message, such as a 2015 Doodle telling the story of Nellie Bly, a pioneering nineteenth-century investigative journalist.[76]

The potential for animated experiential news is just emerging, but it holds promise as a new means to increase user engagement.[77] Vice News, which produces an animated news channel on YouTube,[78] has been a pioneer in developing animations in news reporting, as one example produced in collaboration with HBO illustrates. The animated story provides an audio-video explanation of how the technology known as blockchain can provide a secure, almost unhackable environment for digital cryptocurrencies such as Bitcoin and other digital exchanges as well as experiential news.[79]

Content interactivity and the user experience derive from far more than just the visual elements of a story. Other modalities are vitally important in creating compelling content. "Audio is often more important than video," explains media pioneer and educator Adam Clayton Powell III.[80] He adds that people are beginning to rediscover the power of sound in story telling. Natural sounds, or environmental acoustics, are particularly effective tools to set a scene and advance the narrative. In a VR context, spatial (3-D) audio is key to creating realistic, immersive user experiences. Google announced in 2016 that its Cardboard VR headset would support spatial audio; since then, spatial audio has become the standard for VR headsets.[81] Spatial audio is distinct from surround sound because it not only encircles the listener but also tracks according to the movement and orientation of the user's head, creating a sense of audio presence by keeping a sound accurately aligned with its corresponding source in the narrative.

Audio also plays a key role in user navigation and interaction in an experiential media environment. A user in an immersive space may not have access to traditional mechanisms such as a keyboard or mouse to control the experience. Instead, audio cues or voice commands can be effective. Sound is the mechanism that directs the user's attention in a short VR production titled "Wild—The Experience."[82] The immersive production derives from the 2014 movie *Wild* in which Reese Witherspoon portrays a woman hiking the Pacific Crest National Scenic Trail. The VR experience puts the viewer into the wilderness when Witherspoon's character appears. A voice out of sight and off to the side prompts the user to turn and encounter actress Laura Dern, who portrays the mother of Witherspoon's character.

With funding from the Knight Foundation and Google, Ainsley Sutherland is developing a platform to enable media-makers to record location-based audio in virtual reality. A former fellow at Buzzfeed's Open Lab, Sutherland says that Voxhop will be "a tool that would allow journalists to upload, generate or construct a three-dimensional environment and narrate the scene from multiple perspectives."[83]

A key component of audio-driven immersive content involves the use of natural sounds from a local environment. This would be particularly valuable for experiential stories featuring on-location reporting. Such sounds can evoke the image of a unique place or situation. Authentic sounds from the environment are especially effective in giving listeners a sense of presence, engaging them in the story, and leaving them with lasting memories.

The impact of using audio effects to enhance a story can be appreciated in the many on-location stories reported by NPR. In these stories, reporters often make highly effective use of locally captured ambient sound (sometimes combined with digital visualizations), especially to establish location. As NPR notes on its story-telling Tumblr page, "On Friday, August 28, two stories on Morning Edition achieved the same thing: They painted effective scenes of single, emblematic streets."[84] In the first, NPR's Nathan Rott uses sounds from a Los Angeles street to help tell a story "about Californians limiting their water use. With a small amount of ambient sound, audio of people talking about their lawns, and a few directional details ('on the corner,' 'a couple houses down,' 'across the street'), Nate began his piece with a 360-degree view of the street."

In the second, NPR's Steve Inskeep uses authentic ambient street sound to help tell a story about post-Katrina life in Arabi, Louisiana.[85] NPR sets the scene: "Schnell Drive, which was inundated after the hurricane." The story continues, "Listen to the ways Steve (with producer Rachel Ward) sketched a human streetscape—not with predictable, static sounds (lawn mowers, cars passing)—but by capturing their interactions with residents—knocking on doors, introducing themselves, entering homes, engaging people spontaneously on the street."[86]

Advances in immersive audio technologies are enabling new story forms. They also signal the advent of media experiences that are increasingly indistinguishable from reality. Tomlinson Holman, chief of audio direction at Apple, has developed the concept of sound "envelopment."[87] As an immersive audio experience, envelopment engages how people process sound, especially directionality and depth. With audio envelopment, stories might even convey for the listener something beyond perceived reality.

Adam Clayton Powell III, a former news executive at CBS News and NPR, explains how this might work in an audio-based journalism story. When we hear, Powell notes, our mind can fill in many gaps by drawing upon past experience. In fact, this is a perceptual phenomenon called synesthesia, in which stimulation of one sensory pathway generates involuntary experiences in a second sensory pathway.[88] To illustrate, Powell points to an anecdotal case of an NPR listener from Texas who heard audio of an actual rainstorm in a story. Because of the enveloping nature of the high-fidelity acoustics, the listener was convinced she could actually smell a West Texas rainstorm. In this manner, audio envelopment may provide story tellers the potential to create impressionistic and cross-sensory experiences. Listeners may be able to get not just the specifics of an individual story, but also an impression of the bigger picture. Such capabilities are illustrated in the final segment of a long-running CBS News television program, *CBS Sunday Morning*. Each week's show concludes with a narration-free audio and video segment of an outdoor location such as one of the American national parks. The creator and original producer of the program, Robert Northshield, has described the sublime segment as simply "letting a piece breathe."[89] It is a technique that foreshadows the growing capacity in the digital age to design experiential narratives, especially through ambient sound.

Powell notes that producers at NPR have sometimes constructed entire segments using natural sounds. One award-winning production exemplifying this is a twenty-minute feature on the centennial of the birth of twentieth-century media titan William Randolph Hearst. The segment features twenty minutes of natural sounds of San Francisco (where Hearst lived), Powell says. "The end had a cable car starting to move, and listeners would hear the bell ring. It prompted many listener requests about the cable car, when it ran, where, and the like."[90] Although it would be a topic for research, it is quite possible that such a news experience could change how the listener thinks about Hearst, shaping perceived connections between the media titan—who is perhaps best known to many today through cinematic portrayals such as Orson Welles's *Citizen Kane*—and the city. Listeners to the NPR acoustical segment might perceive Hearst as a more organic part of the urban landscape where he once lived and shaped twentieth-century journalism.

In early 2017 Powell continued to advance innovative news story telling by working with students from the University of Southern California to cover President Trump's inauguration and the Women's March in 360-degree and augmented video.[91] NPR has published some of the experiential reporting, as has the *New York Times*.[92] In these reports, users can virtually stand "between supporters and protesters as Donald J. Trump is sworn in as the 45th president of the United States." Ambient sound helps give the listener an authentic sense of presence on the National Mall.

Advances are continuing in the arena of audio recording and reproduction, which are key to the immersive nature of experiential news. Musician Neil Young's PonoMusic is a case in point.[93] Funded through a Kickstarter campaign, PonoMusic offers musical recordings in digital form but at a much higher level of audio quality than typical digital recordings. Digital audio recordings are made by sampling from the original audio performance and recording it onto a digital storage medium. The audio is then compressed and typically made available as an MP3 file. The sampling rate determines the quality of the audio reproduction; faster rates capture more of the entire audio frequencies. Sampling involves the conversion of continuous audio waves to discrete signals.[94]

PonoMusic samples at a much higher rate than the standard MP3 format, potentially capturing more of the actual audio performance and recreating higher audio fidelity for the listener. PonoMusic aims to deliver music as it sounds "during studio recording sessions," with high-resolution audio instead of the compressed audio format that MP3 files provide.[95] PonoMusic "has received mixed reactions, with some describing Pono as a competitor to similar music services such as HDtracks, but others doubting its potential for success."[96] Experiential news in audio format, such as a new generation of podcasts, could utilize the higher-quality format exemplified in PonoMusic to design more engaging sound experiences for listeners.

Tactile formats are also on the horizon as tools for telling news stories that enhance the user experience. As physical computing increasingly fuses with media, tangible story telling will likely become an increasing part of the news narrative form. Haptic technologies include tablets that simulate a sense of touch. Touch can contribute to the user's sense of presence in immersive media.[97] Further, 3-D printers or even 4-D machines are entering the consumer market that generate printed objects capable of self-adapting to environmental changes. These could be used to print downloadable 3-D digital objects as part of an experiential story, much as an audio sound bite or video clip can be downloaded in 2018. Among other things, contemporary 3-D printers feature a variety of capabilities and formats, including one that prints 3-D objects via paper. This means that news consumers would have access to low-cost and higher-speed and flexibility in the printing of objects that will potentially be part of future experiential news. This is important for experiential journalism in that it could make tangible story engagement available to a much wider public relatively quickly. Much as low-cost (five-dollar) Google Cardboard devices made VR headsets available to millions of news consumers in 2014, low-cost 3-D printing capabilities can substantially increase user adoption of the requisite platforms to make tangible experiential news possible on a mass scale.

A growing number of VR platforms support the use of haptic interfaces to engage users and give them tactile control and feedback in a game or narrative experience. On the Oculus Rift, the user experience is delivered via the Oculus Touch, a handheld game controller that enables the user to navigate and interact physically in the 3-D virtual environment.[98] Some haptic-enabled VR experiences for the Oculus are performance based, such as *Rock Band VR*, where the user can virtually become a musician while playing a peripheral guitar controller device. Journalists might use such an approach to engage users in reports involving physical activity or performance, such as new techniques for mindfulness or meditation.[99]

Another example of a haptic, performance-based VR experience is *The Climb*,[100] which "uses the Oculus Rift's motion-controller technology to let the player control the hands of the protagonist." The haptic VR experience is "based on Vietnam's Halong Bay," and the interface becomes increasingly intuitive. An observer notes, "You learn to scan the rock face for available holds, you learn to plan ahead, using the correct arm to lurch up with, based on its position to your body and the location of the next hold. Eventually you build up a rhythm where you start to scamper up the cliff like Spider-Man." The haptic engagement offers additional authenticity. "You also have to watch a grip meter in the corner of the screen: if it gets too low, you need to chalk up your hands, or your fingers will start slipping from the ledges. It's a small addition, but it just keeps that sense of physicality—that sense that you're actually out there dangling from a 200ft cliff."

The potential to build haptic, performance-based user experiences in the realm of entertainment is apparent. In the future, haptic experiences might also be put into a journalistic use, as 3-D printing and other tangible media develop. A news story, for instance, might offer the user the ability to feel a virtual object, such as a 3-D digital representation of a piece of lava expelled from an erupting volcano in Hawaii or of an ancient Aztec turquoise tile like one that was recently studied in reference to early Mesoamerican history.[101] Or, integrating the performance capability of VR, a future haptic sports news story might let the user engage a football (i.e., soccer) goalie in a free-kick simulation based on the parameters of an actual match.

Innovative journalists are envisioning ways to incorporate such haptic engagement in experiential news. The AP is developing plans for haptic reporting to allow users to touch virtual 3-D objects in news stories.[102] In a story about the discovery of an ancient human skull, *Radio-Lab* produced a 3-D printed copy of the skull and made the file available for download for any interested audience member.[103]

Experiential journalism stories featuring haptics could apply to any subject, although some topics are more immediately amenable to the sense of touch. Illustrative are stories about subject matter with tangible dimensions including science, the environment, health, medicine, technology, culture, fashion, food, or the arts. A story about climate change, for instance, might examine the impact of rising sea levels on wetlands. Mangrove forests, such as those in the wetlands of the state of Florida, are greatly threatened by the sea-level rise resulting from climate change, and a story about research in this important arena might include a 360-degree video shot in the mangrove forest with ambient natural sounds. It might allow the user a tangible interaction such as virtually touching a mangrove tree, feeling through a data glove or other haptic interface the texture of its bark (before and after rising seas lead it to rot), and thereby gaining a more authentic sense of the potential impact of climate change on a threatened species. Similarly, seagrass, such as eelgrass, is indigenous to the coastal Great Bay wetlands of the state of New Jersey. An experiential story about the potential impact of climate change on Great Bay might offer an immersive, 360-degree video inside the marsh ecosystem, ambient natural sounds, and a tangible experience that enables the user to virtually feel the texture of eelgrass or a kinesthetic experience virtually feeling the eelgrass as it moves in an ocean current.[104]

FIRST-PERSON PERSPECTIVE

Journalism stories are increasingly utilizing a changing voice or perspective alternative to the third-person voice that has long been heard, read, or seen in U.S. news and entertainment media. Much as in early twentieth-century radio plays, first-person voice is increasingly providing twenty-first-century citizens with an opportunity to see or hear narratives from the perspective of a central figure in a story. First-person perspective facilitates audience members imagining being in a particular location and experiencing something for themselves. Once a staple of old-time radio plays, first-person perspective is increasingly common in immersive, multimedia, and social media forms.

First-person perspective is also increasingly employed in independent video, radio, and other audio (such as online or podcast) stories.

Among the best examples are podcasts from Podbean, an online provider of free podcasts and podcasting software. Podbean has combined third-, second- and first-person perspectives in its *Leid Stories*, with narratives such as "Columbus: Uncovering the Myth of His New World 'Discoveries'" and "The Pre-Debate Debates, Right Here on Free Your Mind Friday!"[105]

In the spirit of Orson Welles's early radio classic *First Person Singular*, the public radio program called *The Moth Radio Hour* typically uses first-person singular, and sometimes plural, narrative techniques. *The Moth*, which is also available on demand online and as a podcast, frequently delivers quality original nonfiction audio stories. Also in the tradition of great radio story telling, *The Moth* won a Peabody Award for excellence in broadcasting in 2010.[106] "Storytelling, likely the oldest art, is revered and reinvigorated by this hour for everyday raconteurs," said the Peabody judges about *The Moth Radio Hour*. *The Moth* describes its story telling as "true stories told live."

On *The Moth* individuals tell their own personal stories in words spoken aloud. The oral story tellers reflect on emotionally or intellectually engaging elements from their own experience. Radio futurologist James Cridland suggests that this type of personal story telling via radio is growing in many parts of the world, although *The Moth* is among the most well known and highest quality.[107] Individuals use the first-person audio form to recall things from their lives. A compelling example is *The Moth*'s May 5, 2015, broadcast. The story, "Mothering in Captivity,"[108] features actress Molly Ringwald telling the story of her own experience of being a mother whose daughter, Matilda, was accused of possibly becoming a bully at school. Such first-person perspective is a key element of effective narrative structure in experiential news. Reporters going on-site to the demolition of North Korea's nuclear test site in Ponggye-Ri in May 2018, for example, might produce a VR experience that would allow users to witness the demolition virtually.[109]

Withholding selected information can be an effective technique in building dramatic tension including in first-person narratives. Revealing key information slowly and to the surprise of the audience can help to keep listeners' attention, observes Hudson Valley story teller Jonathan Kruk.[110] This is a technique employed in the true-crime podcast *S-Town* that was launched in 2017.[111] By withholding key aspects of the narrative and effectively using foreshadowing, the sometimes-first-person podcast (e.g., "I'm told fixing an old clock can be maddening") keeps its audience listening to each chapter of the series until its conclusion.[112] Experiential news stories might use this technique of revealing key elements of a story gradually, but not linearly, as the user explores a 360-degree scene.

Another popular first-person story-telling podcast from NPR is *Snap Judgment*. *Snap Judgment* invites its audience members to tell their own stories, which are produced in audio format as podcasts or sometimes via text. An example of a successful text-based *Snap Judgment* listener story is "Marooned in the Mojave." In it, a story teller going by "cjross" tells his story about being alone in the Mojave Desert:[113] "Here I was, just where they'd warned me not to end up. I was stranded on foot in the middle of the Mojave Desert in August in the dead of summer. I was at the National Training Center (NTC) at Fort Irwin, California. NTC was desert warfare school."

Snap Judgment asks listeners to first pitch their story ideas for review by *Snap* editors. *Snap* offers guidelines on how to put together an effective pitch so that potential contributors can see whether their stories are right for the show. The guidelines include (1) having a character who tells the story, (2) brevity but enough detail to make it interesting, (3) plot points to keep the story moving, (4) a twist to add surprise, and (5) a solid ending to bring satisfying closure. Story tellers should avoid common tropes or clichés, such as saying, "Something really sad or tragic happened to me and I got over it by doing something positive."[114] Above all, *Snap* editors say, stories need to be true, an essential element of nonfiction and journalism, two sometimes overlapping domains whose boundaries seem to blur in much emerging experiential content.

In most mainstream journalism, news tends to feature facts drawn from a limited range of sources, especially those seen as authoritative.[115] Journalists often interview business leaders and government and elected officials and often only rely on average citizens when they are eyewitnesses to news events or in feature stories. Consequently, research shows, mainstream journalism has tended to lack diversity in its news sources. People of color, women, and members of LGBTQ groups, for example, are often underrepresented.

With experiential journalism, the voices of marginalized groups can find a more open environment in which to tell their stories or have their voices heard in the form of truthful, nonfiction content that is more commonly found in social networking media. In this way, the nature of what qualifies as journalism, and its diversity, can expand in an era of experiential journalism. Illustrative are recent VR productions that allow users to experience the isolation of solitary confinement from the point of view of an inmate, the fear experienced by victims of domestic violence, and the awe-inspiring experience of journeying through a forest of giant sequoias.[116]

Independent video productions illustrate the first-person approach as well. The documentary video work of Kelly Anderson of Hunter College's Integrated Media Arts MFA program makes effective use of first-person narrative. Her digital film "My Brooklyn," available on demand on Vimeo, provides an intriguing nonfiction, first-person perspective on the impact of gentrification in an urban New York landscape.[117] One of the techniques employed by the documentary that can be applied to experiential journalism to good effect is integrating the documentation of change that occurs in gentrification as observed through a personal narrative. In particular, in this story the film examines the redevelopment of Fulton Mall, an African American and Caribbean commercial district in Brooklyn, and on top of it are layered the actual experiences of the director on her personal journey living there.

Nonfiction experiential content can also blur the boundaries between education, journalism, and entertainment. Such is the case with the groundbreaking 2018 VR production "Hold the World" from Sir David Attenborough in which users can pick up, hold, and examine many of the eighty million artifacts contained in the Natural History Museum of London.[118] It illustrates compelling nonfiction experiential story telling and points the way for multisensory, interactive, and immersive journalism.

Virtual travel is another emerging VR genre, including virtual space travel, such as *Adrift*. These genres also suggest possible approaches that might effectively be used in designing news or journalistic VR narratives, especially in the realm of journeys that explore distant real-world venues.

Not only is VR useful in this regard. AR can also be highly effective in providing journalists the tools to layer information into visually compelling, interactive, and multisensory content and do so wherever the user finds him or herself: at home, work, or play. Illustrative of this potential is an AR project called AstroReality Earth, which is now in development. The AR app enables users to overlay a virtual view on a physical globe to learn a wide range of facts about the planet, such as information about the earth's flora, fauna, geology, anthropology, and meteorology. Journalists might use such an AR app to design interactive content that lets users explore the nature and ramifications of global warming, humans' role in it, possible solutions, or dire consequences of it if left unabated.[119]

Telling the same story or set of facts from more than one perspective is another option increasingly available in experiential journalism. This technique is more common in fiction story telling, perhaps most famously in the 1950 classic *Rashomon* in which Japanese film director Akira Kurosawa depicts a rape from multiple perspectives, including that of the victim, the assailant, and the witness.[120] Producers of linear-format video stories on television have experimented with offering alternative perspectives on single incidents or narratives. One effort that has captured much attention is Showtime's *The Affair*. Through various creative techniques, the series offers viewers different sides of the stories presented in each episode. Viewers can contemplate the complex perspectives, motivations, interpretations, consequences, and causes of the actions depicted onscreen. The multiperspectival technique could be employed to considerable effect in experiential journalism. Mainstream journalism has often tried to provide a single spine or narrative structure to any story or set of facts, and this single-viewpoint approach may fall short in revealing the complexity of truth in many situations or conflicts.

A compelling example of an online, multiperspectival, nonfiction narrative is *Highrise: Universe Within*. This interactive story invites users to explore the hidden but true digital lives of residents of high-rise apartments around the world. A user chooses from multiple vantage points by clicking on an onscreen avatar who acts as a guide. One option is an adult white male, another is a teenage boy, and a third is a nine-year-old black girl. I initially selected the girl as my guide and learned about how high-rise residents had organized via the internet to save their building in Mumbai, India; to start a labor movement in Singapore; and to prevent war in Baku, Azerbaijan.

The simulation model can be employed effectively in experiential journalism, allowing users to experience the same set of facts but from multiple points of view to learn how circumstances affect different persons in various ways depending on their circumstances and choices.

NONLINEAR NARRATIVE

As first-person, participatory narratives become more common, structural elements of stories delivered through the media are also shifting. Complex narrative approaches and structures are increasingly a part of the experiential content environment where viewers or users can choose which narrative path to follow and interact with in a variety of ways within the story. The *New York Times*, for example, has produced a report using augmented reality to enable users to engage in a three-dimensional exploration of the character and quality of the costumes of the renowned late artist David Bowie. Via a smartphone app, users see a 3-D, photorealistic, and interactive display of Bowie's costumes. Among those featured are costumes that Japanese designer Kansai Yamamoto created for Bowie on his Aladdin Sane tour.[121] Users can explore the details of the costumes and how they intersect with gender norms, among other aspects, all in a nonlinear manner; there is no set pathway through the narrative, and users can explore on their own.

Evangeline Morphos, professor of film at Columbia University, has conducted research that helps advance understanding of interactive video or film story telling.[122] She has noted that a growing number of video story tellers are using the internet to extend the viewer experience online, including adding interactive content that is possible over IPTV but is unavailable in standard TV. Program producers are also experimenting with extending content online in journalism story telling. However, the narratives are often only additional segments or stories, not necessarily interactive content—with the exception of interactives and interactive documentaries, which I discuss in detail in chapter 5.

Many of the narrative techniques and structures emerging in experiential media story telling were also explored in the 1960s and '70s as part of the new journalism movement.[123] Journalists such as Tom Wolfe used novel and novelistic approaches to narrative structure, first-person perspective, and other techniques to create a compelling form of journalism to engage the reader in a story.

Such stories similarly often feature narrative structures that are non-linear and may not contain an implied beginning, middle, or end. Cause-and-effect relationships may be unclear. Each individual may consume or experience the story in a variety of arcs or narratives or even contribute to the story, in some ways making the story a dynamic, living thing. News users may bring or add their own meaning to such a story. Missouri's Reynolds Journalism Institute is experimenting with telling news stories in nonlinear format via 360-degree video tools such as those of Viar360.[124] With Viar360, users can create VR stories on any subject. They can be designed as simulations, training, or informational narratives for journalism or education. In one case, a small Slovenian news organization, Večer, used Viar360 to create local sports coverage in VR format.[125] Users engage 360-degree video and photographs to explore the local soccer stadium and to watch the soccer match between NK Maribor and HŠK Zrinjski Mostar from omnidirectional perspectives. Such stories enable users to more fully understand for themselves the experience of being at a European Champions League qualifying match.

NATURAL USER INTERFACE

A natural user interface (NUI) enables intuitive human control over a computer or digital content. NUI features user actions that are natural, familiar behaviors, such as a spoken word, a nod of the head, the glance of an eye, or the wave of a hand. These controls are, in a sense, invisible to the user, as their use requires virtually no prior training, computer skill, or even awareness. Advanced VR platforms such as the Oculus Rift, the HTC Vive, and the Microsoft HoloLens employ NUI technologies such as head or eye tracking. NUI design brings significant advantages in how users interact with immersive content.

In one trial during the 1990s, I worked with Tobias Höllerer and Steven K. Feiner to develop a prototype of an immersive news-content navigation system based on user gaze approximation.[126] In this head-worn system, head position and orientation tracking enabled gaze approximation with virtual mouse control over virtual objects in the user's field of view. While in the system's VisualSelect mode, the user could navigate and select objects in the field of view by looking at an object for one-half second. Research indicates that this approach, like voice command, is an intuitive, natural user interface, particularly in a field setting.[127] This design especially supports hands-free content interaction in a mobile environment, which has particular value for persons experiencing news in a mobile environment because it does not require them to touch or click on content in order to interact with or navigate it. For journalists, this is a crucial design element to enable news consumers who increasingly rely on mobile technology to access and engage with immersive news more intuitively and with fewer physical actions.

In another project I directed a research group using a format known as video as input (VAI) to examine the use of digital imaging systems to identify users and then virtually immerse them into a computer-generated story environment.[128] User movements control the story narrative. Such natural user interfaces offer several advantages in that they require little in terms of user training, language use, or technical skill, providing a valuable experiential platform for children or across cultures. Such interface design is particularly empowering for persons with disabilities. A wide variety of stories can be told using this approach. For the study, we developed three. One is a cultural-discovery virtual tour of a Buddhist monastery in Tibet in which the user meets and interacts with a lama, or spiritual leader. A second allows the user to enter and explore a virtual evidence room for the then-unsolved murder case of JonBenet Ramsey. A third, which allows the user to approach and explore a virtual haunted house for Halloween, is meant for children to learn about safe trick-or-treating. This approach offers advantages for both the user and the story teller to improve their work. Users access content that they explore as desired. A journalist can create layered, multimedia content that reflects the complexity of a narrative that may be as of yet unresolved (as in the unsolved murder case) or the nuanced characters of diverse cultures. Such approaches enable news consumers to investigate the facts and draw their own conclusions rather than rely entirely upon the reporter. It is an approach that can engage crowdsourcing to help analyze and interpret evidence in complex, indeterminate, and evolving news situations (for instance, breaking news, such as during a natural disaster or humanitarian crisis involving migrants or refugees). This can help to foster an engaged public discourse, one of the long-standing goals of contemporary journalism.

NUIs, especially those that engage physical movement to control content interaction, can also support more active user participation. Nintendo's Wii and Microsoft's Kinect game systems operate in a similar fashion to enable game play through user movements, which can suggest directions for the design of more intuitive user control in experiential news. Some of these directions include designing news that allows news consumers to use simple gestures such as the wave of a hand or tilt of the head to interact with or navigate content or to design immersive news in which the user's physical activity is part of the story experience. For instance, VR treadmills that are now available allow users to physically move (e.g., walk) through virtual environments without actually moving in a 3-D space. Experiential news stories that journey to remote locations (a refugee camp, a UNESCO World Heritage site, a political protest) could enable users to virtually walk alongside the reporter or news source as if not only present at that location but physically engaging with it. The user could gain a better understanding of a location or event and gain the benefit of physical activity while consuming news.

Advances in voice-based audio interfaces have begun to transform the user media interaction experience in substantial ways. Speech-recognition technology dates to at least 1952 when Bell Labs developed Audrey, a machine that could recognize spoken digits.[129] Bell Labs scientists also invented Voder, an electronic speech synthesizer, even earlier, in 1936.

Contemporary voice-based systems include the Amazon Echo, introduced in 2015, and Google Home, in 2016. They are AI-enhanced, internet-connected, interactive microphones and speakers. Some forty-seven million Americans have bought a smart speaker as of 2018 (with one hundred million of the Echo devices sold; many homes have more than one).[130] Operating via the cloud (internet-connected remote data storage and processing), these platforms permit users to speak to the audio device and hear almost instant responses via a sophisticated speaker and microphone array. Users can engage media content or control intelligent home features via the systems by speaking. My interaction with the Echo indicates an effective audio experience that operates with a relatively good rate of reliability and audio fidelity, especially compared to voice-recognition systems I tested in the 1990s. Echo features the Alexa digital assistant, which understands many commands and usually does not require users to repeat or reformulate statements. It is important to use the syntax Alexa uses. This syntax is similar to how a human might speak to another human and is reminiscent of the human-computer voice interaction simulated on the 1960s television series *Star Trek*; Alexa's voice is even that of a woman (perhaps reflecting a sexist design assumption). Other technology companies have audio-interface digital assistants, including Microsoft's Cortana, Apple's Siri, and Samsung's Bixby. Facebook's voice-based digital assistant, Jarvis, features the voice of actor Morgan Freeman.

The devices are typically placed in the users' homes and are a few inches in height and diameter. Each is shaped in a cylindrical or spherical form to maximize the omnidirectional audio capacity of the device and contains multiple high-fidelity speakers and microphones. Each requires some initial setup to connect the device to a local Wi-Fi network. Google Home and Amazon Echo can recognize individual voices and support multiuser customization,[131] adding a layer of security and customizability. The Echo Show has added a camera and a touch-screen interface, making it an interactive and multisensory media platform. News media have taken increasing interest in this technology as a new platform.

Among the news media experimenting with the Echo Show are Scripps, Time, the BBC, the *Telegraph* and the *Evening Standard*. The *Telegraph*'s editorial team places five stories on its Echo Show daily bulletin, which are accessed by the user via voice command or touch. The *Evening Standard* showcases its "Going Out" section with both audio and video features that are accessed on demand, profiling shows, restaurants, and exhibitions in London.[132] Scripps's Food Network features audio- and video-formatted recipes for users who often engage the hands-free Echo while in their kitchen.[133]

Unless disabled, each device is always listening for its activation word. For the Echo, "Alexa" is the activation word. When the user says

"Alexa," the digital assistant "awakens" to listen for instructions and follow commands or interact with the user via voice. Users can request a particular song or station by saying, for instance, "Alexa, play Pandora," which the Echo then plays via streaming platforms such as Prime Music, Pandora, Spotify, or TuneIn.[134] Alexa can conduct limited internet searches, read Kindle e-books, deliver audio news from various news sources such as NPR or CBS News, report customized traffic conditions, give weather forecasts, provide information on local businesses, or supply sports scores and schedules. Voice and audio interaction via Alexa will soon operate in a wide spectrum of venues, from autonomous automobiles to the workplace, anywhere users might desire media engagement. Also, the Echo includes buttons on the top: one mutes the system's listening capacity, and the other engages the system in setup mode. The mute feature is especially significant as a means to protect user privacy, a crucial topic examined in chapter 7.

In journalism, a voice interface could enable new story experience formats. Users might explore stories interactively through conversation with a digital news assistant designed like Alexa. In the near term, such audio interaction would likely take the form of commands from the user. But as algorithms and artificial intelligence advance (as it is doing rapidly, which I discuss in chapter 4), the interaction would become more of a conversation. The *New York Times* has launched an interactive news quiz in which Alexa poses questions related to current items in the news, and the user responds orally, immediately finding out if they are right or wrong and tallying a score. New software tools such as NoHold enable developers (including journalists) to upload a text document on a topic, such as a news subject, into the software,[135] which then automatically generates a voice chatbot to engage a user in a conversation about that news story, answering questions about who is in the news, what happened, when, or where. Any news organization, large or small, could use such an approach to create voice-based, audio news interaction.

Combining audio and 3-D design within the user interface is a key component to a convincing immersive experience. As such, thoughtful design based on the six principles this chapter has laid out will make experiential news effective as a new, more engaging journalistic form. Integrating the interactive, immersive, multisensory, first-person perspective; nonlinear structure; and natural user interface into experiential news will give users satisfying news experiences and will maximize the potential impact of those experiences on the user's news engagement and comprehension of complex facts. As I discuss in the next chapter, research is beginning to test, document, and demonstrate how these design principles heighten the effectiveness of experiential news.

CHAPTER THREE

The News User Experience

Immersive, Interactive, and Multisensory

Digital design elements are converging in a news user experience that increasingly features immersive, interactive, and multisensory content. Digital stories, especially the experiential, immerse the user in 3-D audio, video, and imagery and encourage user action. These stories often offer a 360-degree, spherical field of view that can surround the story's user in an interactive and multisensory digital environment. This experience can make the user a participant in the story, and it signals a significant shift in the nature, form, and degree of public engagement in journalism.

In this chapter I examine the concept of a news user's experience and the principles that help to define it. Research suggests that the notion of "user" rather than "audience" is increasingly relevant to understanding how the public experiences and engages with digital journalism and media.[1] Three core principles are essential to the news user's experience. First, enabled by technological developments, news content can increasingly provide an enveloping, 3-D, 360-degree, immersive user experience. Whether experienced on a head-worn or other wearable display, in a room, or on a handheld mobile device, content is surrounding or enveloping users or giving them the ability to observe (see, hear, or touch) an entire spherical field of view or multisensory environment.

Second, through VR, AR, and other techniques, the digital, experiential story is evolving away from a traditional narrative, analog story model that assumes a passive user (a public who merely consumes a story) and toward active user participation. In the analog age, reporters or other story tellers would typically tell or show the reader, listener, or viewer what happened and to whom. They would describe the parameters or consequences of the issue or events. In place of this one-directional and fixed narrative model, more immersive and participatory story-telling approaches are emerging. These include, for instance, simulations in which audience members become more akin to users of software or mobile apps and experience the events for themselves through role-playing or making decisions as if a character in a nonfiction or fiction play.[2] The journalist's role evolves toward guide or sense maker, selecting (and verifying), organizing, and presenting the facts and helping the news consumer understand the context, implications, and significance of the environment being explored. Beyond journalism, game formats pit the user against or in tandem with others or a computer algorithm in an attempt to explore and understand the circumstances, people, and issues presented in the digital materials. Algorithms help generate models of alternate worlds in real time as a player acts or reacts to circumstances or other players, human or machine. Sandra Gaudenzi describes this new approach to the telling of the story as a transformation from "representing reality" in traditional film or analog documentaries to "co-creating reality in the digital interactive documentary."[3] Such an approach could be used in experiential journalism to allow users to see or hear what will likely happen if one or another course of action is taken, for instance, to explore how the Trump administration's suspension of the EPA clean water rules will likely impact America's drinking water supply.[4]

Related to this structural shift is the increasing use of first-person perspectives in news stories. In this sense, the user engages the story or content as a participant in or witness to events. Then, through social media, users converse with others about that story or news content, creating a new layer to the experience.

Third, the news user experience is multisensory. Content delivers not just sight and sound but increasingly can engage other senses, including touch, smell, and motion. Immersive media engage users in three-dimensional audio and video environments. None of these three dimensions is dichotomous. Each varies along a continuum or degree of immersion, interactivity, and multisensory engagement.

In the remainder of the chapter I consider the lessons that research and industry practice reveal about the increasingly immersive, interactive, and multisensory nature of the news user's experience. I begin with an examination of the development of the core experiential media technologies of virtual reality and augmented reality and then turn to what research tells us about the roles these new media forms can play in journalism.

VIRTUAL REALITY

Computer scientist, mathematician, and musician Jaron Lanier coined the term "virtual reality" in 1987,[5] but the historical roots of VR stretch much deeper. A. M. Turing Award winner Ivan Sutherland and his student Bob Sproull developed the first VR head-mounted display (HMD) in 1968, calling it the Sword of Damocles.[6] Among the first working VR platforms was the Sensorama, an arcade-style cabinet. Martin Heilig's 1957 invention allowed up to four people to experience "the illusion of reality using a 3-D motion picture with smell, stereo sound, vibrations of the seat, and wind in the hair."[7] His 3-D movies included *Dune Buggy*, *Motorcycle*, and *Helicopter*.[8] Three-dimensional photography, or stereo photography, traces back to at least Sir Charles Wheatstone's invention of the stereoscope in 1833.[9]

Science fiction writers have long imagined virtual environments enabled by advanced technology that could create virtual user experiences. In 1950 Ray Bradbury imagined an electronic virtual nursery in which children could simply use their imaginations to telepathically generate highly realistic and multisensory 3-D, interactive virtual environments.[10] Stanley G. Weinbaum described VR goggles in his 1935 story *Pygmalion's Spectacles*.

Researchers have defined VR systems as computer-generated simulations "of a three-dimensional image or environment that can be interacted with in a seemingly real or physical way by a person using special electronic equipment, such as a helmet with a screen inside or gloves fitted with sensors."[11]

Although most contemporary VR systems involve some sort of wearable technology, some volumetric VR systems enable the user to enter into a digital environment in which interactive content is projected onto and around the user typically via holography. One early volumetric system is called the cave automatic virtual environment (CAVE) and was developed in the 1990s at the University of Illinois. Still requiring the user to wear 3-D glasses, the CAVE is an immersive VR environment in which projectors direct still and moving images onto the walls of a room-size cube. The CAVE acronym is also an allegorical reference to the cave in Plato's *Republic* in which the philosopher considers how we perceive reality and illusion.[12]

VR offers journalists a powerful platform in which to re-create news events, taking the idea of photographic documentation of reality or acoustical recordings to an entirely new level in which the user can be virtually present at a news event and experience it as a virtual witness or even as a participant.

Experiential media can also trick the brain into sensing physical movement when, in fact, there has been none. In *Ripcoil*, a VR game produced for the Oculus Rift, the user becomes a virtual giant robot, interacting with visual objects such as flying discs, almost like being embedded in a huge game of ping-pong. Despite being anchored to a fixed location, the game creates a compelling sense of movement for the user. How journalism might use such an approach is an interesting question. In a science story about research in physics, a VR story might take the form of allowing the user to become an atom and virtually feel the pull or push of an electron.

AUGMENTED REALITY

Complementary to VR is augmented reality. It is a concept that was envisioned a century ago by science fiction writer L. Frank Baum, who is otherwise famous as the author of *The Wizard of Oz*. In a 1901 novel Baum describes an electrically generated "character marker" superimposed on others via HMD.[13]

In contrast to VR, AR systems layer digital information onto real-world scenes, for instance, visually, as seen through the camera in a smartphone or head-worn device in real time. AR uses a combination of technologies including motion tracking (of the user and the device), environmental understanding (enabled by computer vision), and lighting conditions to integrate digital content (audio, video, etc.) into the user's perception of the physical world. In exterior venues, AR can be geo-located via the line-of-sight-based global positioning satellite system (GPS). In indoor venues, Wi-Fi or other wireless technologies can be used to generate position-tracking or other locational information.[14]

Pattern recognition can be employed in either context. For example, via the camera app, an object can be visually identified, and associated AR can be displayed. In journalism, a user's camera running an AR app might recognize a visual pattern in an object—such as a photograph printed in a magazine or newspaper, a sign, a statue, or a building—to which some AR news content is digitally attached. The user might see, hear, or otherwise experience the AR content overlaid onto that object, augmenting the user's real-world engagement. For instance, a user standing near the Ambassador Hotel in Los Angeles might engage an AR-based story about the assassination of Robert F. Kennedy, which occurred there on June 5, 1968.[15] The AR narrative could be engaged via pattern recognition if the AR app recognizes the building or by geo-location if the app recognizes the GPS coordinates, either automatically triggering the narrative or doing so at the user's request.

Slow to develop, AR got a major boost in public recognition and adoption in July 2016 when Niantic's *Pokémon Go* introduced a mobile, geo-located, AR version of its popular video game. In the game, users of mobile devices engage interactively with AR digital objects that are geo-located throughout their own geographic spaces. One nonfiction feature of *Pokémon Go* is the PokéStop, a location in the game that is tied via algorithm to a real-world place of historical or cultural interest. One in the Hudson River town of Peekskill, New York, marks where in 1780 U.S. President George Washington gave official command of the nearby West Point military academy to Benedict Arnold. Newspapers today could populate their geographic communities with such AR content based on any past news coverage with a geo-location.

In 2018 Niantic introduced a new ability in AR called occlusion.[16] This capability allows virtual objects to hide partly or fully behind real-world objects. Occlusion may prove valuable in experiential news so that augments that are overlaid onto or behind real-world objects could seem more real (or for virtual games of hide-and-seek). For example, in a story about the World Cup, an augment such as a soccer ball placed virtually onto a pitch would disappear (at least in part) if a player stepped in front of it.

There is great potential to use AR in journalism and other nonfiction stories.[17] Digital humanities pioneer Bryan Carter of the University of Arizona has conducted extensive research on using AR and VR in culturally engaged stories.[18] Among Carter's most intriguing work has been his virtual exploration of the African American diaspora across the United States and around the world. In the 1990s he used VR to re-create the Harlem Renaissance of early twentieth-century New York City. More recently, Carter has advanced AR and VR experiential narratives to tell the stories of the many African Americans who traveled to Paris in the twentieth century and often made notable cultural contributions such as actress Josephine Baker. Carter is experimenting with AR tools to geolocate 360-degree and other imagery to give users a location-based, immersive, narrative experience about African Americans who lived or worked in different parts of Paris at different times. When the AR project is complete, "people will be able to relive those stories from anywhere."[19] Carter adds that users will be able to experience those stories across "multiple platforms, devices, and media, giving people the opportunity to express themselves and engage stories flexibly."[20]

Narratarium, an AR story research project at the MIT Media Lab, augments printed or aural stories with immersive AR experiences while making the user interface invisible. In the Narratarium, a table lamp "projects imagery on walls and ceilings to augment a variety of activities and products. For example, with a children's book, the system would know the page that was being read and provide appropriate sounds or animation."[21] In journalism a reporter might develop a Narratarium-style news experience that interested people could engage simultaneously in a group setting without the encumbrance of a mediated user interface. In other words, people could attend a news event virtually as if actually present and without an apparent user interface, just as people at the actual event would not have a user interface. As a point of comparison, the reader might consider a Narratarium-designed news experience based on the May 2018 arrest and tasering of NBA star Sterling Brown in Milwaukee for illegal parking. Students in a course on criminal justice could be virtually present within the video projected in their classroom as digitally transformed into a digital version of the parking lot where Brown was tasered and arrested.[22] Such a news narrative could give student users a highly empathetic shared experience in racial justice in America and a basis for a more informed discourse on the issues it raises.

A similar research project at Microsoft uses holographic AR "to project a life-size person into a room" with the user. The goal of the investigation is to determine whether such a virtual presence can make remote communication seem more intimate.[23] Preliminary evidence suggests that for users, the emotional impact of interactive 3-D experiences is profound and compelling. For journalism, producers should design enveloping 3-D news experiences to engage users deeply while resisting the temptation to design emotionally intimate and powerful 3-D news experiences that could overwhelm or detract from reasoned consideration of the underlying issues.

HAPTIC MEDIA EXPERIMENTS

Research on haptic technology also suggests important directions in immersive stories. One such research investigation at the MIT Media Lab is called the ListenTree. The project features tactile audio in a natural environment. Sound technology is embedded through a solar-powered transducer (power converter) into natural settings, such as a living tree, which, while unharmed, transmits the sound through small vibrations. Users lean their heads against the tree and thereby hear live audio communications. The tree becomes what the researchers call "a living speaker."[24] People "are able to both feel and hear crystal clear sound through bone conduction," project investigators report.[25] Bone conduction is likewise used in a variety of head-worn audio devices. The role of physical movement, or kinetic motion, in story formats is also an important aspect of inquiry such as this. Journalists might incorporate a haptic approach into their reporting on a range of topics, including the Japanese mindfulness therapy known as "forest bathing," which is based in part on sounds found in nature.[26]

Other research involves the integration of haptic technology into VR. Investigators are carrying out one such project at the Human-Computer

Interaction (HCI) lab at Germany's Hasso Plattner Institute. Researchers there have developed functioning prototypes of a device called Impacto,[27] which features an electronic band the user wears on the arm, leg, or foot. "Impacto simulates contact on the wearer so that he or she can actually feel objects virtually." Examples include a boxing game in which users can feel punches on their arms or a soccer game where users can feel the ball impact their feet or heads. Such simulated contact could be developed for a wide range of media experiences from entertainment to education to news.

Haptic bodysuits are also in prototype form. Building on the early exoskeletons of several generations ago, these digital, body-worn suits give the user a platform for a complete physical encounter in VR, AR, or MR (mixed reality, discussed below), feeling and interacting with virtual objects and environments.

Also in development is the use of "ultrahaptics." Ultrahaptics use focused ultrasound to project a sense of touch wirelessly, enabling AR or VR users to have a haptic experience with virtual 3-D objects.[28] Journalism could employ this approach to let users feel, through their mobile devices, virtual versions of objects in the news, for instance, the texture of microbatch textiles in fabric for clothing.[29]

WHAT THE RESEARCH TELLS US ABOUT EXPERIENTIAL MEDIA IN JOURNALISM

Much digital story-telling innovation arises from a growing body of academic research on immersive and interactive approaches to digital story telling as well as news industry experiments.[30] Researchers at the University of Southern California, for example, are among those developing immersive journalism and nonfiction games where users enter into the story and participate as a character in the digital narrative.[31] Researchers at the Tow Center for Digital Journalism at Columbia's Graduate School of Journalism are examining the nature and impact of VR journalism.[32] This growing body of research suggests several important implications for experiential news, as I discuss in further detail below. Overall, these investigations suggest that the users are apt to gain increasing empathy from experiential news, especially when that news features the type of design parameters outlined in the previous chapter.

Comprehension and learning are also heightened for those users engaging experiential news, and users are increasingly inclined to share their experiential news interactions via social networks.

Part of the motivation for journalists to create experiential stories is their potential to heighten user engagement in the subjects explored. In an international multimethod study of 1,916 nationals and expatriates in Qatar and the United Arab Emirates, Everette E. Dennis, Northwestern University's Rachel Davis Mersey, Qatar University's Justin Gengler, and I found that immersive media forms such as AR and 360-degree video are related to user engagement, including interest in sharing immersive experiences with others via social media.[33] Moreover, users are especially interested in sharing locally oriented experiential content. Cultural sensitivity in presenting immersive experiences is also a key to engaging users actively in this regard.

In an experiment with 129 subjects, Pennsylvania State University's S. Shyam Sundar, Jin Kang, and Danielle Oprean found that when users experience a story immersively rather than simply via text-based stories, they have a greater sense of presence in the narrative and heightened empathy for the story's characters.[34] "VR stories provide a better sense of being right in the midst of the story than text with pictures and even 360-degree video on a computer screen," states Sundar.[35] "This is remarkable given that we used two stories from the *New York Times Magazine*, which were high quality and rich in imagery even in the text version."[36] The Tow Center's Dan Archer and Katharina Finger report similar research findings.[37] In a study of 180 users, those experiencing 360-degree video stories showed heightened empathy, improved recall, and increased likelihood of taking political or social action, especially when those stories featured a single protagonist.

Immersion may transcend engagement. Frank Rose, author of *The Art of Immersion*, writes, "Immersion takes place when the audience forgets it's an audience at all."[38] Frank Rose is a senior fellow at the Columbia University School of the Arts, where he leads an executive education seminar in digital story-telling strategy. His approach suggests that immersion in a story can facilitate the user entering the psychological state of flow, which is often characterized by a sense of losing oneself in an activity.[39]

Research on immersive stories is beginning to reveal new insights into the nature and impact of experiential media content. "Certain types of television and cable/satellite programming may lend themselves to more immersive viewing," California State University's Pete Seel explains. "Sports, travel, action films, adventure and reality series are types of programs where viewers could viscerally experience being part of the action by sitting close to a UHDTV screen that fills their peripheral vision." Stories about health, science, and the environment might similarly exploit these capabilities. For instance, UHD could enable viewers to see invisible motion, such as the subtle color changes in a person's skin as blood flows beneath it.[40] Research suggests there is a great deal of motion in the world that is imperceptible to the unaided human eye. A glass vibrates from sound waves, and so does even a bag of potato chips. The naked eye cannot see these micromovements, but advanced video cameras can record the movement, and when the video is played back slowly or in close-up, the movement becomes apparent to the human viewer. The visual possibilities are almost endless and may be limited largely by only the imagination of the story creators.

Among the possibilities is creating experiential news that allows the user to engage medical or science stories in a much more participatory fashion than ever before. For example, an experiential story about an advance in cardio-pulmonary health care could allow the user to virtually enter a human body precisely rendered from data, much as the holographic human anatomy platform that has been developed using augmented reality for medical education at Case Western Reserve University.[41] Once inside, the user could see and interact with elements of the narrative at a cellular level to see exactly how a new medical technique could work.

Research also underscores how quality is an enduring priority for experiential content, especially in journalism. Studies show how quality intersects with both the principles of design outlined in chapter 2 and the impact that experiential news can have on the news user. Quality becomes even more important in an experiential news environment because experiential news can have such a profound impact on the news consumer.

Quality ensures the credibility or believability of experiential journalism. As such, quality has at least two dimensions, and these are especially critical in experiential news, as it can become increasingly indistinguishable from reality. First is the substance of the content, particularly its accuracy, truthfulness, and public relevance. Second is the level of production value, increasingly in the form of high-resolution and 3-D audio and video. High production value allows users to interact with the content, zoom in for a closer look, and move about virtually without experiencing degradation of the imagery (e.g., pixelation). For instance, a user might zoom in to a video shot from an extreme distance to examine small objects that are not even visible in the wider view or see details that are otherwise invisible. A nature documentary shot in UHD, for example, could allow the viewer to zoom in to wide-angle video of a lake and perhaps see a dragonfly buzzing just over the surface of the lake. In this sense, high-quality experiential media content can enable users to access the truths that are hidden in or layered into the larger narrative. The fundamental criteria of quality do not change in the new immersive environment, but they do become more complex and amenable to detailed user examination. They also become potentially problematic. In particular, as experiential media become increasingly multisensory and lifelike, the possibility that users will be convinced that what they are experiencing is real—which is the imperative for quality and especially truthfulness—is even more intense. Moreover, the lure of technology might distract producers and users from maintaining a critical eye, especially when encountering powerful, interesting content. Ethics and integrity must be paramount considerations for both users and producers of experiential journalism. Producers must resist the temptation to use these new tools unless they advance the quality of the reporting and presentation of the story.

AR JOURNALISM TRIALS AND DEVELOPMENTS

For nearly a decade, innovative news organizations have experimented with the use of AR in their content. Early efforts such as those at the *New York Times*, the *Philadelphia Inquirer*, and *USA Today* integrated AR overlays into printed content. For instance, on May 6, 2012, the *Philadelphia Inquirer* adopted AR as a vehicle for story telling by embedding a series of videos and other forms of hidden content throughout the newspaper. Readers using iPhones, iPads, or Android smartphones or tablets could install the *Inquirer*'s customized AR app, InquirerAR, to access AR content. The paper tagged several photos and advertisements in a special twenty-four-page section about the relocation of a renowned local arts organization, the Barnes foundation, featuring the art collection of Albert C. Barnes. The photos and ads were labeled with a miniature version of the *Inquirer*'s old-English-type *I*. Pointing the reader's digital device at a photo of Albert C. Barnes activated (through the device's camera) a video about the art scholar and collector who created the arts institution. In another instance, users pointed their digital devices at a photo of the west wall of room 23 in the Collection Galleries to activate a panoramic video, in the center of which is Henri Rousseau's *Unpleasant Surprise*.

News organizations have used a wide variety of off-the-shelf software tools and apps to create AR content and to enable users to access it. Among these AR tools are Aurasma (now called HP Reveal), which has been used by the *New York Times*, the *Wall Street Journal*, and the BBC; Junaio, used by *USA Today* and the *Boston Globe*; and Layar, used by the *Financial Times*, the *LA Times*, the *Philadelphia Inquirer*, Sky News, and the BBC.[42]

Media have also experimented with extending AR into the wearable arena. Vice News, based in Brooklyn, New York, has developed AR news reports that the user can experience virtually either in real time or recorded on demand.[43] In one case, Vice News's Tim Pool used Google Glass to report live, first-person video news coverage of protests and other news events via LiveStream technology.[44] Users could either travel along virtually with Pool on their mobile devices or desktops, or they could don their own Glasses to have a simultaneous immersive news experience as if present with Pool at the news events, seeing and hearing exactly what Pool saw or heard.

Building on the tradition of radio and television broadcasters delivering live coverage of breaking news and sporting events as well as others who have curated live reporting via social networking media, this technology may play an increasing role in twenty-first-century news reporting. Journalists may increasingly don wearable audio and video devices to stream immersive news reporting in real time. News consumers will be able to walk along virtually with those reporters as if on scene together. They may be able to use social media to message the reporter in real time and potentially ask questions that could be reported on in real time. Or news users might share their experiences via social media, widening the news-experiencing public. As Facebook expands its live-broadcasting capability, such real-time reporting may increasingly permeate the social networking environment, bringing with it the pitfalls and the potential of users who live stream violence whether as citizen reporters or as provocateurs.[45]

Advances in mobile technology have enabled developers to create 3-D AR content anchored into the user's physical environment, sometimes called mixed reality, or MR, a hybrid of AR and VR. Paul Milgram, H. Takemura, A. Utsumi, and F. Kishino argue that these forms lie along a continuum of virtuality, which delineates how the qualities of the real world can be represented artificially for user experiences.[46]

Anchoring AR or MR content into the user's physical space is rapidly becoming an important part of experiential news. Coinciding with the 2018 Winter Olympics in Seoul, South Korea, the *New York Times* launched its first anchored AR journalism experience. The *Times'* AR Olympics coverage allowed iPhone users to interact with a life-size, 3-D version of U.S. figure skater Nathan Chen, who appeared virtually before them. Users learn, through the experiential story, facts that are beyond direct human perception but decipherable in 360-degree and 3-D imagery delivered via AR: "From this view, you can see Chen's arms and legs are tight to his axis of rotation, which helps him spin faster than 400 r.p.m."[47] The extent of public engagement with this AR content is still to be reported, but external news media reports on the *Times'* new anchored AR content have been generally positive. One report of the AR coverage said, "*New York Times* readers may be watching with an extra level of appreciation for these athletes and everything they must do to win—or even just to land on their own two feet." One of the limitations for users of the AR story, designed using the Apple ARKit 2, is that access currently requires an iPhone.[48] The Android AR experience is still in development at this time.

CBS This Morning has also begun to integrate anchored AR approaches into its TV broadcasts. In early August 2017 the program broadcast live video of a 3-D animated AR visualization anchored in the CBS studio to help explain to viewers a rare total solar eclipse that would occur on August 21.[49]

AR also represents an opportunity for innovative news media to reach an audience they often have neglected: youths and children. Data shows that youths and children are interested in the news but rely largely on interpersonal communication, social networking, and mobile and school media to get news and information. Historically, mainstream professional journalism has targeted adults, assuming that citizens become news consumers as they age and develop adult concerns and responsibilities such as home ownership and families and start paying taxes. This assumption held for much of the twentieth century, but it has collapsed in the twenty-first century with the rise of social media and a new philosophy among millennials that if it is important, the story will find them.

Media observer Damon Kiesow underscores this point on his blog, writing, "Millennials like news. They just don't like you—the legacy newsroom."[50] He adds, "While much of the journalism being produced by legacy news organizations is of value to younger readers, it does not entirely speak their language nor fully reflect their lives." Research by the American Press Institute (API) confirms this growing disconnect between legacy news media and youths.[51] The data shows that most millennials are interested in news, including hard news. Almost all millennials, 89 percent, say that "keeping up with the news is at least somewhat important to them." Two-thirds, 69 percent, say they keep up with the news daily.

"Much of the concern has come from data that suggest adults aged eighteen to thirty-four—so-called millennials—do not visit news sites, read print newspapers, watch television news, or seek out news in great numbers," the API study finds. "This generation, instead, spends more time on social networks, often on mobile devices." More specifically, "Social media and mobile play a large role in millennial news consumption. 94% of those surveyed own smartphones. The average millennial gets 74% of her news from online sources."[52] These online sources include news content that is produced by legacy organizations but is distributed via social networks.

Usage of social media platforms is nearly ubiquitous in the United States and elsewhere. Nearly all (97 percent) of U.S. adults aged sixteen to sixty-four use social networks.[53] This is roughly a "tenfold jump in the past decade," reports Pew.[54] Pew Research reports document that Americans are increasingly using social media for a wide variety of purposes, including to access news and information that was once exclusively available through content media such as newspapers, television, and radio.

People use social media to get and share information about health, politics, communities, teenage life, and much more.[55] User engagement with experiential media on social networks is rapidly growing. Since the 2015 launch of 360-degree videos on social networks, users have demonstrated a growing appetite to both experience these videos and upload their own. In the first year of their availability on social media, users uploaded more than twenty thousand 360-degree videos on Facebook.[56] The number of 360-degree videos has doubled on YouTube since then.[57]

With demonstrated interest in mobile and wearable media and game formats, young people seem primed for an immersive news experience. And this is exactly the model NewsKid CEO Eva Dominguez is implementing.[58] A veteran Spanish journalist and an experienced digital story teller, Dominguez describes NewsKid as "innovative journalism for kids using augmented reality."[59]

Dominguez explains the challenge of doing experiential journalism for children. She says it is vital to explain the news so that children can understand it, so it is essential to provide context, but that must be done without making things too emotional.[60] To do this, Dominguez explains, NewsKid has built an adventure-story world featuring a character on a mission. NewsKid's focus is hard news. The NewsKid story world in 2015 explored why refugees were crossing Europe. "Children can enter and encounter news in an immersive experience," Dominguez says. "Children can play with objects, with each other, and interact with the character." The character will ask children for help. "This is empowering for the children," Dominguez says. The NewsKid experience includes print, animation, and other media including AR with a haptic interface. For the adventure-story world, Dominguez's team built a physical object of cardboard. "It is a cube that kids can interact with, and it has AR embedded within, accessible through handheld or wearable devices," she says. Children manipulate the cube to reshape it, and it becomes a spaceship. It serves as a vehicle through which the children enter "an exploration scenario where news happened."

NewsKid is international in orientation, Dominguez adds. Children can explore multiple international stories, including the Ebola crisis in Africa. Dominguez describes another animated NewsKid story as "an experiential interactive narrative that allows the user to control the climate history and destiny of six persons around the world."[61]

VR JOURNALISM TRIALS AND DEVELOPMENTS

VR news reporting dates to at least the late 1990s, which was when I worked with computer science colleagues and with my students to produce some of the first news reports using early, experimental versions of 360-degree digital cameras.[62] Produced in collaboration with APBNews .com, my students used 360-degree photography to report on the 1999 police shooting of Amadou Diallo in the Bronx, New York. While users could view the 360-degree photos via HMD, they could also see and navigate the spherical content on desktop computers. HMDs were not yet widely available and offered only low-resolution experiences for the user. Moreover, HMDs were very expensive in the 1990s, at $10,000 or more per unit. Among the challenges we confronted in these trials were the low resolution and limited portability of the early 360-degree cameras. The cameras had never been used outside their computer science developer's laboratory, they had no portable power source, and lacked a mechanism for holding the camera. Moreover, there was no stabilizer to ensure the video would be smooth upon viewing, there was no built-in microphone to capture audio, and there was no viewer to see what the video looked like in real time. It could be viewed only after being recorded, and then it appeared as a sphere. Special software was needed to unwrap the video, and this took several minutes initially due to the limited processing power and storage capacity of the laptop being used. In Rube Goldberg style, my students jerry-rigged a mechanism to carry the camera on a monopod, including a portable battery-powered source of DC electricity, a synchronous and omnidirectional microphone, and a backpack computer that was linked to the camera to record the omnidirectional video.

Reporting on stories required additional communication with sources to explain how the 360-degree cameras worked and what they saw. The intention was to use the system ethically and effectively as a reporting tool, and the newness and novelty of the 360-degree cameras required first educating the sources so they could give their informed consent to be video recorded in 360-degree video and photographic format.

Since these pioneering efforts, a growing number of news organizations have introduced VR journalism, or at least 360-degree video reporting, including the *Wall Street Journal*.[63] Using the Samsung Gear VR headset as a viewing platform, one *Wall Street Journal* VR report is the immersive feature, "Virtual Reality Video: Backstage with a Lincoln Center Ballerina."[64] Another, titled "Japan is Changing How We'll Grow Old," explores the demographics of an aging Japanese population as well as its impact on society and life in its diverse communities.[65] A notable aspect of the VR report, like most other contemporary immersive journalism, is that it does not require the user to don VR goggles to experience the 360-degree video report. Instead, a smartphone can play the immersive video, with the user moving the phone left, right, up, or down to view any portion of the complete scene or using a touch-screen interface to move about the panoramic image by sliding one's finger left, right, up, or down. On a desktop or laptop computer, the user can navigate the video by moving the mouse in similar fashion. A reporter provides audio narration to give interpretation and analysis to the video accompanied by ambient audio captured on location along with the 360-degree imagery and video, overlaid graphics, and text.

The *New York Times* introduced its first VR journalism story in 2015 with the production of "The Displaced," which uses VR in the form of 360-degree video to tell the story of three children displaced by war in Sudan, Syria, and Ukraine.[66] In "The Displaced" viewers see and hear the displaced children speaking in their own voices, in their own languages, and with the ambient sound of the refugee camp. The reporter does not provide any voice-over narration. Instead, the reporter's role is that of editor and videographer. The words spoken by the children are translated into English and displayed as subtitles on the screen. The viewer can look around anywhere in the spherical video and gain visual appreciation of the devastating effects of war. The VR reporting is compelling. The *Times* has produced related immersive productions on stories from the Middle East, including "Pilgrimage," which invites users to experience Mecca and Medina, Islam's holiest cities.[67] Through VR, users can "journey along the pilgrimage destination of Earth's 1.6 billion Muslims."[68] The production was recorded in partnership with leading Italian photographer Luca Locatelli.

To enable its readers to experience the new VR story, the *Times* shipped one million subscribers free Google Cardboard devices. Users then inserted a smartphone into the device and ran the NYT VR app or the VRSE app to access the 360-degree video stories.[69] In late 2016 the *Times* expanded its use of 360-degree video reporting, launching the Daily 360.[70] Produced in collaboration with Samsung, the Daily 360 provides users with 360-degree video reports on a wide range of topics.[71] The 360-degree stories are typically short in length, about one to two minutes, with audio narration or the voice of the subject, ambient sounds, and textual overlays to help advance the narrative. Stories on the Daily 360 have included "Lascaux Caves, Paleolithic and New Again" about early cave paintings in France; "Agony in a Venezuelan Mental Hospital" about the horrifying existence in medical facilities without medications; "The Deadly District in Chicago" about gun shootings in Chicago; "Standing Rock Celebrates Halted Pipeline" about the protests by Native Americans and others in opposition to construction of the North Dakota oil pipeline; and "Inside the Trump Immigration Ban Protests."[72]

Journalists creating 360-degree video news have faced a number of challenges. The platforms continue to evolve, and the requisite hardware and software tools keep advancing, so editorial and production staff have needed to learn and master new skills. There has been a significant need to develop a narrative grammar for 360-degree video news stories as well. The breadth of hard news and feature news coverage using 360-degree video is also helping develop news consumers' familiarity and comfort with immersive journalism. Donning a VR headset does not come naturally for many news consumers, and it requires them to take an extra step to experience news in 360-degree format. News consumers are gradually developing new news habits that are compatible with experiential media and their technological requirements, and the overall framework will continue to evolve. Just as television developed greatly from the late 1940s to the 1960s and news production and consumption patterns shifted toward early-evening viewing, behavioral patterns for those inclined to experience immersive news formats will take time to develop. Producing experiential news across a wide spectrum of story types will help to bring the format into the mainstream of both news production and consumption.

The editorial leadership of the *Times* is convinced that experiential story telling is a key part of creating "journalism that stands apart."[73] *Times* executive editor Dean Baquet has explained part of the rationale for his news organization's commitment to immersive stories. On *CBS*

This Morning he described his paper's VR report about a shooting by a U.S. Border Patrol agent of a teenage boy standing on the Mexican side of the border structure in Nogales, Texas.[74] Baquet said the paper could and did provide a verbal explanation of the situation and its context as well as photos and standard videos. But, he noted, nothing could provide such a compelling sense of the complete story as a 360-degree video. It permits the user to grasp the towering size of the existing border structure and the likelihood that the boy, armed with a rock, could have posed a realistic threat to the agent standing about forty feet away on the U.S. side of the fence and separated by the slatted-steel structure some eighteen to thirty feet in height. Experiencing the VR report, the user gets a clearer sense of whether the use of deadly force by the border agent was justified.[75] José Antonio, the sixteen-year-old Mexican boy, was shot ten times and died.

Editors at the *Times* report a surge in demand for experiential content since the debut of its VR story-telling initiative.[76] Editors said, "NYT VR had the most successful app launch ever at the *New York Times*. Throughout the weekend, and in the days since, the #nytvr hashtag on Instagram has been filling up with photos of people of all ages with our cardboard V.R. viewers stuck on their faces." Comments on social media about the VR experience have been overwhelmingly positive. One Tweet was "OMG THE FUTURE" while another was "Blew my grandparents' minds."

Journalism with 360-degree video is generating traffic. As of August 8, 2017, "Walking New York," a 2016 *New York Times* feature-oriented VR production was among the ten most viewed 360-degree videos on YouTube, with 3.8 million views of the six-and-a-half-minute video. Similarly, *USA Today*'s "Experience the Blue Angels" 360-degree video has generated 7.8 million views on YouTube since the eight-minute video's release in 2016.

Meanwhile, hard-news-oriented 360-degree stories have generated significant, though somewhat lower, viewership. For instance, the *Times'* "A Harvest Underneath the Ice," in early 2017 generated seventy-four thousand views on YouTube by August 8, 2017. It examines the challenges that Inuit fishermen face in harvesting blue mussels in ice caves, and audio of the cracking ice enhances the user's sense of presence.

Other major news providers are also experimenting with VR story telling, at least in the form of 360-degree video reporting. Among those news media are the Associated Press, CNN, the Gannett Company and its flagship *USA Today*, CBS News, and Univision.[77] To create its VR reports, the AP partnered with the LA-based firm RYOT, a company aiming to "Build the world's largest 360° news network," according to CEO Bryn Mooser.[78] Among the AP's VR productions is "Seeking Home: Life Inside the Calais Migrant Camp," an immersive report that gives audiences a 360-degree view of the Calais camp, presenting migrants and refugees preparing for a dangerous journey aboard freight trains heading across the English Channel into the United Kingdom.[79] The AP has also produced an animated 360-degree report on the latest scientific theories of how Alzheimer's disease develops in the human brain.[80] With its initial success, the AP launched a VR news channel in 2016.[81] Since its launch, the AP has produced and published more than one hundred VR news reports, which have been met with growing public interest.[82] As of this writing, 1,271 people have subscribed to the VR news channel. Some of the most-viewed VR news reports include "Mars on Earth: Simulation Tests in Remote Desert of Oman," with more than 9,700 views; "Superfunds: Harvey's Toxic Sites Underwater," with more than 1,100 views; and "Hurricane Irma Prompts Miami to Remove the Homeless Against Their Will," with more than 7,600 views. The VR news reports are typically about one to three minutes in length and feature linear, navigable, 360-degree footage and audio with text and graphic overlays.

A growing number of news organizations both large and small as well as regional and local news media such as Seattle's KING5 television are producing 360-degree video. These experiential news reports tend to be locally focused and of similar length to those of the AP VR news channel.

Among the larger news organizations with a dedicated VR news unit is CNN, which live streamed a 2016 presidential democratic debate via 360-degree video that viewers could watch on Samsung Gear VR headsets, which were then available in an estimated 200,000 U.S. households.[83] Following on this success, in March 2017 CNN launched a dedicated VR news production unit, CNNVR, which tends to offer a blend of feature and hard news productions.[84] Among those produced and published in 2018 are "The Capital in Full Bloom," a land-based tour of the cherry blossom festival in Washington, DC; "Rocky Mountain Rescue," a helicopter flight in Steamboat Springs, Colorado, from which a rescue training session is carried out on the snow-capped mountain; and "A City Runs Dry," a look at the increasingly dire water situation facing Cape Town, South Africa.[85] Like those of the AP, the reports are linear, navigable, 360-degree videos with audio, running about two minutes in length, that are viewable on a mobile device, desktop computer, or VR headset.

Gannett is among the largest cross-platform news conglomerates in the United States, operating newspaper, television, and online enterprises across the country. Reflecting the immersive nature of experiential content, in 2015 Gannett produced a report titled "Bringing You into the News: The State of Virtual Reality in Journalism."[86] The report looks at a series of case studies in VR use in news media around the world, including the BBC, *Frontline*, Fusion, and Gannett. It also provides the results of a VR usability study in which "a researcher presented four VR clips to nine frequent news users between the ages of 25 and 52. The users watched the first three clips in a Gear VR headset and then saw the fourth on a Cardboard viewer." The "impressionistic findings of this survey show that people enjoyed being able to witness stories first hand and that they found the content highly engaging and rewarding. However, the participants also noted that the experience is isolating and all-absorbing." Gannett plans to make VR story telling a part of its daily news coverage.[87]

Although the impressionistic findings offer some positive signs as to the effective production and use of VR journalism, there are a number of potential problems or limitations worth noting. First, the study looking at user reactions was based on only four total VR news clips and involved only nine subjects. Moreover, the nine were frequent news users. This small sample size and the fact that the subjects were frequent news users limits the generalizability of the findings. Second, three of the clips were experienced on a Samsung Gear VR headset and one on a Google Cardboard viewer. The state of the technology (as I will discuss in detail in chapter 7) has advanced far beyond these very limited VR headsets, so users' experiences today could be far different than at the time of the study. Again, this limits the generalizability of the findings, although it is likely that viewers using the much-higher-resolution VR platforms of today would react even more positively or at least more strongly. Finally, the limited topicality of four clips also restricts the generalizability of the findings.

A host of other VR and 360-degree video narrative initiatives are underway, many featuring documentary content. In the forefront of such efforts is the Sundance Institute's New Frontier Story Lab.[88] In 2015 New Frontier began experimenting with the nonfiction story-telling potential of ocular evolution, that is, the development of human vision from the earliest visual ability to that of the fully formed human eye.[89] New Frontier curator Shari Frilot says, "Ocular evolution really is a leap in the ability of storytellers to bring the viewer inside the frame of the story world." It is possible that with immersive visual forms, there will emerge new possibilities for story tellers to tap into the full capabilities of human vision. One New Frontier project is *Assent*, a VR documentary about the Chilean dictatorship of the 1970s. Oscar Raby, producer of *Assent*, explains that the VR project tells the story of his father, who was an army officer in the Chilean military during this period: "In 1973, my father witnessed the execution of a group of prisoners by the military regime in Chile, the Army that he was part of."[90] *Assent* takes the viewers virtually into this story space, where they can witness what happened for themselves. The VR simulation allows viewers to witness an execution, an emotionally powerful experience. Raby explains that the VR documentary engages the viewer in a deep intrapersonal conversation. As the VR documentary unfolds, viewers can reflect on how their bodies react to different types of stimulation. As VR, *Assent* enables viewers to consider how their thought processes are constructed through the experience.

Journalists will confront fundamental decisions when designing emotionally powerful VR experiences and should take care to not blur the boundaries of fact and opinion. It is essential to label re-creations or simulations as distinct from strictly factually based immersive content that draws on archival footage so that users are not confused. Research indicates that the public cares about the entangling of fact and opinion and values the clear demarcation between the two in news content.[91] A 2018 example from the *New York Times* illustrates the effective and ethical use of AR to re-create a virtual crime scene.[92] In its report, the *Times* used verified evidence from multiple sources to create in AR an interactive, multisensory digital version of an apartment in Douma, Syria, where military forces of President Bashar al-Assad executed a chlorine attack on April 7, 2017. Among the materials and sources the *Times* relied upon, which are articulated in AR re-creation, is a report from the United Nations, which states that forty-nine people were killed in the attack. Also, the *Times* states that it drew upon "visual evidence unwittingly provided by the Russian reports." The *Times* then combines those pictures with "other videos filmed by Syrian activists." Finally, because of the complexity of creating the AR in precise, accurate fashion, the *Times* collaborated with Forensic Architecture, a research agency of Goldsmith, University of London, to build the AR experience. In sum, the *Times* clearly labeled its experience as an AR re-creation of a crime scene, sourced its work extensively, provided detailed transparency on its reporting, and ensured the accuracy of its AR content by collaborating with a partner that possessed the requisite technical skill both in AR and in architecture (a dimension central to the story).

Many 360-degree video or VR productions emerge as a product of the increasing popularity of transmedia content production, that is, presenting the same story or experience across multiple platforms including games, books, cinema, television, and interactive multimedia content. There are many examples in which journalism has been produced first in one medium, such as for a newspaper, and then reproduced for other media. This process is common in traditional mainstream news media, where newspapers often first publish stories using text and photos and then radio and television stations or networks translate those stories to more audiovisual formats, usually adding some original reporting featuring recorded audio and video. This is distinct from the concept of transmedia story telling in which a multimedia product "communicates its narrative through a multitude of integrated media channels."[93]

The transmedia pattern is increasingly apparent with experiential media. For example, in 2016 the *Washington Post* published its first hard-news AR story, an experience that enabled users to better understand the death of Freddie Gray at the hands of police in Baltimore.[94] The AR report followed the *Post*'s earlier coverage of the Gray killing that had been published in the paper and online in more traditional formats. The *Post* now uses AR regularly as a reporting tool.[95] Likewise, the *New York Times* designed a 360-degree video titled "Life on Mars" that lets users explore the lives of NASA astronauts training in Mars-like conditions on the Mauna Loa volcano in Hawaii.[96] Produced in 2017, the 360-degree transmedia report is based at least in part on more traditional content that the paper published in 2014.[97] It is unclear at this point whether such transmedia VR content will prove valuable and sustainable for journalism or will remain simply more of a promotional gimmick that exploits a new technical capability.

International journalism pioneer Eva Dominguez says a key challenge confronting journalists in creating immersive, 360-degree photo or video stories is determining precisely when and how to use the technology.[98] Panoramic images can help the user feel or experience a story, she explains, but sometimes they may be a distraction. Journalists should avoid using these tools simply because they are available, Dominguez warns. She cautions against the overuse of 360-degree images in news reporting and explains that using 360-degree images requires thoughtful execution. To illustrate this, Dominguez points to a report in which a journalist provided a voice-over to a 360-degree photograph, simply repeating what could be seen. The narration added little value to the image and thereby might even have detracted from audience engagement.

"Immersive media are so sensorial," Dominguez explains, that journalists must be careful in how they use them within a story. Looking back in time since the advent of electronic media such as radio, Dominguez reflects, "We as storytellers have evolved from telling to showing to experiencing." Immersive media allow the audience or user to experience a news event. With a 360-degree photograph, it may even be annoying to hear someone telling you what you can already see for yourself. A key notion here is that journalists using experiential media forms should employ them when giving users the ability to witness events or circumstances or when the issues can increase understanding. If the only gain is heightened emotional impact, then the preferred option may be to not use experiential formats.

Dominguez also notes that there are important differences in various forms of immersive media. Panoramic photographs and video are different from VR, she explains. A 360-degree photograph or video is a photographic or video record of an actual event or location. The user might look around the scene in a 360-degree photo or video, but unless it was recorded with stereoscopic cameras, there is no real three-dimensionality, only directionality. The distinction between 360-degree directionality and three-dimensionality is worth noting here. In a typical 360-degree photograph or video, users can pan left or right and tilt up or down in the omnidirectional field of view. But they cannot move forward or closer to the subject or objects in the field of view (except to click on a hot spot or link to move to a new position). The user lacks the ability to move about in the 3-D space. I discuss this notion in detail in the paragraphs that follow and consider the tools needed to capture and produce such 3-D news content.

Unlike 360-degree photos or video, VR is typically a computer-generated representation or simulation of a real or imagined world, although advanced 360-degree cameras with position tracking are capable of generating photographic or videographic VR environments. Full VR has three-dimensionality, and the user has six degrees of freedom (DoF) of movement within it. DoF refers to "the ways an object (or person) can move within a space. There are a total of six degrees of freedom in a three-dimensional space. The six DoF can be divided into two categories, rotational movements and translational movements. Each category has three DoF. Both orientation tracking (rotation) and positional tracking (translation) are required to have a fully immersive VR experience."[99] Photos and video in 360 degrees provide users with rotational movement, meaning users can look about in all directions. Users are in a fixed position within the spherical image but can turn their head left and right (yaw), tilt it up and down (pitch), and lean it side to side (roll). But, because of the fixed position, they lack translational movement, meaning users are unable to move about the 3-D space. They cannot move forward or backward, up or down, or side to side. Creating six DoF in the user experience requires substantially more investment in video acquisition, production, and postproduction.

As such, the role of VR in journalism is very different from that of spherical photography and 360-degree video. VR with six DoF gives journalists the opportunity to design stories where news consumers can look and move in three dimensions. These might be stories that allow the user to virtually visit and explore a remote site. Photos or video in 360 degrees that feature only three DoF limit the journalist to creating stories in which the user can look around but not move about a scene.

Mixed-reality and AR formats in which digital objects are layered into the user's real-world experience present the possibility of blurring the boundaries between the artificially generated and the directly recorded. MR can fundamentally redefine the user experience in journalism and challenge editors and reporters to reconsider the parameters of ethics in an experiential environment.

ROOM-SCALE VR, SHARED EXPERIENCE, AND BEYOND WEARABLES

For much experiential media, the user is stationary, often seated. This is both for safety and because the content and the technology may not support user motion. When fully installed, however, the Oculus Rift and HTC Vive headsets and similar systems support room-scale VR and user movement. This means the content is anchored to the user's physical space, and the user is not restricted to sitting. These VR systems include geo-tracking technology that enables the user to move about in a room and interact with the immersive content. For instance, "by placing two Oculus sensors on opposite sides of a 5-by-11 room," the Oculus system permits the user to engage the VR content while moving about.[100]

Similar in user experience is the Taiwan-based HTC Vive VR system: "Third-party developers can tap into the Vive programming environment to develop their own applications." An HTC spokesperson says, "Its software can map 3D space, which would let virtual objects respond to real-world ones—similar to Microsoft's HoloLens room-scanning tech."[101] The HTC Vive also has two hand controllers and a front-facing camera, which allows users to see the real world around them, bringing the experience closer to mixed reality.

VR journalism pioneer Nonny de la Peña, founder of Emblematic Group, has developed full-room-scale VR journalism content.[102] From exploring the melting glaciers of Greenland to the day Florida teenager Trayvon Martin was killed, her VR stories put users inside the story and allow them to move about in a 3-D space. In one experience, the user finds out viscerally what it is like to walk "in the shoes of a patient entering a health center for a safe and legal abortion."[103]

Full-room-scale VR can be a vital element of experiential news. Journalists can design narratives that allow users to experience an interactive scenario that involves moving about a space, such as a crime scene, a news venue (for instance, Sentosa Island, the location of the Trump-Kim summit in Singapore June 12, 2018), or some even more remote location that is pertinent to the news (such as the International Space Station).

Also entering the experiential market are Magic Leap and Avegant, both of which use an approach based on light-field technology.[104] Light-field technology uses cameras that capture and process light intensity and direction to generate 3-D images that allow user-controlled perspective, such as peering around a referee in live-action MR sports.[105] Light-field technology also allows users to move any distance from a virtual object and still see it and interact with it in a 3-D format. Other MR approaches often limit the distance from which a user can see or otherwise engage virtual objects, which can disappear if users move too close to them.[106] For journalism, this will enable the design of news content involving 3-D objects, such as an artifact in a story about an archeological discovery, a rare museum piece, or the molecular structure of a rare virus, which the user can explore in extreme-close-up high resolution.

Next-generation display systems may extend VR, AR, and MR capabilities beyond the current head-worn individual-user experiences. One approach involves the use of volumetric displays, which can project virtual 3-D objects into a space or volume without requiring the user to wear a headset.[107] They can present to the viewer lifelike 3-D objects—either animated, photo-realistic, or interactive—that appear physical or solid in a 3-D space or volume, such as a room, where a user or group of users might view and interact with the objects.[108] Volumetric displays offer the potential to design news stories that give users a convincing level of presence without requiring VR headsets and that extend the capability from the individual level to an interactive group environment where multiple people can simultaneously engage in networked, immersive media experiences.

Researchers are experimenting with various technologies to create volumetric displays, ranging from lasers to fast-moving light-emitting diodes (LEDs) that fuse multiple images into one visually solid 3-D object. The development of volumetric displays has been slow due to technical challenges and cost, but they are gradually progressing toward the commercial marketplace. At least one early market entrant has introduced a consumer volumetric display platform in beta form.[109] Lightform is a commercial platform whose technology uses light to project AR into a space.[110]

One volumetric design may blend AR, MR, and VR into a convergent form dubbed extended reality (XR). Holographic projection is one approach to XR. In development at the MIT Media Lab, Holo-video is an example of one such prototype XR system.[111] Employing holography, Holo-video displays 3-D virtual objects that the viewer sees without wearing a headset.

Volumetric display technology presents significant implications for journalism. By enabling immersive user experiences without the encumbrance of a headset, news consumers who are reluctant to don HMDs could still engage with fully immersive and interactive experiential news. Built around original real-world reporting using volumetric capture—video that captures a full 3-D space and all the objects within it—experiential stories presented on a volumetric display platform could give news users a compelling sense of collaborative presence at news events from press conferences to political protests.

ADVANCING EXPERIENTIAL NEWS CONTENT

Mediated content is increasingly interactive, participatory, multisensory, and nonlinear. Advanced media platforms, including AR, MR, VR, XR, 360-degree imagery, UHD video, and immersive audio increasingly give the user the ability to step literally and figuratively inside a story. Digital enterprises such as Google and Facebook are developing consumer-friendly and professional systems for creating and experiencing such immersive content. Audiences are transitioning to the role of users or participants in mediated content. This is a significant departure from much of the previous century, when news consumers were generally passive receivers of news content and were framed at least in part as potential targets of advertisers seeking to sell them goods and services.

News media are increasingly offering their audiences the opportunity to enter into and interact with experiential journalism. Industry pioneers in journalism and other media domains are experimenting with experiential story-telling formats in news and beyond. These efforts represent a rare opportunity to reinvigorate the core mission of journalism with content designed to engage the public in a robust and interactive exploration and discourse on the issues and events that are central to democracy.

CHAPTER FOUR

Encoded Content

It is almost tautological to say that digital content, including experiential journalism, is encoded, or programmed for computerized devices and systems. As such, it is designed for digital platforms and distributed digitally, usually in compressed format, and accessed via a variety of devices, from mobile phones to tablets and desktop computers, as well as presented on digital TV and wearable displays. When converted back to analog form, audio is played back for human listeners on various types of speakers, from ear buds to sound-canceling headphones to stereophonic sound systems that accompany TV displays. Compression is used to enhance digital content storage, search, retrieval, and distribution.

But the encoded nature of digital media implies far more than simply a representation of the actual content in pixels, bits, and bytes. The code rests on or derives from an entire language of computerized instructions that enables new functionality. Moreover, this functionality intersects with both the design and substance of the content. The impact of code on journalism and media content is apparent in at least four arenas: geo-location, algorithms, Big Data, and artificial intelligence. Each of these has important implications for the development of experiential journalism.

GEO-LOCATION

Many digital stories incorporate geographic location. This is facilitated in the digital domain by the fact that most mobile devices that are connected to a network can automatically tag photos and video with geo-location information as metadata, that is, descriptive data about the content, such as time, date, place, or creator.

Increasingly oriented to mobile technologies, a variety of social media are utilizing the geo-located nature of much internet usage to generate geographically anchored content and communication. Snapchat, for instance, has utilized this capability by creating and offering user story tellers "geofilters" that can place "snaps" for those viewing the stories.[1] Likewise, Facebook's "safety check" is a geo-location feature: during disasters, the network uses the location data reflected in the mobile user's access to Facebook to send the user an alert as well as its safety-check message and a brief textual description of the crisis. The Facebook safety-check homepage offers this example of the message: "You appear to be in the area affected by Typhoon Ruby (Hagupit)."[2] Facebook users are invited to click on either a green button indicating "I'm safe" or another button indicating "I'm not in the area." The safety check is a way for users to tell family and friends that they are safe, how many friends or family are in the affected area, how many have reported they are safe, and how many have not yet marked that they are safe. "Paris Terror Attacks," the safety check message alert on November 13, 2015, marked the first time that Facebook deployed the geo-located app during a terrorist attack. Some critics have questioned whether Facebook's safety-check app may represent an incursion into user privacy. While the safety-check app gives users the opportunity to apprise family and friends of their whereabouts and status during an emergency, it also signals the possible new normal of being tracked continuously in a mobile, increasingly virtual society. Both governmental agencies and industries conduct this type of tracking, and the data could be subject to subpoena or might emerge as a source for news stories.

Needless to say, journalism has a long tradition of creating geographically based stories. News stories often begin with what is called a dateline, a brief statement of when and where the story originates (or where the reporter filed it). In the twenty-first century, the advent of so-called hyperlocal journalism amplifies this tradition. Hyperlocal news is particularly common in the online and mobile platforms, where coverage can focus on the very local, such as a neighborhood, small town, or village.

Content creators across a broad range of media are exploring how to use emerging digital tools such as AR to tell experiential, location-based stories. The National Film Board of Canada (NFB) has created a mobile app called BarCode (CodeBarre in French, a reference to digital bar-code scanners) that enables users to find stories in everyday objects in the world around them.[3] Thirty directors created the app's one hundred multimedia stories, some of which are nonfiction and others more fanciful. Users can employ the app on their mobile devices, which they point at an object in their immediate surroundings—such as a house, a coffee maker, or an egg—and see a video that tells a story about the object. Users can find stories in a wide range of subject domains, including culture, entertainment, food, sports, work, and home. Users can also employ the app to contribute their own location- and object-based stories.

Such linking of mobile content algorithmically to location-based news is an AR capability that news media might increasingly pursue.[4] There are several reasons for journalists to utilize this capacity in their news reporting. A large portion of reporting, perhaps even the majority of it, includes pertinent location information, such as where a meeting took place, the site of a news event, or where a photograph or video was captured. The location information is typically automatically included in the metadata about a photo or video, including spherical images, unless this feature has been turned off in the privacy settings. Therefore, attaching those images to locations via algorithms is an efficient process and requires no additional effort on the part of the reporter. News consumers can then access geo-tagged AR news on location or remotely with their mobile or other networked digital devices. This locational-aware news can give news consumers greater understanding of the context for what is being reported. Moreover, it can help situate the news so that consumers will understand the potential links between various stories or events, even where news has occurred—or at least has been reported—in their communities. Over time, geo-tagged AR news reporting could be used to automatically generate news maps for entire communities. News consumers could begin to glean a better understanding of how the news media are reporting, or not reporting, about an entire community; for instance, are certain parts of a community being neglected or more heavily reported over time?

BIG DATA AND CODE

In addition to geo-location, several other code-related factors are reshaping news content as it shifts toward an experiential future. One of the most significant factors is the advent of Big Data. The term Big Data refers to vast sets of data, often numbering in the millions, billions, or even trillions, that are increasingly available for journalistic inquiry and media production.

The confluence of this Big Data with computer algorithms, or programming code, is fueling a significant shift in the story telling of journalism and the media. This includes dynamic, data-driven visualizations and narratives that can shift in real time from one user to the next and across platforms. Journalists also are increasingly able to anchor their often-anecdotal stories in a data-driven context, thereby simultaneously providing a close-up with a view of the bigger picture.

Stories built on data increasingly enable journalists to place current events and circumstances into wider context. An example of data-driven contextualization in news comes from a 2017 report from New Jersey Advance Media on gun violence in the state.[5] Readers see both a textual narrative and an interactive map of all gun violence in New Jersey in 2015. By clicking on a location on the map, readers access summaries of each shooting, including the date, exact location, and victim. Clicking again gives the reader access to even more detail drawn from the national gun-violence archive.

Big Data, including in the form of social media, can provide a valuable resource for journalists seeking to report on a wide range of stories. In one case, Laura Holson, a reporter for the *New York Times*, noticed that Donald Trump Jr. is an avid angler who posts to Instagram. Hobson asked herself just how big the fishing crowd on Instagram was. Parsing through the data, she found that "it is indeed an active community; #fishing alone has nearly 20 million posts."[6]

Integrating such data into experiential news stories is a natural next step. Journalists could allow users to access and interact with the data themselves in 3-D data visualizations based on the social media posts, for example, enabling more user engagement and potentially greater understanding.

The vastness of the data sets necessitates that news and other media increasingly rely on well-articulated instructions, or algorithms, implemented via computer programs or code to carry out their analyses. The data comes from a wide array of sources, including social media as well as public or governmental transactional records (voting records, financial transactions, and the like). There is also a growing volume of multispectral sensors and other devices connected to the internet precipitated by the rise of the internet of things, which networks an increasing portion of all things human made from security cameras to atmospheric chemical sensors.

Algorithms and Big Data usage are enabling innovative media organizations to restructure both internally and externally to develop new and qualitatively different content. News media are also hiring increasing numbers of programmers, or people with expertise in creating computer code and in conducting data analysis.

Consequently, news media are investing increasing resources in creating code, such as algorithms in the form of APIs, and sometimes sharing that code across the industry in open-source forums. GitHub has become a valuable open-source online resource for the sharing of code for journalism including in experiential form.[7]

Among the leading examples of the computation and data-driven approach to journalism is the *New York Times'* unit called the Upshot. Launched in 2014, the Upshot features journalists and data scientists working collaboratively to develop and apply algorithms to data sets to generate stories and provide context to news stories. The Upshot has produced a series of notable reports, including analyses of data on social injustice and inequality in the United States, the long-term decline in public trust in government, and employment trends in the United States. The Upshot has emerged as an innovative platform for journalism using large data sets to both identify trends and issues in society and also to place breaking news and other developments in a wider, more meaningful context.

A 2015 report from the Upshot provides detailed data on the heavy incarceration rate among black American males and the decimating effect it is having on society. Titled "1.5 Million Missing Black Men," the provocative data-driven story stimulated a national discourse on the policies that have contributed to this dire situation and what might be done to remedy it.[8] Part of what made this journalism so provocative is that it provides data-based evidence that criminality is at least in part a product of the prevailing social system and the public policies that shape it, and it indicates that American justice is not color-blind. Adding more interactivity to let users drill deeper into the data by region or other factors could make this an experiential story with even greater public engagement.

The University of Arizona's Bryan Carter adds that the location-based nature of modern mobile communications may help build public awareness, use, and knowledge of Big Data.[9] Some of these Big Data sets are generated directly by our mobile devices. "Digital devices are usually location-aware," Carter notes. Mobile devices are network connected and, unless the privacy settings are turned off, are automatically generating location data and attaching it to any of the apps we use or photos and videos we take and share via social media. In many ways, networked mobile devices have enabled people to tell stories about "what's happening to them," he observes, often without those individuals even knowing it. As people explore their worlds, they are often unaware of the data-based stories or digital trails they are leaving behind and the stories they may be telling unintentionally.

In a sense, as the public learns about location-based media, "the public will be introduced to Big Data," Carter explains. People will be "engaging stories by location." They may see their own stories—narratives about "where you've been, what you've done." The data we share may be in the form of health information, commercial transactions (purchases), or travel and transportation. When Carter takes his students overseas on research projects to Paris or elsewhere, he admonishes them to be fully aware of location data: "Think about what you are telling others." Although we may know that our friends are following us via what we share through social networks, we may be much less conscious of how marketers, government agencies, or even criminals may be tracking what we do or say.

To understand how Big Data could affect experiential news, the reader might think of a pointillist painting, such as the nineteenth-century masterpieces by Georges Seurat. When viewed up close, a painting such as Seurat's *A Sunday Afternoon on the Island of La Grande Jatte* might appear to be nothing but a series of random dots of color.[10] But from a distance, the bigger picture comes into focus, and the dots create a pattern and tell a complex story. Such will be the case with the Big Data that is collected continuously by mobile and wearable devices. Individuals may not be aware of their stories as they live in the moment (like the viewer of a Seurat masterpiece standing up very close to the painting), but data may let them or others see or experience the bigger, more complex stories they are telling.

People's devices, choices, and actions as collected in Big Data might reveal one's political leaning, sexual orientation, or marketing tendencies. Facebook has algorithms that can estimate users' political leanings simply from observing their online behaviors and interactions such as what stories they share with friends or postings they like and, via algorithms, can automatically filter corresponding paid advertising messages toward or away from them. People may be leaving a digital trail, a complex set of data dots, and telling a story for themselves or perhaps someone else to observe, experience, or even manipulate. Others may find these stories revealing or may seek to exploit them commercially or politically. Researchers and journalists alike should consider the nature, consequences, and ethics of such unaware experiential stories.

For news media, user data represents an opportunity to establish distinct approaches to the ethical use of consumer data with strong privacy protections in place.[11] One important aspect of this is for news media to develop approaches that require users to opt in to, rather than opt out of, sharing data. Moreover, news media should ensure that all personal user identification is stripped out of the data when recorded or used for either marketing or news purposes to guarantee user anonymity. This will distinguish news media from digital enterprises such as social networks and give them a significant advantage in terms of public trust.

Research at the MIT Media Lab is exploring the potential to weave everyday objects and experiences into digital narratives. One project, "Everything Tells a Story," uses pattern recognition to link people's everyday experiences into stories.[12] Journalists could use this approach to develop experiential news stories based on people's everyday lives. For example, Uber collects vast amounts of data on traffic patterns in cities across the nation and the globe, wherever the company operates its ridesharing service.[13] The data is publicly available online and could provide journalists an extraordinary lens into reporting on how we live and travel locally and beyond.[14] Such data could be compiled into interactive visualizations that allow users to interact with and otherwise experience the data, illuminating where and when traffic congestion is greatest and the like.

Journalists and other investigators should advance a model of research on such data-driven stories that sets the highest standards of ethics in the treatment of human subjects of research, whether academic, corporate, or journalistic. These standards should include adherence to protocols that (1) protect the rights of human subjects to control their own data, (2) ensure user data privacy protections, and (3) require informed consent from subjects before they provide their data for others to use.

In the digital age, it is likely that users will be able to design their own personalized story experiences or obtain versions of stories that are customized in a variety of ways, including according to type of delivery platform, geo-location, user preferences, and a host of other data. This could become a new form of citizen reporting, building on earlier social media platforms such as blogs and social networks including Instagram, Snapchat, and Pinterest.

Research is needed to examine the potential social consequences of such personalization, particularly in the context of experiential news. Extreme personalization may increasingly fragment the public and lead to even greater political polarization and culture wars. Yet the personalization that facilitates empathetic experiences may help to make stories and their delivery more efficient, engaging, and memorable. Heightened efficiency could serve users as well as those who seek to reach them, as long as the platform and its algorithms are transparent to both. Perhaps most importantly, news media need to protect user privacy from commercial or political exploitation in an era marked by extreme customization of user news experience.

Ethics in experiential journalism is a far-reaching concern. Tom Kent, AP standards editor and professor at the Columbia University Graduate School of Journalism, contends that visual integrity, especially when dealing with re-creating events, is critical. He asks, "How does a journalist represent competing views of a news event, when various witnesses and images paint alternative pictures? And making decisions about privacy or showing scenes that are graphic and gruesome only add to the layers of complexity."[15]

Investigators at the Poynter Institute for Media Studies have asked how a VR rig changes a situation, including the behavior of those being recorded on video. With regard to the *New York Times'* groundbreaking VR report "The Displaced," Poynter points out, "But the scene also confronts readers with one of the primary ethical dilemmas of virtual reality: how to use obtrusive cameras to document the world without affecting it." In this case, the *New York Times* used 360-degree video to enable users to experience life in three refugee camps as seen and heard through the eyes and ears of children in each of those camps: Oleg, an eleven-year-old boy in a camp in the Ukraine; Hana, a twelve-year-old Syrian refugee in Lebanon; and Chuol, a nine-year-old boy displaced in the South Sudan. In capturing the 360-degree video of Oleg, the *Times* videographer altered the boy's routine slightly by placing equipment on his bicycle before his trip down the street.[16] We just do not know how much or in what way it altered Oleg's routine.

Don Heider, Loyola Chicago professor and Emmy award–winning former journalist, says VR journalism is visceral. As such, he says, there are several vital normative ethics questions regarding the use of VR in journalism. Foremost, when should and will journalists use VR in journalism? A journalist should ask, "What story is so important that I don't just want to provide information but a visceral (i.e., emotionally powerful) experience?"[17] I would say the answer is when the subject at hand is vital to creating informed discourse and debate on matters vital to the public interest.

Heider asks, does a reporter have an obligation to understand the potential emotional or physiological effect of a VR experience on the user? I would say yes, but to do this effectively will require journalists and academics studying journalism to increasingly engage in meaningful dialogue and share their professional and research lessons and insights of relevance to the impact of VR news user experiences.

Should a reporter get the consent of all those potentially in the field of view or audio environment in VR or 360-degree video? I contend that the answer, again, is yes. The privacy implications are profoundly important.

How is the context of a VR story delivered? Journalists should be transparent in their VR decision-making. Are re-creations in VR ethical journalism? Are they or can they be truthful? I suggest that the answer to these questions is a limited yes and that it depends on an essential condition being met: a VR scenario, whether a re-creation or a 360-degree video, should facilitate understanding and not mislead the news consumer. Moreover, the intervention of a 360-degree camera or other experiential news-gathering tool should not substantially alter the behavior of those being observed.

In what ways is it ethical to edit the video shot with a 360-degree video camera? In some 360-degree video reports produced by the *Times*, an editor's note reads: "Images of the V.R. apparatus and its shadow have been removed in some places. This editing, which is common in V.R. production, helps preserve the scene as a viewer on location would normally see it." I would argue that this is an acceptable edit as long as the essential meaning of the narrative is unaltered or is presented truthfully and viewers are informed of the editing.

TYPES OF ALGORITHMS AND EXPERIENTIAL NEWS

At an abstract or conceptual level, algorithms are well-defined computational procedures that transform input (data or variables) into output (new values or variables). More concretely, algorithms operate as a sequence of computational steps (e.g., adding, subtracting, and multiplying data or variables or contingencies such as if/then conditions) that change the data entered into a new set of values or output.[18] In the context of experiential journalism, a news organization might use an algorithm to generate an interactive visualization of the predicted results of an upcoming general election. The algorithm could combine the results of various election polls with statistical weightings derived from the previous accuracy of each of those polls to generate a new set of values or output, that is, the likely election results depending on certain variables such as voter turnout.

Algorithms that are relevant to experiential journalism generally fall into five broad types: (1) predictive models largely based on mathematical formulas (predicting election outcomes, data mining); (2) descriptive statistics (social media analytics, descriptions of census data); (3) critical analysis (to identify anomalies, outliers, things that are newsworthy or unusual); (4) direct manipulation of content (automated writing or video editing, generating data-driven visualizations); and (5) metrics to automatically measure audience engagement and link to content (to sell targeted advertising). Each of these has important implications for experiential news.

Among the most well-known examples of predictive algorithms in journalism is the work of Nate Silver for the site FiveThirtyEight, which was founded in 2008 as a polling aggregation site and then acquired in 2010 by the *New York Times* and is now part of ESPN.[19] Silver initially used a combination of historical election outcome data, current voting patterns, and probability forecasts to estimate the outcome of future elections.[20] He captured considerable attention when his model accurately predicted the outcome of the U.S. Senate elections in 2014. One of the important elements of Silver's model was the use of weighted polling results. The weights themselves depend on a number of factors, including the sample size of the poll, how long ago the poll was conducted, and pollster rating based on accuracy in previous polls.

Such algorithms are far from perfect, as the outcome of the 2016 U.S. presidential election made clear. Virtually all the predictive models employed and reported by mainstream Western news media predicted a clear victory by Democrat Hillary Clinton. J. Donald Trump ultimately won the election, shocking much of the electorate and the Big Data pollsters and predictors and evoking memories of the 1948 *Chicago Tribune* headline "Dewey Defeats Truman," which had been predicted by the polls of the day. The resulting news media navel gazing has led to a reconsideration of the use of predictive models and the data and algorithms upon which they rest. Many now recognize that qualitative factors must also be taken into consideration, and journalists cannot simply rely on mathematical models in isolation from larger or more nuanced historical or contemporary cultural factors.

Predictive algorithms could be used effectively in experiential news in a number of ways, such as news models that allow users to explore possible future scenarios based on trends in the data. We see this potential today when forecasts of rising sea levels are incorporated into reporting on climate change. In an experiential format, such a story could enable the user to explore an interactive scenario that contrasts predicted outcomes based on the U.S. remaining in the Paris Climate Agreement with the likely long-term outcome if the U.S. withdraws from the agreement as President Trump has indicated.

Algorithms are valuable in developing statistical descriptions of large data sets such as U.S. census data or social media activity such as Twitter posts. An example comes from the U.K.-based news organization the *Guardian*. Once known primarily as an important newspaper in the United Kingdom, the *Guardian* has become a recognized global force in journalism, largely due to the advent of Big Data and online news. The *Guardian* was among the first news organizations to effectively use descriptive algorithms to transform its news reporting. In 2011 the *Guardian* applied descriptive algorithms in its coverage of that year's Tottenham riots.[21] *Guardian* journalists employed algorithms to sift through large volumes of Twitter and other social media resources to break down patterns and developments in how the riots began and spread.[22]

Key to the *Guardian*'s use of the data were three elements. First, the news staff compiled a list of each incident in which there was a verified report. Second, they mapped the verified incidents using Google Fusion tables (a free data visualization web application to collect, visualize, and share data of any type).[23] Third, this digital mapping allowed the staff (or others, including the public) to download the data and conduct further analysis.[24]

This three-part model could be employed more widely in experiential journalism to create data sets for journalistic analysis and for users to conduct their own independent analyses, much as crowd-sourcing works more generally.

A third type of algorithm that potentially can be of great value in journalism involves techniques for conducting critical analysis of data sets. Thus far, this approach has been relatively rare in journalism but ultimately may have the greatest value, at least in the sense of journalism as an independent check on government. This kind of reporting, which requires less labor and is potentially less expensive, may be especially valuable for journalism and society in an era of news media cutbacks and the erosion of investigative journalism. Using well-designed critical algorithms, human journalists could augment their investigative potential. Critical algorithms could play a key role in the journalistic research or reporting process.

This algorithm-driven investigative approach involves using well-articulated instructions to comb through massive data sets to identify patterns, exceptions to routines, or outliers that suggest potential problems or areas for closer examination. For instance, a reporter might receive an anonymous tip that there is corruption in the leadership of an international sports organization. The organization may have vast resources, both economic and transactional, in digital form. The data may involve massive volumes that could take a team of investigators years to unravel. The time needed may be far more than any typical news organization can commit to an investigation that ultimately might not yield a story. The data might include vast collections supplemented by data dumps of documents. To analyze such massive data sets, investigators could make efficient use of algorithms that carry out the instructions in the form of if/then queries or metatags designed by reporters. The if/then instructions might identify exceptions to normal patterns, suggesting when or where more focused and detailed examination is warranted.

Of course, the actual algorithms used in journalism and elsewhere add more layers and complexity to the processing of data. The algorithms may include mathematical factors that weight different variables or combine them in various ways (additive, multiplicative, etc.). The challenge in understanding the algorithms and their accuracy or effectiveness is that most news or other organizations treat their algorithms as proprietary software and have little transparency in revealing to the public how they work. The public (or anyone outside the news organization) often must accept on faith the reliability of the algorithm. For news organizations to build trust in the experiential age of journalism, the transparency of these proprietary algorithms should be greatly increased. If the public can see and understand how these algorithms work, why they are reliable, and how they do not encode bias, they will be much more likely to trust them and rely on their use in the news-production process.

Humans generally make the algorithms, although this is changing, too, and humans have their own biases and assumptions. When these biases and assumptions are built into the algorithms, the analyses they produce may be just as deeply flawed, if not worse (given the potential speed or magnitude of the data involved).

Beyond these methods of journalistic work, algorithms have important implications for the automatic processing of data into news stories or media content more generally. Foremost, data-driven visualizations, created by algorithms, are increasingly common in all forms of journalism. Assuming the data is reliable, the visualizations will be equally accurate and may also lend themselves to layering, interactivity, and multimedia.

The *New York Times* has employed algorithms to the processing of reader comments to generate in real time a visualization that identifies the tone of those comments. The algorithm is "the Perspective API tool developed by Jigsaw (part of Google's parent company Alphabet)." The API (application programming interface, or digital algorithm that interacts with the remote Google server where the data resides) sorts reader comments "interactively so that viewers can quickly see which ones they may find 'toxic' and which may be more illuminating. Viewers can read comments by sliding a bar across the top of the page from left to right. The closer the bar gets to the right, the more toxic the comments become."[25]

As such, algorithms offer the potential to facilitate the level of interaction between the public and reporters and editors and to develop content based on that interaction. As members of the public participate in social media networks revolving around news and issues of public importance, algorithms can help news media process the large volume of conversations, create summaries for reporters and editors, and direct such summaries to reporters working on relevant beats. These summaries might help reporters identify new story ideas for enterprise reporting as well as potential new sources to help expand diversity in reporting. For instance, like most news media, the *Guardian* allows viewing online comments either in temporal fashion (oldest or newest first) or by thread. In a study of user comments on the *Guardian*'s website, researchers in the School of Informatics at the University of Edinburgh used an algorithmic approach to sort and summarize comments.[26] In particular, they examined 161 comments posted over two days in response to a story about gang violence. Topical clusters included comments that criticized gang culture and comments that reflected an interest in hearing more from victims of gang violence. Reporters could use such information to pursue areas of coverage that would resonate with readers, such as more reporting about gang culture, or new leads, such as interviews with victims of gang violence. News media should consider implementing such algorithm-enabled systems to facilitate sorting and summarizing reader comments in a timely and efficient manner to help better inform readers as well as enable experiential news reporting opportunities (e.g., a virtual visit inside a gang or a community impacted by gang violence, incorporating reader comments).

Research indicates that it is also important to assess and account for any bias that reader comments might reflect. Studies indicate that readers who are more to the right, or conservative, side of the political spectrum are more apt to post comments than those in the middle or even to the left.[27] Journalists should exercise caution when interpreting summaries of reader comments as accurately reflective of the views or opinions of the broader population. Experiential stories based on algorithmic analysis and synthesis of reader comments should be especially attuned to potential bias to avoid exacerbating the problem.

Data-driven visualizations are increasingly common and customizable via algorithms. For instance, news media across a variety of platforms from television to online to mobile frequently use Google Earth and Google Maps to provide customized, data-driven visualizations for stories to place news events in geographic context. As journalism embraces formats such as AR, VR, and games, algorithm-driven visualizations are especially germane for creating new patterns on the fly or based on the individual news consumer's location, actions, or context. These new patterns might take a variety of forms, such as illustrating the tone of reader comments in the above example or some other characteristic of the data (e.g., sea level rise around the world, refugee migration patterns, or shifting economic indices).

News media may be greatly interested in next-generation interactive visualization approaches that offer new content capabilities and expanded levels of user engagement. One such project at the MIT Media Lab is called the BigBarChart,[28] which uses data and algorithms to generate immersive 3-D bar charts. Future generations might enable interactive visualizations on a wide spectrum of subject matter that are displayed in three dimensions and that allow the user to explore the data in an immersive, customizable, and haptic fashion. For instance, in early 2018 it was reported that a robot called the Remus 6000 operating on behalf the Woods Hole Oceanographic Institute had apparently discovered a 310-year-old shipwreck in the Caribbean worth an estimated $17 billion.[29] An experiential news story about the discovery could enable news consumers to explore in interactive fashion how the Remus 6000 works, how it sifts through data, the treasure thought to be inside the wreck, and what may have caused the ship to sink three centuries ago.

News media are also increasingly using algorithms to automatically generate news stories and are doing so across a variety of topical domains. From sports to finance, science to crime, algorithms are writing increasing numbers of stories. Sometimes algorithms even directly link reporting with content, particularly when the data is structured, meaning organized into fields or meaningful categories, as in a spreadsheet.

Chicago-based Narrative Science has an interdisciplinary team of data scientists who have created Quill, a system of automated writing based on data-driven algorithms.[30] As of this writing, Narrative Science's code-based system was already producing extensive numbers of journalistic stories (more than one million) with many paying clients such as *Forbes*.[31] To illustrate the writing and reporting quality of algorithm-based experiential news stories, following is the lede sentence from a Narrative Science–written story published July 22, 2015, on Forbes.com: "Despite an expected dip in profit, analysts are generally optimistic about Xerox XRX—1.30% as it prepares to reports [*sic*] its second-quarter earnings on Friday, July 24, 2015."[32] It might not win a Pulitzer Prize, but it is readable, despite the typo. Experiential stories could utilize such capabilities to efficiently generate interactive content localized by community.

The *Los Angeles Times*, for instance, used its Quakebot algorithm to capture in real time a data feed from the U.S. Geological Survey about a 4.2 magnitude earthquake in Southern California.[33] Designed by a human reporter, Quakebot "wrote" the story, alerted a human editor to the breaking news, and electronically delivered the story for publication on LATimes.com, all within moments of the earthquake event. Quakebot is perhaps the news organization's most visible robotic reporting tool. LATimes.com uses similar code-based software tools to report on an increasingly wide range of topics, including crime news.[34] Readers can even follow Quakebot on Twitter, demonstrating the story-telling potential of algorithm-driven social media narratives. News algorithms in the future could generate experiential news that is customized on a wide range of topics for each individual reader.

AP is similarly making growing use of computer code and algorithms to report financial news stories. By using automation, AP has been able to expand by tenfold its coverage of financial news stories based on corporate earnings reports.[35] AP previously could report just three hundred earnings stories in the final quarter of the year, and now it can report more than three thousand without hiring any new human staff. Algorithms cull through the reports and generate narratives summarizing the key elements of each report. Increasingly, computers are able to create code, so conceptualizing algorithms may be the most valuable human activity. Seeing potential in the technology, AP hired an automation editor. AP announced in July 2015 that it would fully automate its corporate earnings reporting and in 2016 that it would soon begin using a similar algorithm-based approach to automatically create broadcast news stories.[36] It is still a work in progress, but the expectation is that by 2020 stories produced for print or online could be automatically converted, at least in part, to broadcast format. Such conversion involves a number of components that are labor intensive—including shortening stories, making each sentence more concise, placing the attribution at the beginning of a sentence rather than at the end, and rounding numbers—but they could be performed by a well-designed robot, freeing the human journalist to work on new stories and reporting that is not amenable to automation. Such an approach might be extended to the realm of experiential news, with news robots helping in the process of converting more traditional news content into more interactive and immersive forms and creating that content tailored to each person's investment portfolio and presented interactively or via multimedia depending on user preferences.[37]

Other news organizations are on the same path as AP. Tribune Publishing Company (formerly Tronc, the convergent digital organization that emerged from Tribune Publishing in 2016 and then was renamed in 2018), announced plans to produce some two thousand videos daily via AI protocols.[38] Although these early adopters tend to be large-scale operations, there is also potential for smaller media organizations to employ automation in in experiential news. For instance, the Norwegian news agency NTB is developing an algorithm to generate stories for each of the twenty-thousand league soccer games played in the country annually by drawing on data from the Football Association of Norway, and that process could extend to experiential formats.[39]

Data- and algorithm-driven reporting and analysis are also leading to qualitatively different news reporting. Algorithms enable news media to place current developments and trends into broader context. While much traditional reporting often emphasized anecdotal evidence, algorithmic, data-driven reporting is helping journalists identify trends, patterns, and broad developments, giving the much-needed context that was often missing in the past. In 2014 Craig Silverman, a journalist and fellow at the Tow Center for Digital Journalism at Columbia University, developed Emergent, an algorithm-based tool that tracks the online dissemination of rumors.[40] In some ways Emergent presaged the fake-news crisis of 2016. One rumor that Emergent analyzed and found to be false—that a female United Arab Emirates pilot who was helping to bomb ISIS had been disowned by her family—started on September 25, 2014, and within forty-eight hours, 10,951 people shared the rumor. Although this is at least partly an organizational or systemic consideration, it represents an essential element in the overall news ecosystem in which experiential news will operate in the twenty-first century.

Data-driven, interactive, and dynamic reporting is growing in journalism and often deemphasizes narrative in favor of presentations using data-driven graphics and animations. The *Guardian*, for example, published an interactive map revealing the type, location, and casualties resulting from sixteen thousand improvised explosive device (IED) attacks in Afghanistan.[41]

Among the possibilities emerging from the intersection of Big Data and algorithms are new personalized interactive stories such as the Surgeon Scorecard created by ProPublica, which applies a complex algorithm to public data on surgical records to rate seventeen thousand surgeons operating in the United States.[42] Anyone can access the Surgeon Scorecard and find surgeons in their selected areas who have the highest ratings for particular surgical procedures. It is controversial because some surgeons have objected to having their medical records subjected to such easy and widespread scrutiny, and they criticize the algorithms, which place an emphasis on the frequency of complications in surgical procedures.

Among ProPublica's notable innovations in telling the story via data and algorithms is Dollars for Docs produced in 2015.[43] This provocative interactive report allows readers to examine and search an interactive, data-driven investigation of how industry dollars reach medical doctors. As reported on ProPublica, "Pharmaceutical and medical device companies are now required by law to release details of their payments to a variety of doctors and U.S. teaching hospitals for promotional talks, research and consulting, among other categories. Use this tool to search for general payments (excluding research and ownership interests) made from August 2013 to December 2014." The algorithms used in producing Dollars for Docs received critical acclaim as well as objections from some in the medical industry, but in combination with the underlying data, this suggests a powerful approach to nonnarrative telling of the story to deliver personalized medical news.

In some ways, this represents a different kind of journalism focused on putting facts in the form of customizable data into each user's control. It is a form of public-service-oriented journalism that can serve the public at two levels simultaneously. First, it gives individuals the ability to make decisions based on reliable information personalized to their exact situation. Second, because it is scalable via algorithm, it is public-service journalism that can serve the entire population. In the future, a vast array of stories could enable news consumers to see and experience almost every story at both the general and the specific level, gaining insight into what each story means for society or a community at large as well as for themselves on an individual level. In a sense, this has been a long-term goal of journalism, but one that has been beyond the reach of most news operations—until the advent of contemporary tools for news and data analysis and presentation.

Northwestern University's Nicholas Diakopoulos, assistant professor in the School of Communication and director of the Computational Journalism Lab (CJL), has conducted research that helps to illuminate the inner workings of algorithm-driven journalistic investigation. The computer scientist reverse engineers algorithms to see how they are being used in a variety of arenas, including experiential journalism.[44] He describes his work as "the process of extracting knowledge or design blueprints by studying and then emulating the behavior of an algorithm." Diakopoulos analyzed "five case studies in which journalists used reverse engineering to examine algorithms, including a story in the Daily Beast, on the iPhone's language-related algorithms; ProPublica on the 2012 U.S. election campaign and targeted email strategies; the *Wall Street Journal* on website pricing differentiation and on stock trading by executives; and one story by Diakopoulos himself."[45] He "identifies the scenarios journalists typically encounter in their reporting on algorithms as well as the challenges emerging from these investigations in terms of human resources, legality and ethics."

A central ethics issue in experiential journalism that this example illustrates is making algorithms in journalism more transparent. By critically examining the inner workings of the algorithms used in journalism, Diakopoulos's investigation can help advance understanding of a key part of how journalism will function in an experiential age.

The rise of Big Data, algorithms, and code has led growing numbers of news media to employ data scientists to help or even lead their data analysis. This shift signals an evolution in how we think about the journalist. Interviewing ability, skepticism, and concise writing once served as the foundational skill set of great journalism. Today, these skills are increasingly being supplanted by digital abilities such as writing code (such as hypertext markup language, or HTML, to design web pages, or algorithms to help analyze data), participating in social media, and designing and presenting a multimedia and interactive narrative of events.

For some observers, the fusion of computing and news content represents a threat to journalism. Automated reporting and writing technology may further erode the role of the human journalist. Critics question whether merging computing and content will lead to better-quality journalism. HuffPost has labeled automated news reporting "robo-journalism."[46] HuffPost's Magda Abu-Fadil reports that automated journalism is both "funny and scary: A robot writes literature, akin to churning out copy for news organizations, thereby eliminating entry-level newsroom jobs and alarming future journalists."[47]

Although this negative impact is certainly a real possibility, especially as newsroom management seeks further cost-cutting measures, the potential to use these digital tools to augment human capabilities offers a positive scenario. Algorithm-based news systems should augment, not supplant, human journalists in the production of experiential news. News organizations need to move forward carefully and consider the full impact of automation in the experiential newsroom. Management should balance the cost savings and increases in efficiency in automated experiential news production with possible human costs such as newsroom layoffs and any potential erosion of the quality of news content in the form of errors that might accompany the integration of algorithms into news workflows. Although algorithms may operate tirelessly and rapidly, they have little capacity for empathy or critical insight, and they are susceptible to mistakes that simple human common sense could detect. The goal for news organizations should be to employ algorithms to assist in the routine tasks needed in news production while giving human journalists greater opportunity to develop investigative, in-depth, and multisensory experiential news. Editorial oversight needs to be maintained especially as the role of algorithms increases. Potential problems of errors in news reporting could be amplified to dramatic proportions if algorithms begin to operate on a large scale and at nanosecond speed, which could cause devastating and irreversible erosion of public trust.

Digital technologies of various forms may enhance or support the human journalist, including as an aid in creating immersive and interactive VR visualizations into which the user can enter and engage the data. E. T. Meyer writes,

> There are many examples of technology that have become sufficiently advanced that the previous need to develop expert-level skills before being able to perform at a high level is either vastly reduced or eliminated. For instance, digital cameras can create sharp, beautiful photos with essentially zero technical skill, and high-definition video recordings are available on smartphones and iPads. The question is not only whether these technologies eliminate the need for expertise (thus substituting engineering for expertise) but also if in doing so they foster the development of

new types of creative expertise (such as an ability to use photography as part of a social media strategy).[48]

Perhaps the combination of human journalistic intelligence and data-driven algorithms can produce an experiential form of news that helps reengage an increasingly alienated public whose trust in mainstream media and journalism has reached historic lows.[49] In the weeks following the 2016 U.S. presidential election, subscriptions to the *New York Times* surged by 276,000.[50] This surge is likely due to a combination of factors, including public response to President Trump's accusations of "fake news" in reference to mainstream news media. But also likely playing a role is the *Times*'s innovative use of data-driven reporting and experiential story telling; chapter 7 provides further details.

The surge in subscriptions at U.S. news media since the Trump election, what some dub the "Trump bump," has not been limited to the *New York Times* and the *Washington Post*. The *Wall Street Journal* has also seen its subscriptions climb substantially, some 200,000 in the six months after Trump's election.[51] Traffic to these sites has grown substantially as well, not just in terms of subscribers. "By October 2017, the *New York Times* moved ahead with a total digital audience of 93.5 million per month, compared to the *Post*'s 88.9 million unique visitors. In page views, the *Times* is also still ahead with 1.2 billion digital page views, compared to 821 million for the *Post*, according to the *Washington Post* PR blog."[52] The *Times*, the *Post*, and the *Wall Street Journal* have all committed substantial resources to creating quality experiential journalism, including 360-degree video reporting and augmented reality content. The *Post*, for example, has hired more than one hundred reporters and editors in recent months, many of them helping to produce AR and VR news content.[53]

Likewise, CNN has seen its ratings climb since the Trump election. February 2018 was the network's second-best-rated February in a decade.[54] CNNVR has been a major push of the network since the 2016 campaign. Although it is hard to parse how much of this increased audience engagement is due to the network's public feud with the president and how much is a product of better, innovative journalism in the form of experiential news, the network's efforts with VR reporting do not seem to have detracted from its recent ratings success.

MEASURING AUDIENCE ENGAGEMENT
VIA ALGORITHM

Measuring audience engagement can help those who design or deliver digital content to refine their efforts. Those who would fund the media can also benefit from better information and knowledge about their audiences or potential consumers. Software tools can measure almost every aspect of digital content and its distribution, consumption, or interaction. In broadcasting, Voltair measures radio listenership by tapping directly into the watermark embedded into digital radio transmissions, whether played back in a car, home, or other environment.[55] A watermark is a unique piece of data inserted into the metatags associated with digital content, whether audio, video, or other emerging formats. Using these digital watermarks, other programs can be used to measure video consumption or interaction.

Many news media use commercial data analytic tools such as Chartbeat to measure the audience for news items published online.[56] Some innovative media organizations are applying algorithms to social media and content customization to assess, engage, and build audience. NPR employs an algorithm to tweak its mobile app to deliver customizable, on-demand audio programming, including experiential news content. Metatags on program elements facilitate automated customization. Overall, NPR was able to use this algorithm-based approach to double the time audiences spend listening to NPR programming via its mobile app.[57]

Increasingly sophisticated and highly atomized algorithm-driven metrics allow media organizations and researchers to assess audience engagement in many forms and on many levels. Almost every aspect of digital content consumption or interaction can now be measured, including reading, listening, watching, sharing, liking, clicking, contributing, and commenting.

Preliminary research findings indicate that interactive content is stimulating high levels of engagement.[58] Metrics such as those described here are available virtually instantly, giving story tellers and distributors vast amounts of data and the potential to adapt news stories and other types of content such as advertising in a highly dynamic fashion. Some might not see this as a good thing, but the tidal wave of data seems virtually unstoppable.

A media ecosystem where news stories are increasingly ubiqui-tous, interactive, and measurable brings potentially serious negative consequences that merit attention and research investigation. Such a measurable future might pose significant threats to personal privacy, security, and health as well as bring about extreme forms of commer-cialism and globalism. Constant measurement and use of data analytics may reduce experiential story production to a formulaic approach, no matter how complex. Such thoroughly far-reaching and instantaneous measurement may lead story delivery systems to increasingly empha-size or highlight only those experiential stories that maximize audience or engagement through systems such as social networking media. This drive for maximum audience reach and engagement can work counter to quality, emphasizing economic efficiency over journalistic excel-lence or vigilance. Thus, in place of more complex investigative report-ing, we may be confronted with experiential click bait.

ARTIFICIAL INTELLIGENCE

Somewhat further on the media horizon is a digital tsunami known col-lectively as artificial intelligence. AI has been a field in development for decades, since before even the work of British computer scientist Alan Turing in the early twentieth century. Turing posited that if humans interacting with a computer could not determine whether they were communicating with a machine or a human, then that machine had artificial intelligence. In other words, it would pass the Turing test. AI researchers have sought throughout the intervening decades to create a computer that could pass the Turing test. In 2016 Amazon announced the Alexa prize, a $2.5 million award to researchers who could create a chatbot that would allow the Echo to engage in a sustained dialogue with a human for up to twenty minutes on a range of topics, thereby passing the Turing test in the experiential arena.[59] Google engineers have devel-oped a similar application called Tacotron, which is available online for Turing test assessment.[60] The BBC and other news organizations are experimenting with AI-powered voice assistants for news and could make direct use of a chatbot for news.[61]

AI has developed along several dimensions, including robotics, vision, machine learning, language processing (natural language), and Big

Data analytics. Each dimension is relevant to journalism. Robotic devices might be used in news reporting or writing.[62] Algorithmic robots can cull through data and craft news stories. Robotic software devices are taking the form of automated natural language writing programs and could soon be designing experiential news content. They are also entering the realm of the physical. Digital cameras can scan roadways or other areas, utilize facial recognition tools, and help initiate news-gathering and conduct surveillance.

From New York to London, many cities around the world have installed intelligent surveillance cameras to aid in law enforcement. One of these cities is Chicago, which has installed thirty thousand surveillance cameras enabled by facial recognition and other AI technology.[63] Preliminary evidence suggests that installing video cameras can help reduce crime or aid law enforcement, at least in limited circumstances, for instance on the subway.[64] At the same time, the impact of ubiquitous AI-powered cameras on privacy is potentially profound. For Chicagoans, it means living in an Orwellian surveillance-state environment where thousands of cameras equipped with facial recognition technology and algorithms may be tracking their every outdoor movement, processing each person via AI for suspicious activity, matching each face against a database of known felons, and recording the data onto the cloud. For citizens anywhere, news media access to these cameras could enable the production of real-time experiential news that lets anyone walk virtually around the city streets on Chicago's South Side and come face-to-face with at least a bit of life there.

Taking the concept of digital facial recognition even further, MIT professor Chris Csikszentmihalyi has developed the idea of a news robot.[65] Such an intelligent news-gathering machine could go into battle zones to conduct field reporting, recognize people and places, ask questions, record answers in audio and video, transmit from the field, and reduce the potential for casualties among human journalists.

Machine learning is highly relevant as a type of AI system that can observe the behavior of human reporters and then model or even refine certain actions to increase reporting efficiency. Such a system could observe human reporters monitoring social media, selecting items that are newsworthy, and crafting interactive content based on what's trending. A deep-learning system could quickly model that reporting and writing behavior and scale it up to monitor all social media continuously, instantly, and efficiently, generating vast numbers of stories ranked according to importance or likely audience appeal or engagement. AI systems for social media monitoring and reporting could potentially replace the need for human reporters on such a social media beat, or at least supplement them. By extension, as other sources of Big Data emerge based on a vast array of other networked sensors, AI reporting and news-writing systems could be developed on an even wider scale in generating a nonstop flow of adaptable experiential news.

There are at least three sets of issues and opportunities in this application of AI to Big Data in experiential journalism. First, AI could help journalists identify and develop new stories hidden in vast troves of data that are far too large (zettabyte size, for example) for a human to process alone and on deadline. One such story might be based on an AI-driven analysis of the zettabytes of data that will soon be generated by autonomous driving vehicles.[66] If, for instance, one-third of the 470,000 registered automobiles in San Francisco are autonomous, the data generated annually will exceed that of all three hundred million internet users in the United States. Important transportation stories will no doubt lie in this data, but the volume of data will far exceed the ability of even the most adroit team of human reporters to process in a timely fashion unless they are AI assisted. A branch of AI known as deep learning uses advanced statistical techniques to process vast troves of data and might be an ideal tool for such a journalistic investigation. Experiential news could employ this approach to give users real-time access to interactive traffic reports that are personalized to each individual's location and travel plans.

Second, AI could help journalists design and produce new experiential news formats. One possibility would be to allow the user to journey into a data set such as those described above and interact with the data in a dynamic simulation, seeing how adjusting a variable such as the number of autonomous vehicles on the road could impact for a better or worse life in a city such as San Francisco (e.g., averting accidents, reshaping demand for parking, reducing carbon emissions, affecting air quality).

An interesting opportunity in this regard involves the application of AI to the arena of video games for news. Video games have emerged in the twenty-first century to rival Hollywood and other major media industries in popularity and economic power. Increasingly, video games utilize AI-based programming tools that support machine learning, thereby allowing game play to feature intelligent digital opponents who face off against human players. Journalism has been developing news games as a way to engage news consumers more actively, especially younger members of the public who are among the most devoted core component of the video game community. Advancing AI as a new frontier in news games could help produce even more complex and sophisticated news games based on current events with multiple players in geographically distributed communities. It could make interactive news games such as quizzes, roleplaying, and simulations scalable by featuring AIs (AI news agents, rather than human news staff) that act as guides, competitors, or game collaborators in environments that can be operated 24/7 and on a national or global scale.

Finally, ethical considerations need to guide journalists as they develop AI-assisted Big Data capacities. Among the core considerations are protecting user privacy while effectively mining data for stories, avoiding potential conflicts of interest, and ensuring that the imperatives of press freedom (maintaining open access to information housed in Big Data), independence, and the pursuit of truth remain central to the algorithms that frame the AI priorities.

Future news media may be able to field robotic reporters, perhaps with drones operating via cloud computing using robotic vision combined with advanced, centralized digital intelligence and control to capture and analyze high-quality video of news events and sources.[67] AI authority Martin Ford explains in *The Rise of the Robots* that the robotic replacement of human workers is more about the predictability of tasks and the availability of data than it is about a work routine. Radiologists, Ford suggests, will likely be replaced by auto-vision and AI systems. Photojournalists and others might follow, he adds, and I agree. Many of journalists' activities are relatively predictable and data driven. Reporters have beats, such as covering city hall, police, and the courts, and much of what these institutions generate is increasingly in the form of data published on predictable schedules and in predictable form. Perhaps the most significant limit regarding the tasks that robots can accomplish when it comes to journalism in this context is asking the important follow-up questions when an initial lead, story idea, or source is identified. Human reporters of the future may work with a large team of AI assistants, intervening as needed to redirect them, much as human operators intervene from remote locations with the operation of autonomous vehicles when they encounter unpredictable situations, such as unexpected construction or police activity on a roadway. Experiential news could especially benefit from this approach to mitigate the potential problems that ever-increasing data vastness and transmission speeds can present.

Ford argues that automation via data and algorithms likely will put about 80 percent of the U.S. workforce out of work by the end of the twenty-first century if not before. This is equally likely for journalists, with forecasts suggesting that as many as 90 percent of news stories will be automatically generated by the mid-twenty-first century.

To this point, AI-reporting has focused on crunching data. Illustrating the role and impact of AI reporting is how it has begun to reshape election coverage at the *Washington Post*. To report on the November 2012 elections, four human reporters required about twenty-five hours to produce stories on a handful of election results. By November 2016, Heliograf, the *Post*'s AI data platform, quickly generated more than five hundred articles using almost no human assistance, and the stories also attracted more than 500,000 clicks from readers. "We're naturally wary about any technology that could replace human beings," says Fredrick Kunkle, a reporter with the *Washington Post* and cochair of the Washington-Baltimore News Guild.[68] So far these bots have mostly done the grunt work that many reporters will gladly not have to perform, but developments on the horizon may take bots to the next level in experiential journalism.

Emerging is an AI-related discipline known as cognitive computing— AI that is applied to data-driven analysis, decision-making, and problem solving. Cognitive computing is emerging as a transformative technology for experiential journalism on multiple levels.[69] It enables digital devices to solve problems, communicate, and potentially automate decision-making in situations that involve high levels of ambiguity or uncertainty. Such ambiguity or uncertainty often characterizes human communication and public engagement with the news. Once powered by cognitive computing, digital devices from smartphones to wearables may feature enhanced adaptability, interactivity, and contextualization, all of which are key elements in experiential news production and consumption.[70]

In 2015 researchers at IBM under the direction of Benjamin Fletcher, the product head of cognitive consumer experiences, explored the potential for cognitive computing in journalism, and they found that potential to be transformative.[71] A highly knowledgeable cognitive computing system called Watson, which is capable of nimble human communication and critical analysis, might serve as a powerful assistant to an investigative reporter or in the realm of fact-checking and experiential reporting.

The 2016 Wimbledon tennis tournament, a major sporting event spanning nineteen courts and covered by some 3,500 journalists, featured a Cognitive Command Centre powered by IBM's Watson, a cognitive computing platform running on the cloud. Watson's performance at the tournament illustrates the potential of cognitive computing in experiential journalism. Employing its cognitive computing capability, Watson monitored and analyzed tournament play for impending upsets, rallies, and other breaking news while simultaneously monitoring Twitter, Facebook, YouTube, and Instagram, which supplied a total of eleven million pieces of content about the tournament. Within six seconds of developments observed in tournament play and in social media posts, Watson would alert online spectators to news and other information, including new tennis records such as Roger Federer's 307th grand slam win. "Watson's understanding of what content was relevant, and what was most likely to get and keep people's attention, actually improved over time," notes Sam Seddon, who headed the Watson Wimbledon team.[72] Extending these capabilities to the experiential realm could enable tennis fans to engage in interactive dialogue with Watson about tournament news and analysis.

In 2011 tens of millions of television viewers in the United States and around the world witnessed the power of cognitive computing when Watson successfully played the TV game show *Jeopardy!* Watson drew upon its natural language-processing abilities and massive database to understand and correctly respond to even the most challenging queries on *Jeopardy!* Immediately following Watson's convincing *Jeopardy!* triumph, IBM scientists and other AI experts anticipated future possible applications for the expert system and began developing interactive applications for medicine, weather forecasting, and beyond.

IBM's Watson is not alone in developing such cognitive computing applications for experiential journalism. Spanish news innovator Chequeado has been developing an automated fact-checking system and anticipates that the algorithm-based system will serve a vital purpose in today's fact-challenged era.[73] Chequeado proves effective at tasks such as culling through streams of digital data to spot the most significant news items. It also might succeed at rapid fact-checking and even story writing or multimedia production as well as answering the questions of news consumers on demand. A digital assistant such as Chequeado might one day have a profound impact on the world of experiential news. For instance, it might prove highly valuable during a presidential debate or a political campaign as a means to vet an onslaught of potentially false or fake news or propaganda and to give audience members interactive and personalized political news analysis.

One way a system such as Chequeado might work is to use an advanced form of machine learning known as a neural network to observe and then model the behavior of human journalism fact-checkers. Neural networks have proven highly effective at processing massive and complex data sets. In one data analysis conducted by medical researchers at Google, a neural network processed more than 175,000 data points in a patient's medical record and demonstrated predictive power at twice the accuracy of the human medical doctors that the neural network had observed.[74]

In a news context, it is a likewise difficult and complex matter to determine what is true, accurate, or false. Neural networks might prove to be an especially valuable tool in establishing veracity in experiential news, which may increasingly feature dynamic and highly personalized news. Human fact checkers would be unable to operate effectively in an environment where millions of news consumers might each experience a different story. An AI system operating via a neural network could be effective and scalable.

Here is how it might work. In a typical approach to fact-checking, journalists identify the individual facts or assertions reported in the news or by a source. Then they verify these bits of information from additional known or generally reliable sources. For instance, in a 2018 meeting with

Canadian Prime Minister Justin Trudeau, President Trump asserted that the United States had a trade deficit with Canada. This assertion was false, and comparing the assertion with the U.S. government database established so in verifiable, independent terms. The United States actually had a trade surplus with Canada, which Trump's own Council of Economic Advisers acknowledged in their 2018 annual report. "In 2016, the United States ran a trade surplus of $2.6 billion with Canada on a balance-of-payments basis," the report says.[75] Trump even signed the report, agreeing that the United States had a trade surplus with Canada.

A neural-network cognitive-computing AI assistant could observe what data sources a human reporter uses to verify such an assertion. The AI could monitor the method the reporter uses to interrogate the relevant database in order to establish truth or falsehood. Finally, the AI could model those behaviors, or replicate them, especially in future experiential reporting situations, gradually becoming more and more adept at this vital journalism skill.

Cognitive computing and neural networks reflect an increasingly powerful form of AI known as artificial general intelligence (AGI). In this form of AI, computer intelligence is no longer one-dimensional, such as playing chess or *Jeopardy!* Instead, AGI technology may be multifunctional and capable of application to any aspect of human activity or intelligence. Technology leaders such as Elon Musk, founder of the Tesla electric car and other pioneering industry developments, has led a Silicon Valley initiative to create a new AGI institute called OpenAI. Leaders from the technology industry have pledged more than $1 billion in initial funding for the institute, whose mission will be to develop AGI for prosocial purposes.[76]

One of the big questions is the extent to which the views and values of these technology industry leaders and their AGI initiative will align with the views and values of journalists and journalism, especially as the field moves toward an increasingly experiential future. Although their priorities may match up along the dimensions of speed of and access to news as well as the value of accuracy in reporting, the core values of editorial independence and freedom of speech and press may not be well aligned between the two domains. The tension may be especially pronounced in an era marked by experiential journalism that can increasingly link news to public action.

A key unresolved matter is the extent to which an effective AGI approach advances quality experiential journalism that reflects journalism's importance in a democracy according to the principle of the Fourth Estate (which refers to the watchdog role of the press, positing that independent journalism is an informal fourth branch of government, serving as a check on the other three formal branches). If AGI ethics rest on this principle, then it may prove highly valuable to experiential journalism and its function in democracy. If this principle takes a back seat to protecting the commercial interests of technology giants, AGI is not likely to help lead to a better-informed citizenry but rather one that is largely a consuming marketplace intended primarily for profit taking. In 2018 Musk advanced an increasingly hostile view of contemporary American journalism as an institution not to be trusted, and his adversarial view may grow as experiential news becomes increasingly ubiquitous and users act on what they experience by protesting, boycotting, and buying or selling stock.[77]

Table 4.1 provides a summary of the transformative influences that algorithms, Big Data, and AI may bring to experiential journalism. The figure arrays four experiential journalism dimensions: (1) methods of production; (2) content and stories; (3) management, finance, and law; and (4) who is a journalist. These four dimensions intersect with three dimensions of computing technology: (1) algorithms, (2) Big Data, and (3) AI. Each of the twelve resulting cells identifies a consequence of computing technology on experiential journalism.

Not only can these computing developments facilitate new methods of experiential journalistic production, they also foster shifts in story forms, organizational structures, and the notion of who or what a journalist is. Newsroom management, finance, and law may seem less intuitive in this context, but the consequences of computing technology are substantial. For instance, the application of algorithms is facilitating the development of a virtual newsroom in which physical newsrooms are being supplanted by news organizations that exist largely in cyberspace and automatically generate experiential news. For instance, Fusion, Vox, Quartz, Slate, the AP, and the *Times* of London employ Slack, a cloud-computing work-collaboration tool for digital news workflow.[78]

Japan's JX Press is a news start-up using AI to conduct its news reporting in an effort to compete with Bloomberg News. JX Press uses a

TABLE 4.1

Implications of Algorithms, Big Data, and AI for Experiential Journalism

Computing technology	Methods of production	Content	Management, finance, and law	Who or what is a journalist?
Algorithms	Reporting	Automated writing and immersive, multisensory stories	Virtual newsroom	Data scientist role
Big Data	Systematic contextualization	Data-driven visualizations	Convergent research units	Heightened public engagement via citizen reporters and IoT
AI	AI assistants	Fact-checking, filtering fake news	Dynamic news augmentations	Expert-system AIs and neural networks

machine-learning platform called Fast Alert to monitor social media posts and analyze text, photos, and punctuation to identify breaking news in Japan, including fires, traffic accidents, and disasters. Fast Alert's algorithms then write the stories.

Koichiro Nishi, a deputy editor in chief at TV Asahi, says his newsroom now relies upon Fast Alert, which has become a "must-have tool" since they began using it in November 2016.[79] "It's basically a world of 100 million cameramen," Nishi says.[80] Sometimes Fast Alert identifies news events even before the first responders, such as the police or fire departments, Nishi says. Fast Alert also tracks overseas media and Twitter accounts that it determines are trustworthy and sorts out possible false or fake news items. AI-driven news-user interaction and other experiential news formats may soon follow. Among the investors in the start-up is Japanese media giant Nikkei, and paying clients include Japanese public broadcaster NHK, TV Asahi, and Fuji Television.

The question of who a journalist is represents a vital matter and is shifting quickly and dramatically. Data scientists increasingly play a central role in daily journalism, bringing a more quantitative approach to experiential news-gathering and analysis. Citizen reporters are poised to increase in number as well, as more individuals can participate in the news-gathering process via their mobile devices. This could represent a substantial increase in public engagement in the news, including experiential engagement, as more devices add AR and 360-degree video capabilities. Moreover, the rise of IoT can greatly advance the flow of data into experiential journalism and may be fueled by intelligent or at least sophisticated algorithms that can learn from observing human citizen reporters as to what data is most useful or valuable in the news stream. This stream of data and advanced computer processing in the cloud will drive the capability of generating real-time augmentations for the news. Currently, most augmentations (or AR augments) require substantial human intervention to capture, produce, and publish. As computing systems grow in sophistication and capacity, it will be possible for news organizations to rely more directly on automated systems to generate augments and to adjust and adapt them in real time to consumer preferences, changes in the data, and display platforms (such as handheld or head-worn).

At the end of the day, the promise is increased public engagement in a more fluid, contextualized, accurate, and interactive journalism system operating on an increasingly global stage. It will be essential to minimize any potential adverse consequences and to address any ethical challenges that may arise with the advance of computing technology. Identifying and filtering out fake news will likely take a combination of human and machine intelligence such as machine learning. To avoid influencing news events or sources with intrusive 360-degree video camera rigs, well-trained reporters will be required as well as new protocols that ensure the informed consent of the public. Shielding against threats to privacy in the pursuit of addressable digital advertising sales—currently a primary reason marketers spend much of their advertising budget on digital platforms such as Google, YouTube, and Facebook—will require a commitment from newsroom management to place the interests of the public over profits. News media decision-makers must protect the privacy of their experiential news users even if it means fewer advertising dollars. Violating privacy is tantamount to further eroding the public's trust in journalism, and without that trust, experiential journalism will lose all agency, influence, and eventually its audience before the nascent field can mature.

In the near term, Facebook has employed algorithms in a variety of ways including establishing editorial guidelines that use algorithms to generate news feeds.[81] Since the crisis of fake news erupted on Facebook in late 2016, the social network has implemented new methods to help detect fake news items—what it describes as "disputed" posts—and filter them out.[82] Combining algorithmic tools with the human efforts of users and professional journalists, these protocols seek to flag suspicious news items and vet them. Google has likewise introduced a fake-news tagging tool that runs via a mobile app.

An important question for both the experiential-news-consuming public and journalists alike is whether they should trust these technology companies and the fake-news detection, security, and privacy tools they develop and introduce to their platforms. The short answer is that it is too soon to say for sure. Some technology companies have introduced modest measures to heighten user security, privacy, and fake-news protection. But they have not developed any tools especially designed to address experiential news formats such as AR and 360-degree video. For instance, in 2018 Google launched a browser tool called an "incognito" window, which allows a Chrome user to "browse privately." However, this small step toward protecting online user privacy will do little to detect or prevent the distribution of fake experiential news.

The longer-term answer to the question of whether to trust technology companies is that it will be crucial that journalists and members of the public maintain a skeptical eye and ear and not assume that these tools, even if well intended, will be enough to rely on by themselves. It is likely that technology companies will not make their news detection algorithms transparent, and this fact by itself should make any news consumer or producer suspicious. The technology companies are for-profit, publicly traded, global behemoths whose dominant purpose is to make money. The only reason they have instituted substantial new methods to detect and prevent the spread of fake news and protect user privacy is that they have been caught in international controversies in these arenas and, at least in Europe, regulators have forced them to take action. At best, the new algorithms and methods that technology companies develop and implement to protect privacy and detect and prevent the spread of fake news should be viewed as ancillary protections and services, not the core tools to rely on for online safety and the reliability of experiential news and information. News media should independently assert a substantial effort to provide their own tools to protect online privacy and detect and prevent the distribution of fake experiential news. Reporting on the capabilities and foibles of digital companies in this regard should become a staple of twenty-first-century experiential journalism.

CODING THE FUTURE

Journalists and media professionals face an uncertain future. The economic foundations of news organizations, and media enterprises more generally, are in an unstable and rapidly evolving state. Public engagement with the media is in transition, as citizens increasingly use mobile and social media to participate in an interactive news and media environment. News dissemination is highly fragmented and frenetic in pace. Citizen reporting is often vital to the news process, but news organizations have sometimes struggled to fully embrace its potential or recognize its pitfalls.

The code-based nature of digital media is poised to fundamentally transform journalism and media even further. Algorithms, Big Data, AI, and geo-location are all fueling basic changes in news and media content as well as journalistic work methods, organizational structures, and public-media relationships. While some observers see these forces as a threat to journalists and traditional media, it may be more productive to see these developments as an opportunity to reinvent journalism and the media for a networked, mobile, and experiential age. Through this reinvention, innovative journalists and media entrepreneurs can employ AI in its various forms to augment their work, their reporting, and their story telling. Greater efficiencies are possible, and higher levels of journalistic quality (defined in terms of accuracy, compelling story telling, and original reporting) are within reach. Journalists and those in various media organizations can use these tools to increase public engagement through experiential news formats and expand the notion of who, or what, a journalist is. Scholars also face a set of challenges as new research questions emerge surrounding experiential news and may require new methods of inquiry. Meanwhile, journalism educators need to restructure their curricula to provide journalism students with the new intellectual skill set needed to succeed in an AI-driven age of experiential journalism.

Moving forward, all the elements of coding and experiential news content will be increasingly intertwined. Even the concept of what a story is will undergo a metamorphosis. New narrative structures draw upon Big Data, algorithms, and dynamic formats. Users can access stories on demand and obtain versions that are customized or personalized to their preferences, platforms, demographics, or geo-locations. Users can even contribute to those stories or the discourse surrounding them.

For journalism, these developments signal at least three important opportunities. First, innovative journalists and news organizations can transform both their operations and their news content by tapping into the synergies that are possible between content and computing to efficiently produce and distribute experiential news that is built on data and algorithms. Second, news leaders can greatly expand public engagement through the novel application of computing to journalism. In particular, dynamic and data- and algorithm-enabled news content that adapts automatically and in real time to user preferences, media choices, and the IoT can produce reliable, interactive, and multisensory news in efficient and scalable ways that can reach a mobile and active global news public. Finally, encouraging and incentivizing the news-consuming public to share their favorite news experiences can build user loyalty and the total size of the news-consuming public. Incentives have sometimes served journalism well in the past. For example, in the late 1800s Edward Willis Scripps purchased small, financially struggling newspapers, hired capable young editors, and gave them a share of the profits to incentivize them to increase circulation.[83] Some might say this represented a conflict of interest between the business and editorial sides of journalism, yet it helped to build a quality, profitable chain of newspapers whose legacy is still with us today.

A system of incentives for experiential news consumers—perhaps not financial but rather in the form of social capital such as likes or positive ratings on social media—might help build both the quality of citizen reporting and also the size and activity level of the engaged news public. For instance, establishing a rating system that publicly recognizes the quality of the AR and 360-degree video contributions of citizen reporters could be worthwhile. It could be achieved efficiently using a combination of user inputs, algorithmic compilation, and human editor oversight.

CHAPTER FIVE

Interactive Documentaries

Interactive documentaries (I-Docs) are a visually driven subset of what those in journalism industry often call "interactives." I-Docs in many ways represent a convergence of the content developments described earlier in the book. Advances in audio technology also underscore the importance of sound in producing compelling I-Docs and suggest directions in the documentary form that could be aurally driven, as is evident in the popularity of podcasts.

This chapter examines the interactive documentary, or I-Doc, as an emergent form of digital journalism and one that is increasingly experiential. As a subset of the more general interactives format, I-Docs are typically built around a visual frame—often using a panoramic image as an interactive user interface—and video as a central component of the story presentation. Interactives often incorporate visual, video, and audio elements, but they are not the core spine of the story or the interface framework for user navigation. The acclaimed *New York Times* documentary "Snow Fall" is an example of the general interactives format. It incorporates significant use of photography, video, graphics, and interactive features, but much of the narrative is in the form of text. In contrast, the I-Doc subset does not present the user with extensive portions of the story in textual form; rather, they feature extensive multimedia content and other novel techniques to engage the news consumer.

Since the late 1990s, a growing number of news organizations and journalists around the world have created interactive documentaries as a format for telling journalistic stories based on original research or reporting, multiple media, and immersive environments to engage the audience interactively with deep content, the teller of the story, and other viewers. Notably, the I-Doc is a form of digital journalism increasingly produced internationally, and it signals a possible global standard for quality experiential journalism stories. A number of online resources are available for the growing amount of interactive story-telling developing in journalism around the world. The Online News Association (ONA) is among those providing resources, including a number of quality interactive narratives as examples of excellence in this arena.[1] A notable I-Doc from Submarine is "Poppy Interactive."[2] Published in 2017, the I-Doc examines the role of the world's illegal drug trade in funding terrorism and decimating local populations including the people of Afghanistan. The extensively reported I-Doc features quality audio, video, and data in articulating the roles of globalization and drug money in fueling terrorism and destabilizing local economies. The user can navigate through the I-Doc in multiple intertwined narratives, taking the "northern route" through former Soviet states; the "Balkan route," which is the traditional route for heroin production and distribution; or the "southern route," which explores developments in West Africa, including Mali and the drug-funding of Al Qaeda and ISIS.

For journalists, I-Docs represent a compelling story form that can blend excellence in reporting—based on quality audio, video, and data—with user experiences designed to highlight the complexity of many of the world's most vital issues.

"Interactive" has become a news industry label for an emerging form of journalism content that emphasizes user engagement in the narrative through clicking, tapping, or otherwise manipulating or actively engaging the content or visual story elements. For instance, a user who encounters an interactive might begin by clicking on an object within a spherical photo or map to access further information or to explore a data-driven visualization that can be customized to user preferences. Interactives feature deep reporting, are highly produced, and emphasize narrative but not necessarily linear formats. They often use first-person perspective and sometimes employ the present tense rather than past tense. They tend to feature content via organizational structures that are uncommon in journalism and more often found in entertainment media, such as in video games and simulations. Interactives feature rich, immersive media content and contextualization and are especially valuable in explanatory reporting, although they are relevant to all types of stories.

"Snow Fall" from the *New York Times* in 2012 was among the first in the interactive genre to get widespread attention and acclaim for its effective combination of various story-telling techniques, including interactivity, multimedia, in-depth reporting, and narrative.[3] It earned a Peabody Award as well as a Pulitzer Prize in 2013 as a journalism feature story, for which the Pulitzer committee said the story telling in "Snow Fall" was "enhanced by its deft integration of multimedia elements," which included video, animation, and graphics.[4]

The multimedia "Snow Fall" tells the story of an avalanche that struck the Tunnel Creek section of Stevens Pass in the Cascade Mountains, Washington, on February 19, 2012. John Branch is the credited author, but the report involved a large graphics and design team of eleven *New York Times* staffers, including a photographer, three videographers, and a researcher, all of whom who worked more than six months to create the report. Among the innovative reporting resources and story-telling techniques employed, "Snow Fall" features elevation data from LIDAR (a survey technique measuring distance using pulsed laser light) and satellite imagery of the mountain terrain. The designers created a virtual model of the avalanche to generate a precise animation of the catastrophe that resulted in three deaths. Story telling in "Snow Fall" is enhanced by the integration of a bio card to introduce each character in the story. Users click on the bio card to see each character's name, photo, age, and occupation.

Demonstrating the continuing role that interactives are playing in its journalism, the *Times* has since reported other quality interactive and multimedia stories, including "The Heart-Stopping Climbs of Alex Honnold" about a climber who ascends some of the world's tallest and sheerest mountain faces without ropes.[5] Honnold was the first person to "freesolo climb El Sendero Luminoso (the Shining Path), a climbing route in El Potrero Chico," Mexico.

Among the first interactives produced by any news organization was the *Chicago Tribune*'s 1995 interactive crime map based on actual

Chicago-area crime data.[6] Since the groundbreaking report, a growing number of news media have produced quality interactives and have organized units that specialize in producing interactive, multimedia reports. The *Guardian*, for instance, has developed many interactives and captured much attention in 2013 with its "Firestorm," which engages users in an interactive exploration of one family's struggle to survive a violent and destructive bushfire in Tasmania.[7] Like "Snow Fall," "Firestorm" combines video, audio, long-form writing, and interactive elements. One of the qualities that distinguishes "Firestorm" is an organizational structure that offers a series of chapters as in a book. Users can select chapters in any sequence and then explore a blend of content including text, audio, video, graphics, and photographs. Extensive ambient sound from the fire itself and other sources such as first responders adds to the authenticity of the experience and the sense of presence for the user. Small icons associated with each type of content quickly denote for the user what type of experience they will have when clicking on a content item, for instance, a small movie camera denotes a video.

Nikki Usher, associate professor in the Institute of Communications Research in the College of Media at Illinois University, has investigated the emergence of interactive and immersive forms of journalism. In *Making News at the New York Times*, she explains how data-driven interactives are now a core part of everyday news work.[8] Her research suggests that this type of journalism came to play an essential role in the *Times'* journalism as digital in general became increasingly central to the overall nature of the news organization and its production, distribution, and unique online story form. Achieving this transformation required substantial change, including new organizational structures (including creating the Upshot, a unit focused on data-driven reporting), new types of staff (hiring data scientists and the like), and expanded numbers of staff with expertise in design, visualization, and multimedia production. The transition to a digital newsroom also required some difficult cultural adjustments, which frames the integration of interactive, multimedia content into daily reporting. The *Times'* organizational culture was somewhat top down, Usher found, and not all journalists were eager to change their reporting approach. Journalists are often reluctant to change out of concern that new techniques may increase efficiency to the detriment of quality, thinking that increasing speed also means the increased potential for error.

Because of the substantial staff and other resource requirements needed to generate interactives and I-Docs, not every story can feature such rich content and design. At least in the early days of interactives production (Usher was embedded in the *Times*' newsroom in 2010), resources that were needed to develop interactive, multimedia content were most often on major projects, ones typically geared to potentially win a Pulitzer Prize.[9]

Interactive journalism is increasingly integrated into the newsroom and is fundamental to helping newsrooms survive in the highly fragmented and competitive digital environment. Such new story-telling forms are entertaining and engaging multimedia, Usher's research indicates, and she describes the user experience with "Snow Fall" as almost like a video game. She writes, "With a 3D rotating view of the Cascade Mountains, maps that allowed users to point and click and explore of their own volition, videos that were revealed as users scrolled over areas on the page, and integration of audio, this was truly an immersive story-telling experience, one that almost felt like a video game."[10] "Snow Fall," Usher notes, brought in substantial numbers of new visitors to NYTimes .com, comprising up to one-third of the overall visitors to the site at any one time during the story's peak in 2012. For the year, "Snow Fall" brought in 2.9 million visits with more than 3.5 million page views. During the peak period for the story, "Snow Fall" had some 22,000 persons viewing it, and 7,500 were new to the *Times*.[11] Usher adds that in 2014 six of the top twelve traffic generators on the NYTimes.com most-emailed list were interactives.

Usher's research also indicates that interactive journalism requires new ways to think about how to produce and tell stories. Partly in response to the growing role of programmers working in news organizations, interactives bring a "build-it" or "maker" approach that is common to the world of computer programmers or hackers. Interactive journalists are making digital structures and systems via software code that can be reused or adapted for multiple stories. These digital structures include code-based tools that can be used to tell a story such as an interactive quiz or a data-driven calculator that can give each user a view of the story customized to her or his individual situation. Code can thus be used to create an integrated database for use by the entire newsroom via the cloud.

Interactives in journalism also enable the reader to get what Usher calls both a near view and a far view.[12] This can be done, for instance, through the use of geo-located data offered to readers in the form of an interactive map. Readers might see overall patterns across the entire map or community as represented in the map, for instance, crime patterns for a city. Then they might zoom in to their neighborhood or even their block and see the crime rates where they live. Similarly, interactive maps can perform a dual functionality of providing both a wide view and a narrow perspective on stories located anywhere in the world (or potentially beyond its boundaries). A useful example is an interactive map, "Inside Raqqa, the Capital of ISIS," which the *New York Times* offered readers on November 22, 2015.[13] The interactive map enabled readers to see the broader context for ISIS's occupation of the city of Raqqa, Syria, and to examine in closer detail the specific key elements of the terrorist capital.

In the analog age, story structure meant the parts of a written story, including the lede and the nut graph. Interactives still might have the equivalent of a nut graph, Usher adds. But each reader may not find the nut graph in the same place or form; for instance, the thesis of the story might come in the form of a visualization or interactive experience. Yet, the digital or experiential nut graph still gives the core thesis of the story.

STUDYING THE I-DOC FORM

For this chapter, I have developed an analytic framework for critically examining the nature of experiential journalism as reflected in a series of award-winning interactive documentaries. The framework, presented in the following schema, builds upon the analog journalism story model.

- Foundational elements
  1. Extent of evidence of reporting (number of sources cited)
  2. Quality of writing, editing
  3. Production values reflecting quality of audio, video, or other content elements

4. Structural elements
- Use of nonlinear or other narrative structures, including sequencing or layering content or developing braided (two or more narrative threads that initially seem unrelated but eventually intertwine, revealing qualities of each), interrupted, or mutable narrative structures[14]
- Presence of dynamic, data-driven content (customization, data visualizations, fluidity, location-enabled, kinetic/motion)
- Use of immersive, first-person point of view (versus third-person)
- Features unique to the digital media environment
  1. Number of media modalities (text, audio, actualities, acoustic elements, environmental sounds, video, GPS-encoded drone video or satellite imagery, animation, music, voices, color, light, image composition, pattern-making or grouping, shapes and models, user interface, motion, Java, Flash, GIFs, VR, advanced or basic AR using handheld or HMD, haptics, tactile or physical computing such as 3-D or 4-D printing)
  2. Extent of interactive elements (clickable components, or more NUI, with audio command, and even direct brain-machine interface—a direct electronic link between a digital device and the human brain, increasingly used in assisting the disabled to interact digitally—or as part of a video game interface)
  3. Incorporation of social media interactivity (engagement with social networks, engagement of Internet of Things)
  4. Extent or presence of contextualized content (connected to larger-picture data patterns or historical trends)
  5. Approach (narrative exploration, game, simulation, AR, VR)
  6. Mobility (designed for or adaptable to various mobile devices)
- Substance of message
  1. Social meaning, public significance, or news value
  2. Surprise
  3. Vividness
  4. Authenticity
  5. Less event centered, more process oriented

As this schema suggests, there are three core dimensions to experiential story telling in journalism. These are (1) the fundamentals;

(2) qualities of the digital, experiential media environment; and (3) message substance. Although these three dimensions parallel the traditional model of journalism stories, there are dramatic differences in the characteristics and complexity of these three dimensions in an experiential format.

The fundamentals include the extent to which the story draws upon evidence obtained through reporting (the number and diversity of sources cited, for instance). Other fundamental factors include the quality of writing and editing and the overall production values, reflecting quality of audio, video, or other content elements. Structural fundamentals include the use of nonlinear narrative, as reflected in sequencing or layering of content and braided, interrupted, or mutable (participatory) narrative. Also these include the use of dynamic, data-driven content (such as customization, data visualizations, fluidity, location-enabling, kinetics/motion), immersive presentations, and first-person point of view instead of third-person narration. Increasingly, these qualities intersect with the nature and capacities of the digital media environment. Digital formats enable more fluid, nonlinear, and immersive narrative structures, although such approaches are also possible in limited fashion in traditional analog media.

Features unique to the digital, experiential media environment include an array of communication modalities (e.g., text, audio, actualities, acoustic elements, environmental sounds, voice, music, and video including 360-degree, GPS-encoded, drone video, or satellite imagery). Also, these features include animation (including Java, Flash, or GIFs), color, light, image composition, pattern making or grouping, shapes and models, user-interface design, motion, VR, AR using HMDs and handheld devices, as well as haptic, tactile, and physical computing such as 3-D or 4-D printing. Important as well is the extent that interactive content elements are incorporated (clickable NUI or brain-machine interface—which is increasingly used in assisting the disabled to interact digitally—or in videogame interfaces). Social media interactivity is also relevant (content that is engaged with social networks and the Internet of Things).

Message substance is a dimension of unique importance to journalism and especially so in the experiential realm, where the boundary between the real and the artificial can easily blur. The incorporation of more contextualized content is an important element in experiential news that can intersect with the substantive aspects of the message or story. For instance, a story about a particular location, person, or event can include connections to the larger picture, data patterns, or historical trends. Further, a key element is the adaptability of the content across various mobile platforms. Finally, the story approach (e.g., narrative exploration, game, simulation, AR, or VR)—which intersects with the foundational elements of the story—varies widely in the digital media environment.

It is worth reiterating that in many ways, experiential news content, such as an I-Doc, is essentially a piece of computer software that tells a story. In this sense, the audience becomes a user of the software. The user can interact with the software, or story, navigate through the narrative, and otherwise control at least some aspects of the experience. This user control or manipulation is characteristic of many digital media, especially those that engage an immersive, interactive, and multisensory experience.

Social meaning and public significance, which are key aspects of news value, as well as surprise, vividness, and authenticity are qualities that often characterize the substantive aspects of experiential news, including I-Docs. Illustrative of this is a digital story-telling site called the Longest Shortest Time. Although not part of the case studies examined here, the site features stories that emphasize the surprising—such as episode 116, "How to Not (Accidentally) Raise a Racist"—and user engagement and interaction.[15] Stories are produced as podcasts but also include multimedia and user or reader contributions. I-Docs also incorporate elements of surprise or novelty and are typically less event-centered and more process-oriented than traditional news stories.

Here I employ a hybrid content analytic approach to determine the extent to which the elements of experiential journalism are utilized in selected I-Docs. To conduct this analysis I conduct a close "reading" of each I-Doc, involving both qualitative (critical) and quantitative (empirical) analyses of their manifest content characteristics.

The evidence presented in this chapter can help articulate, or unpack, the nature of quality in experiential news stories. It is an arena that is receiving growing research attention. Relevant work includes that of Gifreu Castells, whose research "provides an original conceptual framework and taxonomic study of the interactive documentary and the interactive forms of non-fiction."[16] Paralleling the experiential journalism framework outlined previously, Castells's taxonomy suggests a three-part model based on the subject matter of the documentary, the support or media platform, and the user experience.

QUALITIES OF I-DOCS

The specific interactive documentaries selected here for a close examination, or interrogation, are ten award-winning, original journalistic productions from the first fifteen years of the twenty-first century from around the world, including the United States and six other countries in North America, Latin America, Europe, and Asia. Here I list the ten I-Docs examined in this chapter.

1. *Le Mystere de Grimouville*: a mystery in a French community; FIGRA 2013 Award Inside Web & Doc, SCAM 2013 Brouillon d'un Reve.[17]
2. *Hollow*: an interactive documentary about the economic and cultural decline of an American community in West Virginia; Peabody Award 2013.[18]
3. *Fort McMoney*: a web documentary and strategy video game about the efforts in Fort McMurray, Alberta, Canada, to develop the world's largest oil sand reserves; Best Original Interactive Production Produced for Digital Media at the Canadian Screen Awards 2015.[19]
4. *Inside Disaster:* inside the Haiti earthquake experienced through a multimedia simulation; winner, 2010 Applied Arts Interactive Awards (Gaming); nominated, Gemini Award for Best Direction in a Documentary Program.[20]
5. *A Journey to the End of Coal in China*: millions of coal miners risk their lives for China's economic growth; Prix SCAM 2009 Digital Interactive Artwork Award.[21]
6. *The Reykyavik Confessions*: the mystery of why six people admitted roles in two murders yet could not remember anything about the crimes; produced by the BBC; Prix SCAM 2009 Digital Interactive Artwork Award.[22]

7. *Harvest of Change*: Iowa farm families confront a nation in transition; produced by the *Des Moines Register*; Murrow Award for Innovation.[23]

8. *Gaza Confidential*: an inside look at the Israeli-Palestinian conflict; Klynt Interactive Player mobile app for iOS, designed in France; Prix SCAM 2009 Digital Interactive Artwork Award.[24]

9. *Losing Ground: Louisiana Erosion*: the effects of climate change on Louisiana; from ProPublica; 2014 Gannett Award for Innovation and Watchdog Journalism.[25]

10. *Fukushima*: a nuclear disaster in Japan; from POV; 2015 Webby Award.[26]

These I-Docs were selected for three reasons. First, the productions reflect diverse content in the international context of each I-Doc. Second, the high quality of these productions is reflected in the awards they have won. Third, the free availability online (at the time of this writing) or on mobile platforms—including Apple iOS and Android—makes these I-Docs accessible to students, journalists, scholars, and the public at large for further examination. The preliminary findings of this investigation were presented at a conference in Berlin, Germany, as part of a blind-reviewed research paper competition.[27]

To critically examine these I-Docs, I use a form of close reading (intense examination) known generally as textual analysis, although it is not limited to text (it can include audio or video, etc.). Nor does this method rely strictly on reading (the method can include observation in any mode of expression, including listening to audio, watching video, or experiencing VR or AR). I interrogate each selected I-Doc to assess and measure the extent to which it incorporates each of the dimensions in the model or the presence or absence of particular techniques.

These I-Docs serve as a series of detailed case studies to test the proposed theoretical framework for experiential journalism outlined earlier. This case study approach is employed largely because of the embryonic nature of experiential story telling in journalism. As of this writing, the body of I-Doc stories is on the order of perhaps hundreds of stories worldwide, and only a portion (a few dozen perhaps) are at an award-winning level. In addition, the field is still in a state of significant development, with the experiential story form evolving in substantial ways.

The I-Docs reviewed in this chapter explore a wide range of topics, from an examination of a murder mystery in Iceland to the decline of farming communities in Iowa. Each I-Doc won at least one award or recognition for quality. For example, *Fort McMoney* was named Best Original Interactive Production Produced for Digital Media at the Third Canadian Screen Awards.[28] *Le Mystere de Grimouville* won the FIGRA 2013 Award Inside Web & Doc and the SCAM 2013 Brouillon d'un Reve.

In partnership with my spouse—an artist, educator, and former journalist—I coded each I-Doc in terms of the fifteen dimensions outlined in the schema presented earlier. The coding results were compared to test intercoder reliability. A measure of reliability was generated by assessing intercoder agreement on each of the fifteen dimensions included in the coding framework and then by averaging the combined overall scores. Analysis of the ten I-Docs indicates intercoder reliability of 0.978, or about 98 percent.

STRUCTURAL DIMENSIONS

A textual and multimedia analysis of the I-Docs reveals that journalists use a wide spectrum of digital and experiential techniques to create engaging stories. Table 5.1 summarizes the findings with regard to two of the narrative structural metrics. Most of the productions employ a nonlinear narrative model, but the extent and manner of doing so varies. *Hollow*, for instance, gives the user control over the general episodes to explore, but the specific elements of each largely consist of a series of linear video segments.

TABLE 5.1

Summary of Structural Metrics

Dimension	Low	Medium	High
Nonlinearity	1	4	5
Customizability	9	1	

$N = 10$

The productions enable various levels of user customization. *Fort McMoney* allows the user to customize the settings and is largely a user-constructed narrative. The production presents a series of data points and decisions that the user must make. Each choice can affect the subsequent possibilities and the overall user experience. The I-Doc uses a 360-degree Gigapan (using more than one-billion-pixel panoramic photo) high-resolution photographic image as the basis for its initial interactive interface.[29] Users click on the panoramic image to begin, or enter, the I-Doc.

Inside Disaster: Inside the Haiti Earthquake allows substantial user customization, with options including various choices within the narrative. These include decisions about how to frame a story (e.g., is the chaos best described as "looting" or "scavenging"?) if the user elects to play the role of a journalist.

APPROACHES

There are four main types of story-telling approaches: simulation, game, VR, and narrative exploration. Four of the productions use the narrative exploration approach. Producers have designed their digital content to enable the user to proceed through the elements of the narrative at a largely self-paced and user-controlled fashion but with relatively little interactivity. Each individual piece is largely linear in format. The voice or perspective in these productions is generally the third person, which is, for the most part, in the fashion of a traditional documentary.

Five of the productions employ a role-playing approach in which the digital elements are arranged to provide a virtual simulation of the corresponding real-world subject matter. This is the case in the *Inside Disaster* production, "Simulation: Inside the Haiti Earthquake." Directed and produced by Nadine Pequeneza, who also wrote the complex screenplay, the 2011 digital documentary is a nonfiction, fact-based, roleplaying simulation that allows the user to experience the story in three ways. Users can engage the simulation as a survivor of the earthquake facing difficult decisions about how to manage in precarious times after a natural disaster, as an aide worker making decisions and taking actions to help survivors, or as a journalist on assignment covering the aftermath of the earthquake.

Through these roles, the user proceeds in a first-person perspective, attempting to achieve the goals as laid out for the character, confronting a variety of challenges and problems, making decisions, and attempting solutions. As the simulation states, "What decisions would you make as an earthquake survivor, aid worker, or journalist in Haiti after the earthquake? *Inside the Haiti Earthquake* is a first-person simulation based on documentary footage from Haiti and real-life decision scenarios. Try it now, click the graphic below."

One production uses a game approach in which participants can play against other users or against the computer. *Fort McMoney* takes the user to the real-life setting of Fort McMurray, Canada. There, the user virtually enters a community confronted by major growing pains, environmental problems, and more as industry booms at the Athabasca oil sands.[30]

To implement a narrative exploration, *Harvest of Change* uses VR as a platform for experiencing life in an Iowa farming community. While a web-based version is available, the full experience requires Oculus Rift or a similar wearable headset. *Harvest of Change* was one of the first uses of VR technology by a mainstream or legacy news outlet, but it had problems with using "gamification" in a rendered interactive segment. Moreover, the 360-degree video in this innovative news content could be experienced by very few news consumers at the time because so few had access to wearable technologies needed for a fully immersive experience.

Gaza Confidential uses a graphic novel approach to narrative exploration, layering in animated text and limited user interaction, and is designed for users of mobile, handheld devices.

PERSPECTIVE AND MODALITIES

First-person perspective is a common point of view (four of the I-Docs use this) in the productions as the model predicts. But third-person perspective is used slightly more often (by half, or five), perhaps a legacy from the traditional world of journalism. Some productions (two) allow the user to see the same story, circumstances, or events from multiple perspectives.

Table 5.2 presents the findings regarding the extent to which the I-Docs utilize the unique capabilities of networked, digital, and mobile media.

TABLE 5.2

Summary of Digital Media Metrics

Dimension	Low	Medium	High
Interactivity	3	2	5
Modalities	3	3	4
Social Media	7	2	1
Data Visuals	4	3	3
Context	2	5	3

N = 10

The modes of communication are diverse, and several productions make use of at least eight modes of expression. The modes utilized include audio in the form of spoken words, music, environmental sounds, photographs, artist-rendered graphics, data-driven visualizations, video, animation, immersive video, and location-based media. None of the I-Docs employ emerging modalities such as drone-captured video or other data collected via multispectral sensors that might provide aerial or other, broader perspectives or tactile engagement.

Some journalists contend that stories in journalism should avoid the use of music, with the possible exception of during transitions between segments or at the end or beginning of a news report, as T. Sean Herbert, producer at CBS News, told those assembled at the Quality Journalism in the Digital Age conference on April 10, 2015, in New Brunswick, New Jersey, organized as part of the Journalism and Public Interest initiative directed by Phil Napoli (then professor at Rutgers but now at Duke).[31] "Never use music in journalism," Herbert stated. Music, he argued, can build suspense or manipulate emotion and detracts from authenticity. It is an interesting argument, but there is little research to date to confirm whether it is true. Studies in neuroscience do document that "music activates emotional centers in the brain."[32] Exactly which types of music influence which centers and emotions is still under investigation, Hollywood notwithstanding.

It is perhaps conventional wisdom in established journalism to not use music, but there are notable exceptions, including several of the I-Docs studied here. Moreover, the highly acclaimed podcast *Serial* makes effective use of subtle musical elements. Yes, the music seems to tap into emotions, but it does not seem to detract from authenticity or believability in the message. The music certainly did not diminish audience interest in *Serial*, as the 175 million downloads suggest.[33] Featuring a quickly recognizable piano arrangement, *Serial*'s music is from an original score by Mark Henry Phillips and Nick Thorburn.[34] It may raise the larger issue of whether stories such as *Serial* are, in fact, journalism.

Joyce Barnathan, president of the International Center for Journalists, a nonprofit based in Washington, DC, and a veteran journalist, argues in the *Columbia Journalism Review* that *Serial* is journalism, and that its transparency is the key.[35] "What [Sarah] Koenig does that we (journalists) don't normally do is share our thoughts and views as we research a story," Barnathan writes. "Normally we do all that work *before* publishing. We give our audience the most intelligent assessment we can. We go through the same hard work of interviewing and researching as Koenig—and we suffer through the same anxieties and soul searching. The difference is, we never make that work public. She breaks new ground because she makes journalism more transparent—and in my view, adds tremendous credibility to our field."

Transparency of *Serial*'s reporting and story-telling process allows others to critically examine its methods and rigor, its fundamentals. Perhaps journalists should not use music in breaking news stories unless it is from a source and directly part of the story (for instance, a story about a musician), but in feature-type reports or investigations, music seems to have a useful place in journalism stories in the digital, experiential media age. The popularity of *Serial*'s first season led the producers to create a television version of the program during its second year, which focuses on an examination of the case of Bowe Bergdahl, the U.S. Army sergeant held captive for five years by the Taliban in Afghanistan and who faced a military court-martial for desertion.[36] The internet radio giant Pandora streamed the second season of the popular program and "the public radio show that spawned it, 'This American Life.'"[37]

Several of the I-Doc productions studied provide compelling contextual information. *Hollow*, for example, provides extensive data and historical information on the decline of the county it examines in West Virginia. It situates the county in time and place and uses algorithms to automatically generate animations of the data-driven visualizations. It also places the story of McDowell County in the context of the nation-wide decline of many American counties. In its opening sequence, the I-Doc notes that one in three U.S. counties is dying in terms of shrinking populations.

SOCIAL NETWORKING AND INTERACTIVITY

Most of the I-Doc productions use social media and do so in several alternative forms. First, those that integrate social media, at a minimum, allow users to share or like their experience on social media platforms such as Facebook, Twitter, and Instagram. A few also allow the user to upload information that can be shared with other participants with regard to the story.

All the productions utilize interactive techniques but vary in their methods. Most utilize an onscreen, clickable menu that allows the user to select and navigate through the content. *Le Mystere de Grimouville* extends its visual navigation further, providing an animated, locative map of the community that overlays the user's virtual location in real time. But the map is not interactive; the user cannot click on a location and move directly there by choice.

A small number of the productions utilize mobile platforms, though most of the productions were designed for a web presentation. The newest of the productions utilize a mobile design and app, for example, *Gaza Confidential*. The mobile apps tend to offer less overall interactivity than the web-based documentaries, perhaps due to bandwidth or user-interface considerations. This is likely to change as mobile devices become increasingly powerful experiential media platforms capable of any functionality available on a desktop or laptop computer or other digital device (e.g., flat-panel TV).

FOUNDATIONAL ELEMENTS

Table 5.3 summarizes the foundational elements in the I-Docs. The productions generally utilize original reporting and draw on a wide range

TABLE 5.3

Summary of Foundational Metrics

Dimension	Low	Medium	High
Significance	1	3	6
Novelty	3	2	5
Factual Evidence	1	5	4
Sourcing	4	1	5
Production Value	1	3	6

N = 10

of source types. The writing and editing quality are generally good. Several productions use a wide spectrum of primary sources, including interviews; paper records; digital records; direct observation in the form of photographs, video, or audio recording; and governmental data such as the U.S. census, economic data, and the like. *Gaza Confidential* is drawn largely from secondary sources (previously published) but utilizes some direct observational evidence. The production values are generally good, and some are exceptional. *Le Mystere de Grimouville, Hollow,* and *Fort McMoney,* for instance, all utilize high-quality professionally produced multimedia. Shots are well composed and appropriately lighted. Color and framing are effective, and video and audio are tightly edited.

MESSAGE SUBSTANCE

The significance and novelty of each story's content varies. Most explore a domain that involves elements of high news value, including social or economic injustice, the imbalance of power, and the environmental consequences of large corporate or governmental actions or policies. Some explore topics of human greed and crime, including murder. Several engage the user in a mystery that can be understood only by completing the interactive experience.

Two particularly interesting I-Docs that score highly on nearly every dimension of the story-telling framework are *Losing Ground* and

Fukushima. Losing Ground is an I-Doc from ProPublica that examines the topic of the environmental devastation of development and industry activities in the Gulf region of Louisiana. *Fukushima* is a similarly creative I-Doc, which examines the aftermath of the 2011 catastrophic nuclear accident in Japan. Both productions make extensive use of data-driven visualizations, location-based media, and compelling media perspectives including satellite imagery to provide effective understanding of environmental dimensions of their stories.

REFLECTIONS ON THE I-DOC

At the dawn of the twenty-first century, I wrote about the agency quality of interactive journalism in a hypothetical news story from an imagined space journey to the far reaches of the solar system.[38]

> You're immersed in the evening news of 2010. A ninety-second video bulletin reports an important extraterrestrial discovery on Europa, Jupiter's largest moon. Using your head-worn display, you look around the surface simply by turning your head. You look at the left-hand portion of the three-dimensional omni (directional) video (your gaze acts as a mouse would today) and say "select," and a second window in your immersive environment plasma display reveals a special video inset with detailed animation showing how life began under Europa's frozen hydrogen crust.[39]

In this scenario, the user is an active participant in the story, looking and even moving about in a 3-D virtual world. The experiential story is presented in the second-person voice.

The findings of this I-Doc investigation suggest at least five important sets of implications for the experiential journalism story model, including the quality of agency. First, journalists utilize varied techniques to produce and design I-Docs; there is no single design standard. Creativity in design can support the unique qualities of a particular story, including its facts and sources of information. News organizations increasingly recognize the importance of creativity in stories. The *New York Times* is one such organization; its masthead lists a creative director under news.

Second, the findings confirm three major dimensions of digital journalism stories. Producers of I-Docs are generating quality nonfiction stories based on the following:

1. foundational elements including the research, writing, editing, media production, and structural elements, including nonlinear narrative structure, first-person perspective, and dynamic data-driven content
2. unique qualities of the digital, networked, and mobile media environment, including mixed-media modalities, social networking media, greater contextualization, and novel approaches such as games and simulations
3. substantive dimensions of the message or story, including social meaning and resonance, public significance, surprise, and distinctiveness or vividness

Third, the extent to which journalists employ these techniques and principles varies widely in scope and quality. Each of these story characteristics increasingly intersects across the dimensions of story fundamentals, features of the digital media environment, and message substance. In addition, the advent of mobile, wearable, haptic, and other emergent media forms promises to further transform journalism stories. Journalists have only begun to tap into the story dimensions that may most directly engage the public, such as social media, immersion, and content interactivity.

Fourth, although this chapter has examined ten award-winning I-Docs, quality productions around the world are growing in number. These include *Immigrant Nation*, one in an award-winning series of web-based I-Docs from POV. Other examples of excellence in the I-Doc arena include "Can You Spot the Threat?" an NBC News airport security simulation narrated by Natalie Morales;[40] *Cutthroat Capitalism*, a nonfiction game by *Wired* that offers an interactive story on the nature of the American economic model with the user placed in the role of a pirate;[41] "Roots of the Recent Violence Between Israelis and Palestinians" from the *New York Times*;[42] *Storming Juno*, a World War II I-Doc focused on D-Day, June 6, 1944;[43] *The Last Hijack*, an I-Doc incorporating raw video footage video, animations, and an interactive timeline for navigation to explore "the mind of Mohamed, a wealthy Somali pirate while at sea but just another struggling man while on land";[44] and *Door into the Dark*, an interactive exploration of blindness and winner of a Tribeca Film Festival award.[45] As the interactive documentary form continues to grow in use and popularity around the world, it suggests future directions in experiential journalism, including the use of multiple perspectives, mixed-media modalities, and fact-based virtual worlds.

Finally, it is worth noting that I-Docs are in some ways derivative of traditional documentaries more than hard or breaking news. This has been a bit of a double-edged sword. Although it has helped to ensure that I-Docs are deeply reported, truthful, and professionally produced, it has seemingly limited their incorporation of some more innovative experiential techniques that might increase audience engagement without sacrificing the quality or integrity of the news content. For example, producers of I-Docs and other news content might explore greater use of first- or second-person perspective as a means of increasing user empathy with the subjects being examined. An interesting illustration of the potential is a VR op-doc published by the *New York Times* in early 2017. In "Orbital Vanitas," "you are placed inside an enormous human skull that is orbiting above the earth."[46] Through VR, the user journeys on a meditation on "existence and death."

CHAPTER SIX

Drone Media and Beyond

Humans have long dreamed of flight. Since at least the ancient Greek myth of Daedalus and Icarus, stories of unassisted human flight have stirred the popular imagination.[1] The advent of advanced VR technology promises to transform narratives of human flight. Experiential media systems may enable users to virtually experience flight, not just see, hear, or read stories about it. One example is a VR flight narrative called *Birdly*—an experimental media project supported by the Sundance New Frontier Story Lab—which engages the user in a realistic flight experience via an Oculus HMD.[2]

Creating the video content featured in *Birdly*, however, required a very different technology: a drone equipped with an array of ultra-high-definition cameras. The videos from the cameras were stitched together via algorithm-driven software to create the immersive video displayed on the Oculus headset.

As this chapter will suggest, drones play a key role in the creation of experiential media content, especially journalism. Far from limited to flight simulators, drones have a range of unusual capabilities that enable story creators to utilize this emerging technology to generate compelling, authentic, and unique experiential news content.

AERIAL PERSPECTIVE AND THE MEDIA

The development of modern unmanned aerial vehicles (UAVs), commonly known as drones, presents a dramatic opportunity for television and media organizations and content creators to capture aerial video less expensively and ostensibly more safely than video obtained via helicopter or airplane.

Television stations have been using helicopters since at least 1958 to capture aerial video of news on the ground.[3] Los Angeles TV station KTLA used the first news helicopter, dubbed the Telecopter, to capture news on July 4 that year. In the six decades since then, the use of helicopters for news-gathering and other media productions has grown dramatically. Some of the capabilities fueling TV news helicopter usage include providing unique aerial, wide-angle views of terrestrial news events and locations.

There are also significant drawbacks to the use of helicopters by TV and other media organizations. Chief among them are the cost and danger, especially to those flying on the helicopters. Since the first news helicopter crash in 1966, more than sixty people have been killed and dozens more injured worldwide in helicopter accidents during news-gathering.[4] On March 18, 2014, for instance, two people were killed in Seattle, Washington, when a news helicopter crashed near the city's famed Space Needle.[5]

ORIGINS OF DRONES

Drones have a long history, dating to at least the mid-1800s, when unmanned air balloons were used to deliver bombs from Vienna, Austria, to Venice, Italy.[6] In 1915 inventor Nicola Tesla proposed creating a fleet of UAVs designed for combat.[7] Since then, UAVs, or drones, have become widely used in military operations, both for surveillance and for the delivery of explosives. Drones are particularly well known for their use by the U.S. military in its battle against terrorism outside the United States.

Modern drones come in a variety of forms and types and are increasingly useful in the commercial sector. Their applications range widely from making deliveries to delivering internet access. Broadcasters and filmmakers are making increasing and sometimes innovative use of drones in video production. In one case, the BBC used an underwater drone to capture video by employing a camera-equipped robotic tuna to obtain underwater video of a large pod of dolphins swimming in the sea near Costa Rica. Called "Dolphins—Spy in the Pod," the documentary featured unique video that could be captured only via underwater drone technology.[8]

Of more general value to broadcast journalists and film media is a class of drones called quadricopters or quadcopters. Quadricopters are multicopters that lift and propel via four rotors. Some drones have six or eight rotors, which provide more precise maneuverability, but they are also more expensive and heavier. Quadricopter drones are small, lightweight, and inexpensive. The Parrot AR.Drone, for instance, is a quadricopter that is about a meter in diameter, weighing less than a pound, and costing just a few hundred dollars. Like many drones, it is equipped with two video cameras, one of which is an HD video camera (720 pixels) capable of live streaming on a smartphone or tablet.[9] Chinese firm DJI, which dominates the consumer drone market worldwide, sells the more expensive Phantom drone. It features vibration-stabilized geo-located cameras, which can produce much smoother aerial video.[10] In 2016 several entrepreneurial initiatives introduced miniature drones, some of which are foldable and can fit in the palm of a human hand or in a shirt pocket. They weigh only a few ounces and can serve as autonomous (self-piloting) personal drones, hovering near their human master or journalist, and can record audio and video of a subject being interviewed.[11] Even smaller microdrones are in development in various research labs. These functional drones are as small as flying insects and might serve a significant role in surveillance and reporting. But they also raise privacy concerns, as humans might not notice a microdrone or realize that a spec on the wall is actually a drone watching and recording them.

FOUR EXPERIENTIAL JOURNALISM IMPLICATIONS OF DRONES

Drones present a number of important opportunities for the journalism industry generally. Four areas that video-equipped quadricopters impact are particularly significant for experiential journalism. These are (1) new methods of video production, (2) techniques for increasing audience engagement, (3) emerging economic and regulatory frameworks, and (4) content transformation, including geo-tagged content, novel content types, or data acquired from a broad range of sensors beyond the standard visible light captured via video cameras, which may be a central generator of unique experiential media content.[12]

New Methods of Video Production (and Beyond)

Quadricopters are an increasingly common, inexpensive, and relatively safe form of unmanned aerial vehicle or drone. Quadricopters can be equipped with various sensors, particularly those used in remote sensing, including electromagnetic sensors to capture the visual spectrum and infrared or radiant heat (for nocturnal or low-light situations) or biological and chemical sensors. Drones with night-vision cameras were introduced into the market in 2016.[13] Developed via DJI, these drones feature thermal imaging technology capable of capturing imagery of objects in the dark as well as in smoke (for instance, from a burning building or a wildfire) or while otherwise obscured by environmental conditions such as smog. Combining sensors and AI can also enhance the safety of drone operation by enabling automatic object avoidance, much like autonomous land-based vehicles (self-driving cars or trucks) operate. AI also can be used to analyze vast volumes of drone-captured imagery for newsworthy content.

For journalists and filmmakers, the most frequently used sensors are high-definition video cameras equipped with geo-location tracking. Quadricopters equipped with high-definition video cameras, GPS tracking, and Wi-Fi capability can produce geo-located video (and audio) for real-time viewing or recording. They are emerging as important new tools for experiential journalism.

In addition to the cost savings, drone video is important in experiential news reporting for at least five production-related reasons. First, drones provide more media operations with the ability to capture video, revealing a wider aerial perspective on current events. This can help provide context and before-and-after imagery. Such uses are effectively illustrated in a 2015 AP report on melting glaciers.[14] The AP employed a drone to capture powerful aerial footage on melting glaciers in the Arctic, Norway, and a number of other venues and to thereby explore the impact of global climate change. HuffPost has published a series of remarkable aerial photographs captured by drones around the world.[15] Illustrating the potential to obtain unique perspectives via drones, the photos include "Pink Lake" in Bumbunga, Southern Australia, and "Japanese Van Gogh" (colorful agricultural patterns) in Tosacho, Japan.[16] CNN has used a drone to capture aerial views of Cuba, a country that has long been forbidden to those from the United States (due to the 1959 revolution) but is now opening up to American visitors because of an executive order from former president Barack Obama.[17] Experiential news stories could allow users to virtually visit and explore such exotic venues and environments from a first-person perspective, potentially amplifying the impact of the reporting on viewer empathy and understanding.

Second, drones enable non-government-controlled access to news events, and this may be especially important for experiential journalism. This may be vital in obtaining truthful, nonfiltered documentation of breaking news, such as calculating crowd sizes at protests or observing the aftermath of natural or human-made disasters. This capability was powerfully illustrated on March 12, 2014, when citizen reporter Brian Wilson captured aerial drone video of the devastation left behind after a deadly gas explosion leveled two buildings in East Harlem, New York, killing at least eight and injuring dozens.[18] In war-torn Syria, drone video captured by independent journalists in 2016 revealed that the Syrian city of Homs had been "utterly destroyed after five years of war."[19] Experiential reports could utilize this type of content to enable real-time, first-person user engagement with distant but vital news events.

Third, drones increase safety in news-gathering. While dozens have been killed in news helicopter crashes, drones present virtually no danger to their pilots. And miniature, lightweight models such as the Parrot AR.Drone 2.0 pose relatively little danger to anyone on the ground or in the air (relative to a helicopter crash), especially if used responsibly and according to regulatory guidelines as discussed later in this chapter, although midflight collisions are a legitimate concern (especially considering the possibility of terrorist attack via drone). For journalists already operating in dangerous environments (conflict zones or natural disaster areas), such tools could prove especially valuable in the growing production of experiential news.

Fourth, drones offer the capacity to capture geo-located video from the air. As terrestrial geo-located video has emerged on mobile apps such as Kinomap, aerial geo-located video is an important complementary development extending this capacity into a three-dimensional arena. Drones equipped with a variety of other sensors beyond video cameras can collect additional data that may be useful in news reporting or other forms of experiential stories. For instance, drones might use chemical, biological, or other types of sensors to gather information about air quality or pollution and the like to enable data-driven journalism about the environment. Drones can also be equipped with miniature high-resolution cameras or similar advanced devices to capture high-definition video and still photos.[20] A new generation of cameras mounted on drones can shoot video from six perspectives and stitch together the video automatically to generate 360-degree, immersive, experiential aerial news video.[21]

Beyond these principal uses, drones enable content creators to obtain video and other digital data to generate uniquely compelling experiential news content. Drones are essentially robots. They can be remotely controlled or even operate independently via the application of algorithms, machine vision, automated decision-making, or other AI technologies. Because of their small and lightweight dimensions, drones are capable of tightly controlled maneuverability and even remarkable athletic performance, with the ability to operate in the air, on the land, or in the sea or even to fly under bridges or through an open window; they can even hover over someone's shoulder like a well-trained parrot.

Because drones operate without a human operator on board, they can travel into situations or environments that would be impossible or unsafe for a human to enter. For instance, a drone can fly into a nuclear disaster zone. Equipped with advanced imaging technology or multispectral sensors, drones can obtain video or other data that content creators can turn into powerful and almost unprecedented experiential news content.

Given the advantages of modern drones, a growing number of news organizations around the world have started to utilize drones to capture video. In late 2013, for instance, news media reporting on political protests in Thailand used drones equipped with high-definition video cameras to capture moving pictures of the protests.[22] This video was important in documenting the protests, helping provide an independent means to calculate crowd size.[23] A wide range of videographers and organizations are exploring the use of drones to capture new vantage points on terrestrial events. "Long Island high school experimenters and professionals alike are finding that remote-control aerial shots, like of a fisherman's expression from the ocean side, can expand their perspectives," reports the *New York Times*.[24] Using a handheld device to control a drone, "nature photographer Dell R. Cullum thumbed the inch-long joystick controls, and within seconds, the drone soared to 190 feet," Christine Giordano explains. "It shared its view from a camera about the size of a matchbox to an iPhone screen below. From the elevated vantage point, the trees had a cotton-puff quality, the long spine of the LongHouse's roof could be seen in its entirety and the 20-person crowd—mostly photographers and videographers—looked like a cluster of dolls." Experiential stories could employ this type of drone reporting for expanded first-person coverage in a wide spectrum of localities that are often outside the regular coverage of daily news media.

Despite their cost advantages and technical capabilities that support experiential news production, drones should not be used as a substitute for on-site reporting by human journalists on the ground. Drones capturing video or other data should be a complement to shoe-leather reporting, including eyewitness accounts and interviews. Reporters on the ground may be able to make contextual or other observations and ask insightful questions that may be invaluable in providing additional cues to make sense of unfolding developments. Still, veteran journalist and author Todd Brewster notes, economics may dictate that shoe-leather reporting will be "simply too expensive to compete with drone reporting, driving traditional journalism tactics into history."[25]

Because of their relative safety, small size, and ease of use, a quadricopter can shoot video indoors or in other tight spaces. Documentary makers, for instance (including the BBC), are using drones in the production of a variety of documentaries. Oscar-nominated documentary maker Bayley Silleck used a quadricopter to film under low bridges over the Rappahannock River in the Chesapeake Bay watershed.

Quadricopters could prove valuable in producing experiential stories in a variety of space-restricted venues, such as inside museums or outdoors in a garden such as the maze and the labyrinth at the Schönbrunn Palace in Vienna, Austria.

Broadcasting pioneer Michael Flaster, president and founder of Traveling Mind Productions, notes that sports is one of the first areas to find an effective production role for video-enabled drones.[26] Flaster says, "Surf videographers are already using drones to capture the action from an aerial perspective. That trend seems to be migrating to the documenting of extreme sports as well as climbing and skiing."[27] The potential to integrate such drone footage into experiential stories is substantial and could give news consumers the opportunity to virtually experience real-life extreme sports as if a participant.

Quadricopters feature various capabilities that have increased their ease of use and potential value in the production of experiential news. Most quadricopters, for example, feature Wi-Fi-enabled remote controls via smartphone, tablet, or even HMD. Thus, a freelancer or citizen reporter can easily learn to pilot a drone. Some commercial drones can fly up to fifty miles per hour and thereby offer the potential to create compelling, high-speed news user experiences.

Geo-location in drone video provides at least two benefits in experiential news production. First, geo-location is an important tool for the digital watermarking of video shot by freelance or full-time journalists or by citizen reporters. Providing a time, date, "author," and location stamp independently embedded via GPS into each video frame is a potentially powerful protection of copyright. Moreover, such location tagging can be useful in helping establish the veracity of video. In some cases, authorities or even members of the public may question the authenticity of video of conflict zones, for instance. Having an independent means of authenticating drone video, including that produced by civilian drone journalists, may be especially useful in experiential journalism to help establish the truthfulness of first-person news experiences. Another potential capability for use in experiential journalism is what is known as photogrammetry, which involves taking measurements via the high-resolution imagery available in VR content.[28] Such VR measurements could be compared with samples of direct real-world measurements to aid in the authentication of reporting by drone.

Audience Engagement

Camera-equipped or other sensor-equipped drones offer at least two important means to increase audience engagement in experiential journalism. First, because of their low cost, ease of use, and novelty, drones have become increasingly popular among lay citizens around the world. Paris-based Parrot SA reports selling more than 600,000 of its drones by early 2016, the vast majority of those to civilians. As such, civilian drones represent an important vehicle for citizen experiential reporting.

Citizen use of drones is likely to increase dramatically in coming months and years. In 2014, at least two citizen-oriented drone projects debuted on Kickstarter, the crowdfunding website.[29] In addition, aerial "selfies" shot via drone are already emerging as an increasingly common social media offering.

Second, geo-location offers an intriguing opportunity to enable audience members and journalists to search for and access video by location. Geographic search of videos has not been available historically for news video (except by textual descriptor) and is a new capability via GPS coordinates. Location-based video search has potential utility or value for future investigations both by reporters and news consumers seeking specific immersive aerial experiences.

Economic and Regulatory Frameworks

Most commercial drones range in price from several hundred dollars, up to about $40,000. One high-end UAV known as the Camcopter, which looks like a small helicopter and carries high-end broadcast-news-gathering equipment, runs about $400,000.[30] These costs are in contrast to those required to purchase or contract a helicopter and pilot. Robinson Helicopter Company, for instance, lists the base price for a newscopter at $829,000.[31] Operating costs, including fuel and maintenance, are in addition to the base price and pilot expenses. Accident liability and insurance are pertinent regardless. The dramatically lower price of a drone and its operation opens up the potential for much wider use of the technology for aerial videography and use in experiential journalism.

Although drone journalism has taken off in much of the world, it has developed more slowly in the United States where there have only been scattered uses of drones to capture video of news events. On February 1, 2014, for instance, a photojournalist on temporary assignment to TV station WFSB in Hartford, Connecticut, used a drone to capture aerial footage of a fatal car accident. Police investigating the accident were upset about the journalist's use of the drone, alleging that it endangered the police investigation, and subsequently questioned the reporter. Connecticut's laws regarding the commercial use of drones are in development. The Federal Aviation Administration (FAA) is conducting its own investigation of the reporter's use of the drone.

Authorities also restricted or even banned the use of drones by journalists during the 2016 protest at Standing Rock, North Dakota, where opponents of the Dakota Access oil pipeline clashed with law enforcement and those attempting to construct the pipeline. Such investigations by authorities may have a chilling effect on journalists' use of drones in experiential news-gathering and raise important freedom-of-speech concerns.

FAA regulatory requirements require commercial drone users register their drones.[32] *CBS This Morning* reported that some 914,000 hobbyist drones and 194,000 commercial drones were registered by July 2018 in the United States, and some three million had been sold worldwide.[33] Federal rules require that drones fly below four hundred feet, operate only within visual line of sight, and not fly directly over people. The FAA predicts that by 2020 some thirty thousand drones could be in commercial operation in the United States, both for news-gathering and other uses, and millions more in noncommercial use.[34]

Jeff Bezos, whose empire includes the *Washington Post* and retail giant Amazon, is developing drones to make retail product deliveries to home consumers in fewer than thirty minutes.[35] Amazon started its drone delivery service in India—where the skies were open early for commercial drone flight although they have since been banned—and other international venues.[36] In one of the first commercial field tests of drone delivery, an Amazon drone delivered a product to a consumer in the UK in late 2016 in just eighteen minutes. It is unclear whether the *Post* will utilize drones in the production of experiential news, but they represent an opportunity for innovation that could draw on Amazon's expertise.

The term "drone" also conjures negative imagery to the public, largely because of the vehicles' use in military strikes and spying (threatening privacy). Consequently, there is considerable public concern and correlating political and regulatory reluctance in some countries, including the United States, to legalize widespread drone use, especially drones with sensors such as cameras.

Edward Markey, a Massachusetts Democrat, cochairs the Congressional Bipartisan Privacy Caucus. Markey has drafted drone legislation intended to protect the privacy of people on the ground. The proposed law would establish a public website listing drone licensees and their flight plans, including when and where their drones would fly. How this would affect the development of experiential journalism using drones is an unsettled issue.

Public concern about drones and privacy may increase as the public begins to see drones increasingly often. As I can attest, there is something a bit unnerving about a video-enabled drone coming toward you, especially when it is less than one meter away. In the close presence of a drone, you tend to have an uneasy feeling of being watched. Drones with powerful cameras running facial recognition software can both track and identify individuals in the camera's field of view. While such capability may prove enormously powerful in both surveillance and experiential news reporting, the implications for privacy are equally profound. Naira Hovakimyan of the University of Illinois predicts that drones will be the cell phones of the future.[37] She expects that personal drones will be increasingly miniature (perhaps only a few inches in diameter) and capable of a wide spectrum of tasks, including the capacity to carry out household tasks such as retrieving medicine for the elderly and making video recordings. A variety of scientists anticipate the diffusion of drones will be at least in part fueled by advances in AI, which can enable drones to operate more effectively, efficiently, autonomously, safely, and intuitively (anticipating user needs or wishes) in close spaces. "Roboticists and physicians predict that a new wave of technological advances, including drones, will help older adults stay at home longer."[38] Such developments will also support greater data collection on a variety of fronts, which may contribute to experiential news content production and consumption.

Drones may signal the beginning of a new age of ubiquitous surveillance—a mobile panopticon.[39] Eighteenth-century social philosopher Jeremy Bentham described a powerful system of surveillance that he called the panopticon, which could be used to monitor inmates such as those in a hospital or prison from a central position. In the two centuries since Bentham's proposal, the panopticon has been reimagined as a ubiquitous surveillance technology for the networked digital age. Although many anticipate that such surveillance would be a likely tool of the government (perhaps abused but ostensibly for law enforcement), novelist Dave Eggers describes in his book *The Circle* a potentially even more likely and frightening world in which corporate interests dominate global data collection driven by ubiquitous cameras, social media, algorithms, and the profit motive.[40] The book offers this succinct summary of the corporate view of ubiquitous data collection and distribution via social media: "Secrets are Lies. . . . Sharing is caring. . . . Privacy is theft."[41] Balancing the public's right to know via drones in experiential news against the public's right to privacy may become a twenty-first-century flashpoint.

Celebrities are also raising concerns about the potential use of drones by paparazzi to capture candid shots in both public and private locales.[42] Of course, the public may also become increasingly accustomed to seeing drones and come to accept their presence in the same way that many people have become accustomed to and tolerant of video security cameras in more and more locations. Still, a segment of the population objects strongly to the widespread presence of video camera surveillance. Some have even developed wearable devices, such as customized hats that feature a matrix of infrared LEDs to effectively blind most surveillance cameras.[43] Law enforcement professionals and others, including entrepreneurs, have developed a variety of systems and approaches to disable drones, including in Finland where an eagle was trained to intercept and disable drones in midflight. Journalists seeking to capture drone video for experiential reports may find unexpected obstacles during production.

Federal law is also beginning to conflict with local law regarding drone use.[44] Federal law supersedes local laws, which are often stricter. Yet "more than 20 states approved drone laws this year [2015], as have major cities like Chicago, Los Angeles and Miami, with many of the regulations placing tough restrictions on areas to fly and clamping down on the use of drones to snoop on neighbors."[45] Illustrative of the more restrictive nature of some local laws pertaining to drone use is that enacted in southern Florida. "In Miami, drones are banned within a half-mile radius of a 'large public event,' and the police are able to use jamming technologies to take them down. In Los Angeles, drone users who operate near airports can face up to six months in jail." Journalists investing in drone technology for experiential news stories may face a complex and growing web of legal restrictions.

Various enterprises have also developed software-based platforms that use the digital nature of drone operation as a means to control where drones can fly. Such electronic fences are in place in a variety of venues such as around airports, military facilities, and the White House and can be erected in real time to automatically stop a drone in midflight from entering a restricted space. Digital and networked drones may also become victims of computer hacking. Journalists seeking to use drones in experiential news production will need to develop detailed flight plans to minimize the potential impact of electronic fences, hackers, and restricted air spaces.

Content Transformations

Geo-located video shot via quadricopter also presents new possibilities for experiential stories. Perhaps most significant is the ability to create geo-located aerial narratives. These narratives could be in the form of a first-person perspective that enables viewers to virtually fly through locations, seeing events or venues as if they were present at the time the video was shot. This is in contrast to the third-person perspective that is typically delivered via aerial video shot from a helicopter.

Taking this possibility even further, drone-generated experiential news tagged to precise locations in a 3-D environment (with measures of latitude, longitude, and altitude) could support novel user experiences in precisely measured atmospheric or environmental conditions (for instance, inside a cloud or a volcano or over a distant terrain such as a desert, rain forest, or glacier). This is a capability that is enhanced by the aerial quality of drones as well as the ease by which geo-tagged video can be uploaded to publicly accessible online locations such as Google Earth.[46] Since 2010, Parrot, for example, has provided a drone video channel available on YouTube.[47] It includes a subchannel for videos recorded using an on-board GPS flight tracker, a module that has been available since 2013.

Geo-located video shot over time can also be digitally interconnected to provide a growing matrix of geo-tagged aerial video. Comparative views of the same location shot at two or more points in time are possible. Comparative video would be useful in illustrating before-and-after views of locations, such as sites adversely affected by natural disasters, human-made impacts (deforestation or development), and conflict zones (refugee camps). While similar comparative video or photos might be available from remote-sensing satellites, such imagery is considerably more expensive to obtain and is not generally under the control of media. The miniature and highly maneuverable nature of drones also provides producers with aesthetic opportunities to create unique fly-through videos in confined spaces. The BBC, for instance, has used a drone (a hexacopter, or multicopter with six rotors) to capture unique aerial video shot in a port and on a farm from various angles and in close proximity to objects.[48] This and other drone video can be viewed on YouTube.[49] Video captured simultaneously from multiple drones could generate 3-D, 360-degree views.

Many of the advantages of drone use in content production converged in obtaining unique aerial footage of the eroding California coastline during El Niño in 2016.[50] As one climate scientist notes, drones can fly below the clouds, above the sea, and close to the shore and thereby provide a unique perspective on the coastal erosion.[51] In addition to video, drones can also provide GPS data enabling the construction of a 3-D map of the coastline. Journalists and scientists alike can use the map to analyze erosion, observing and recording the height of the tides with precision on the coast. Moreover, amateur drone operators are capturing and sharing much of the drone video data. Three-dimensional maps could be used as a platform for aerial experiential news reporting about the environment or other stories.

In early 2014 I purchased a Parrot AR.Drone 2.0. Demonstrating the ease of operating a quadricopter, I was able to begin piloting and shooting aerial geo-located video inside my office within a few minutes after opening the box and charging the drone's battery. Still, skillful drone operation requires experience and training, particularly if operating the drone in exterior venues because wind or other conditions can quickly come into play. Parrot and other organizations offer online tutorials for drone operation; such training is essential for all drone reporting, including experiential. Although Parrot does not offer training courses for the AR.Drone, it does provide instructional tutorials for the professional drones that the company sells and offers online video instructions for the safe and effective operation of all its drones.

In an effort to study, teach, and advocate for the use of drones in journalism, two U.S. universities (Missouri and Nebraska) have launched drone journalism education and research programs.[52] Further, the Professional Society of Drone Journalists (PSDJ) was founded in 2011 as an "international organization dedicated to establishing the ethical, educational and technological framework for the emerging field of drone journalism."[53] A news consortium including the *New York Times* has also launched a drone journalism research project in collaboration with Virginia Tech University.[54] To what extent these undertakings will offer specialized research on the role of drones in experiential news is unclear.

The immersive potential of geo-located drone video that can be experienced or navigated via HMD also suggests a new mechanism to engage audiences more fully in site-specific narratives. Some developers, for example, have modified selected drone piloting mobile apps for operation on Google Glass.[55] One developer describes the experience of using Glass to navigate a drone with real-time video transmission capability as feeling "like being a bird" in flight.[56] Glass drone navigation would permit wearers to see in front of them an immersive view of the video captured via the drone in flight. This capacity suggests a new potential form of experiential stories in which journalists or other filmmakers could share live or recorded video feeds of drones in flight with audience members wearing the Glass or another HMD. Users could engage in virtual flight and experience firsthand stories told via drones in flight. These could be recorded and edited for later viewing, with potential geo-location features. For instance, a viewer wearing an AR or VR headset could experience virtual flight as it is simultaneously tracked and displayed on a digital map, possibly with a 3-D format representing topography. Video could be overlaid as AR to provide contextualization or interaction.

Drone video is merging with VR and other experiential forms. The applications are wide ranging. Seattle's Space Needle features a viewing platform where observers can take in a dramatic panoramic view of the city's skyline from more than five hundred feet above the ground. Outside this viewing area is the Halo Walk, a ring accessible only to maintenance workers and window washers. It offers those select few a breathtaking view of the city with nothing between the viewer and the city but air. In 2015 the view from the Halo Walk was recorded in high-definition geo-tagged video via drone. The video has been stitched together to offer anyone interested a potentially powerful VR experience of the Halo Walk. In the spirit of Sundance Institute's *Birdly* and other emerging media, the Halo Walk 360-degree video illustrates the potential to create unique experiential media content from the intersection of drones and other emergent immersive platforms such as VR.[57]

Such experiential media content creation is far from limited to professional video production. A somewhat whimsical example comes in the form of a user-generated version of *Superman*. "Sam Gorsky" attached a GoPro camera to his drone, put on a Superman cape, and took an aerial journey through "Metropolis."[58] Using off-the-shelf video editing software, he created a compelling and realistic video of Superman flying under bridges, over canals and across a real cityscape. He then posted the video to YouTube.[59] This story of virtual flight is enabled by not only a combination of drones and digital platforms but also the ease of production and inexpensive tools for editing that have lowered barriers to entry and content creation by citizens. Anyone with internet access can view this Superman video on any networked digital device. In the future, when VR technology may have taken hold in the consumer marketplace, such drone video may contribute substantially to the growth of citizen-reported experiential journalism.

Looking further into the future, drones portend potentially even greater transformative possibilities in news content creation. In a robotics laboratory at TEDGlobal, Raffaello D'Andrea has demonstrated the extraordinary athletic capabilities of flying drones. D'Andrea's demonstration illustrates how drones as athletes can solve "physical problems with algorithms that help them learn."[60] D'Andrea's algorithm-enabled drones autonomously "play catch, balance and make decisions together," acting in coordination with each other.[61]

As D'Andrea's drone demonstration suggests, drones equipped with cameras or other sensors can travel to locations that are otherwise inaccessible to human-operated devices and perform maneuvers that might vex even the most skilled human pilot. For instance, a drone can fly into an active volcano and obtain video that no human-operated device such as a helicopter could obtain. Such was in fact the case in October 2014 when a photographer attached two GoPro cameras to a drone and flew it remotely via algorithms inside an erupting volcano in Iceland.[62] The cameras melted from the intense heat, but the drone made it back out from the cone of the volcano with the memory stick storing the video still intact. The video was posted to YouTube and aired on *CBS This Morning*.[63] The ability to create, share, and view such unique video in VR or other immersive media illustrates the unique potential of experiential news.

SUMMARIZING THE MEDIA IMPACT OF DRONES

Table 6.1 summarizes the key emerging issues involving the development of drones and the media, especially with regard to their near- and far-term implications for the growth of experiential journalism. In the near

TABLE 6.1
Drones and Experiential Journalism: Emerging Issues

Issues	Methods of production	Content and story telling	Public engagement	Economic and regulatory frameworks
Near term	Primarily noncommercial, innovative reporters	Aerial, geo-located	Citizen-journalist contributions	Local, regional regulation, cost savings
Far term	Increasingly commercial	Immersive, live, interactive aerial reporting on wide spectrum of stories	Social media engagement across borders	First and Fourth Amendment battleground, international, revenue producing

term, drones will be used especially for noncommercial video production, particularly in the United States.

Early sources of drone video are likely to be citizen reporters and innovative professional journalists. Providing aerial perspective, geolocated drone video will play an increasing role in citizen-reported breaking news coverage. News organizations will find that drones can produce significant cost savings over alternative methods of aerial video production. This will encourage even further use of drones as an experiential reporting tool.

Regulations will be a combination of local and federal rules and regulations, with international frameworks also developed. Tensions between the First and Fourth Amendments will likely emerge, especially around freedom of speech, privacy, and security issues. These factors will likely limit the time, place, or manner in which drones can be used in experiential news reporting.

In the long term, new story forms or news experiences will emerge. These will include live and recorded immersive drone video in which users donning wearable technology will experience geo-located video in simulated flight. They will be able to share their drone-based news experiences via social media engagement.

Commercial uses of drones will become increasingly common, and their integration with VR and other experiential media forms will expand. Journalists will use drones to create flight-based narratives that support first-person user engagement on a wide spectrum of stories. These stories will include reporting about the environmental impact of climate change, the world's ongoing refugee or migrant crises, political protests, urban development, agricultural activity, and natural and human-made disasters.

CHAPTER SEVEN

Economic, Regulatory, and Other Contextual Factors

Experiential media are developing on a number of fronts. But the advance of new forms of immersive content is far from an inexorable march toward the future. Nor is it certain that evolving contours of experiential media will ensure that journalism emerges in a form that improves upon the past or the present.

Several significant factors will likely shape the evolution of experiential media and its possible impact on the transformation of journalism. Paramount among these are four contextual forces: (1) economic imperatives, especially the costs of production, distribution, and access, and the associated revenues news media will need in order to produce quality experiential news; (2) the legal and regulatory framework both domestically and internationally, especially regarding concerns about privacy and other potential adverse effects of emerging media; (3) an increasingly intense competition for human attention balanced against the need for accurate news and information; and (4) a robust network infrastructure to support the bandwidth demands of an evolving digital, mobile, and global media ecosystem.

ECONOMIC IMPERATIVES

Economic forces have long been a primary driver in the development of media forms and news content. The economics of media are in an unsettled, rapidly evolving state, with enormous implications for experiential content innovation, especially in journalism, where resources have been in decline. The high cost of experiential content production makes this problem especially acute for the news industry.

At the same time, audiences have turned away from traditional content media, especially newspapers, and toward networked platform media. Advertisers have increasingly put their marketing dollars into those digital platforms, including social networks and news and entertainment media. Newspapers have been forced to lay off staff as advertising revenues have fallen or migrated to digital platforms, and subscription and other revenue models have been slow to develop. Innovation is at a premium, but it often requires significant outside investment.

The economics of television, including television news, is similarly unsettled. Onetime cable TV subscribers have increasingly disconnected from cable or other TV delivery systems. Millennials often do not have a TV set or a radio receiver. Both groups have turned to internet-connected platform media, such as laptops, smartphones, tablets, and other digital devices such as wearables.

The fluid nature of the media marketplace was on full display when Disney CEO Robert Iger publicly acknowledged declines in TV audiences and media-property-generated revenues.[1] His remarks precipitated an immediate and dramatic drop in Disney and Time Warner stock prices as investors realized the implications for future revenue growth.

In the UK this same decline in content media has resulted in a dramatic drop in that country's required TV and radio set license fees; fewer people own TVs or radio sets, and thus fewer people are paying the set license fee. The BBC, which relies on these fees for its annual revenues, has seen those revenues drop significantly, and management was forced to lay off a thousand staff members in 2015.[2] The BBC may need to reinvent itself for the platform age and the rise of experiential news, or it will soon see its role shrink even further.

At least five economic factors will shape the potential for experiential media to develop and therefore for experiential news to move from niche to mainstream journalism. These are (1) pricing and product performance, which directly impact the rate of consumer adoption of experiential media; (2) production costs and the availability of quality content; (3) revenues, both anticipated and actual; (4) investment activity; and (5) ownership patterns.

PRICING AND PERFORMANCE

The likelihood that consumers will adopt new media technologies, including those needed to access experiential news, depends largely on pricing and performance. As prices fall and performance improves, consumer adoption becomes more likely. Driving both falling price and improving performance of experiential media is Moore's Law, which predicts a doubling of transistors on a single computer chip every eighteen months.[3] Gordon Moore—then CEO of Intel, a leading producer of computer chips for five decades now—first posited this formulation in the 1960s after observing the pattern in the early years of chip production. Moore's Law has continued largely unabated since its initial formulation despite questions about the theoretical limits of chip miniaturization at the atomic level. Advances in quantum computing, for instance, suggest radically smaller computational systems that are capable of processing speeds more than one hundred million times those of conventional chips produced in 2018.[4] Processing speed is vital in experiential news for both production and user experience. Among other things, ultrafast processing speeds can reduce or even eliminate what is known in virtual reality as the latency effect, referring to the time delay between a digital simulation and response for the user's experience.[5] It should be near zero to create a user experience that seems real.

As a consequence of Moore's Law, digital devices are shrinking in size (i.e., miniaturization of media devices) yet are more powerful, faster, and cheaper. In turn, these devices have become increasingly ubiquitous. Readers might consider that in the 1930s, radio audio-storage technology came in the form of expensive room-size magnetic recorders. Today, much greater audio recording capacity is available on a single thumb drive like the kind that is often provided as a free giveaway at conferences. Similar advances in digital technologies across all the functions described above are apparent and facilitate the widespread production, distribution, and use of experiential news.

Fueled by Moore's Law, cameras capable of capturing high-quality immersive video are increasingly available in the commercial marketplace. Prices are relatively high but are likely to fall with time. Some low-cost options are already available, but high-quality video is critical to creating an immersive experience for the user that most closely approximates reality. Moreover, these cameras are increasingly convergent digital devices, or devices that are networked, can communicate or share data, and can incorporate metadata (or descriptive tags) embedded into the content, including geo-location information, time stamps, and digital watermarks, which can facilitate both the form and function of experiential news.

Advances in the technologies that are needed to experience immersive news will likely continue to reflect the consequences of Moore's Law as well. For instance, headsets and other wearable devices are likely to continue to improve in performance (with higher resolution of displays), shrink in size and weight, and drop in price. New formats, including bendable, stretchable, and even fluid devices are in the prototype stage.[67] Digital devices might be worn like a Band-Aid and might be similarly inexpensive and disposable yet fully functional as wireless internet devices.

Lessons can be found in my collaborative experiences in the mid-to-late 1990s with computer science colleagues on journalism projects testing AR and VR. These trials included the use of an early prototype of a wearable device for experiencing virtual journalism content. This Mobile Journalist Workstation (MJW), circa 1996, could be used to generate AR content and to experience such immersive media.[89] Developed by Columbia University Computer Science professor Steve Feiner, the 1996 version included a backpack computer that weighed twenty-two kilograms. It also included a differential GPS that could provide locational tracking within 1.5 centimeters. The HMD with orientation tracker weighed about one pound, and the display was low resolution. An experimental version, which cost about $10,000, "had a Sony LDI-100B color display with 800 × 600 triad resolution." Contemporary VR headsets deliver about ten times the resolution at about half the weight and at a fraction of the price.

The MJW also included high-speed wireless (Wi-Fi) communications and internet access and a 360-degree camera and microphone for omnidirectional audio and video capture developed by computer science professor Shree Nayar. Reflecting the technological trends manifested in

Moore's Law, Nayar's 1999 omnidirectional camera system had resolution of about 1,140 by 1,030 pixels, about one-tenth of today's immersive imaging systems, as discussed below.[10]

Over the ensuing two decades, technologies that were needed to produce and experience immersive media fell dramatically in price and improved markedly in performance. Debuted in 2014, Google's low-priced Cardboard viewer helped propel early growth in the VR consumer market. Priced at about five dollars, the cardboard device requires the user to already own a smartphone, which, when inserted into the headset, acts as a computer to access and display immersive content. The *New York Times* implemented a VR journalism unit that was initially based on Google Cardboard.

Google has since launched a mid-price-range VR headset, Daydream View. Made of molded plastic and still requiring a smartphone, the Daydream costs about eighty dollars. A variety of companies launched similarly designed, mid-price-range VR headsets including the Samsung Gear HMD. Like Google VR headsets, the Gear VR headset requires the user to insert a smartphone, in particular a Samsung phone running the Android operating system. One of the notable features of the Gear VR headset is its head-tracking technology that allows the user to control the system and interact with VR content with head movements, such as tilting left or right, up or down. A variety of news media have utilized these headsets for experiential news reporting.

Sony's PlayStation VR takes a different approach to experiential media. The system operates via the PS4, the company's popular game platform, and costs about $400. Few news media have employed this platform for experiential journalism, but it could be an opportunity to engage gamers in immersive news.

Two VR systems stand out on the high end of the VR marketplace both in terms of functionality and price. These are the Oculus Rift and the HTC Vive. Gamers and others who are interested in a quality immersive media experience are among the early consumer adopters of these systems. The Oculus Rift headset cost about $599 when introduced in 2016.[11] In an indication that pricing is not an obstacle to highly motivated consumer adoption, when the Oculus website opened for preorders in early January 2016, high demand caused the system to crash.[12] The price of the Oculus fell rapidly, with a Rift and Touch VR bundle available in 2017 for about half the original introductory price.[13] In 2018 Oculus introduced the Go, a $200 untethered headset that no longer required the user to insert a smartphone or link via a cable to a desktop computer.[14] This relatively low-cost stand-alone HMD may help to propel VR into the mass market, which is typically defined as 50 percent market penetration, meaning at least 50 percent of households have adopted a new technology.[15] This could be a key factor in the development of widespread experiential news usage.

Similarly situated on the high end of the experiential market is the Taiwan-based HTC Vive. In 2017 HTC introduced the HTC Vive Pro for $799 as a high-resolution, untethered, stand-alone VR headset with motion tracking and 3-D spatial audio and a 110-degree field of view.[16] The wider the field of view, the more immersive the experience for the user (emerging platforms may increase the field of view even further). HTC Vive features its technology for use beyond the home; in Taiwan fans can visit Viveland, an HTC Vive VR theme park. Many leading news media have embraced the use of these platforms to design higher-quality (with higher resolution and location tracking) experiential journalism.

Some systems have captured a great deal of market buzz while still in development. Among these is Microsoft's HoloLens, which entered the consumer market in 2018 and offers users a rich MR experience via room-based holography.[17] Expected by year end 2019 the HoloLens 2 system is priced at $3,500, and developer kits run about $3,000. Magic Leap has generated similar attention, with its AR glasses priced at $2,295 upon their introduction in 2018.[18] The long-range potential to employ these platforms may create an opportunity to develop room-based AR and MR news experiences.

Another cost element is the operating system required for experiential content. Windows 10 makes it easier to set up VR gaming experiences, according to one observer.[19] In anticipation of an opportunity in the immersive gaming arena, Microsoft offered its users a free upgrade to Windows 10. Consequently, Windows 10 has been installed on more than 110 million devices since its release in 2015, and Microsoft expects to achieve an installed base of one billion Windows 10 devices by the end of 2018. This could be an important factor in mass user engagement with experiential news.

With low-end pricing, Google Cardboard leads the VR headset market with ten million headsets shipped as of this writing.[20] In the midrange, Samsung Gear is in second place, with five million units sold.[21] On the high end, the installed base of Oculus Rift headsets is about three million, and the HTC Vive is about 2.1 million worldwide. Sony PlayStation VR (a.k.a. Morpheus) has sold about one million units. Industry forecasts predict that more than one hundred million VR headsets will sold by 2021 worldwide.[22] But this pales in comparison to the estimated nine hundred million mobile AR devices in use in 2018, with the number expected to top three billion by 2022.[23] For news organizations planning to develop experiential news content, these are important considerations that may affect or limit potential public engagement.

Pricing will likely play a significant role in the development of experiential media. The first 8K UHD TV displays in 2015 cost approximately $133,000.[24] At this price, the installed base of UHD TV displays is very limited. Still, if the introduction of previous technologies such as HDTV is indicative of future patterns, then it is likely the cost of UHD TV displays will fall dramatically over the next decade. In the 1990s the first HDTV displays also cost about $100,000. But by the early 2010s the price of HDTV displays had fallen to just a few hundred dollars. It is virtually impossible to buy any TV set that is not flat screen and at least HDTV capable, and the once-dominant box-shaped TV set is largely a relic of the past.

Previous patterns of consumer adoption would suggest that by the early 2020s, 8K UHD TV sets will likely cost about one week's take-home pay and consumer adoption will surge. Although 8K UHD sets are presently very expensive, the price is expected to fall rapidly in the next decade.[25] In December 2016, for example, some 4K UHD TV sets had become available for just $900. Strategy Analytics forecasts by the early 2020s about 50 percent of U.S. households will have a UHD TV set at a cost well under $1,000.[26] News media developing UHD content need to account for the potential audience for their immersive content as well as how producing that content may affect or encourage further adoption of the requisite advanced video platforms.

PRODUCTION COST AND DEVELOPING
QUALITY CONTENT

Adversely affecting the growth of the experiential marketplace is the high cost of content production. Producing quality VR, AR, or MR content is expensive, including in journalism. Forrester research estimates that a typical VR production costs roughly $500,000.[27] VR content requires a substantial level of expertise, production skill, creativity, and technical infrastructure. Another essential element for extensive VR content production is high engagement with the developer community, typically using specialized VR programming platforms such as Unity. For Oculus, by year end 2015, there were more than "200,000 registered Oculus Developer Center users."[28] HTC Vive also has thousands of VR developers.

Producing quality experiential journalism also requires a significant level of expertise in news-gathering and editorial judgment. A high price tag can put experiential media production out of the reach of many smaller news organizations, or it may mandate collaboration or significant external investment. Production costs for 360-degree video are significantly lower than full-scale VR, and that can help explain why this has been the entry form for much VR-oriented journalism, especially at smaller news operations.

Beyond journalism, one industry segment in particular is expected to substantially influence the development of VR, especially in terms of the installed user base and the funding needed for the field to expand. "While movies and news are quickly ramping up," reports one analyst, "the PC gaming market is the epicenter of VR development." Newzoo reports that the worldwide PC gaming market topped $137 billion in 2018 and will total more than $180 billion by 2021.[29] Mobile games already total more than $70 billion, more than half the entire market. There are some 2.3 billion gamers globally. These numbers bode well for the potential development of AR and VR games, as they are optimal for mobile and wearable platforms. This can pave the way for possible widescale experiential news engagement, especially if games are part of the news experience.

Estimates are that more than one hundred VR games have been developed for Oculus,[30] more than fifty for PlayStation VR, and several dozen for the HTC Vive.[31] VR game content features a number of genres.

Insomniac's *Edge of Nowhere* is a horror game that incorporates madness in which the user is immersed in a virtual exploration of Antarctica.[32] Other, more surrealistic VR experiences include *Wake-Up*, a VR game in which the user awakens in a mysterious room and is guided by a butterfly. Users try to escape within a limited period of time. Developed by independent Black-Cell Games of Vienna, Austria, the VR experience is available for free via Steam, a popular platform for experiential media content; other VR games typically cost about sixty dollars. News media might employ *Wake-Up*'s somewhat cerebral game design to create immersive content that enables users to explore news events, venues, and issues in an interactive, immersive, and collaborative fashion.[33]

Further underscoring the emergence of immersive content production and consumption is the rapid growth in the number of VR content apps on the marketplace for mobile users. There are hundreds of VR apps available for Apple or Android users. These range from general-purpose apps for content developed for cross-platform domains, including VRSE for the *New York Times*, to specialized apps for specific content domains, including games and travel. Many VR apps are available for free, with content purchases available within the VR experience.

Free VR content apps in journalism include one titled simply VR Journalism. It features a variety of nonfiction sports experiences such as shooting a match-winning shot in soccer or sinking a hole-in-one in golf. Fractured Tour allows the user to experience the economic, racial, and ideological divides that exist in Selma, Alabama. A growing number of AR journalism apps are internationally produced. Canada's National Film Board has launched a nonfiction-based AR app called The Enemy. It gives users the opportunity to meet and engage in dialogue with combatants on opposite sides of a military conflict. The Enemy's AR experience includes the wars in El Salvador and the Democratic Republic of Congo and the Israeli-Palestinian conflict. El País VR delivers VR experiences (shot with fourteen camera rigs) in English and Spanish produced by reporters from the newsroom of *El País* in Madrid, Spain. JMK VR offers student-produced VR, mostly 360-degree video, from the Department of Media Studies at Stockholm University.

Some AR journalism content apps are also citizen reported. One example is the YouAnchor News Cast AR, which offers citizen journalism via an interactive 3-D map of the United States.

Although experiential journalism content apps are available for free download and use in 2018, it is likely that the situation may soon change. Once the market is more established, news organizations may begin introducing revenue models based on user fees or subscriptions just as they have with other forms of digital news content. I discuss below the evolution of revenue models to support experiential news production.

Producing quality experiential journalism requires high-end camera systems costing tens of thousands of dollars. These rigs employ multiple UHD cameras, in some cases up to two dozen optical sensors in a circular or spherical array. The rigs, which can weigh nearly five kilograms, capture 3-D, 8K, 360-degree live-action video at thirty frames per second optimized for a VR headset user experience.[34] Some systems allow the rig operator to don a VR headset to see and hear 360-degree video streams in real time to determine immediately whether the content is usable. Using "dynamic rendering," systems can stitch the video and audio feed simultaneously from the video and audio sensors.[35] Some rigs incorporate position tracking along with the omnidirectional audio and video.[36] This yields a user experience supporting complete freedom of movement (with six degrees of freedom, or DOF) within the 3-D, immersive visual space.

Now in prototype form, 4-D cameras capture through a single wide-angle lens panoramic video with depth and light directionality, potentially providing users up to six DOF in the rendered content.[37] Once commercially available, 4-D cameras could be highly mobile, miniature, and ubiquitous and could propel even greater volumes of immersive news production.

Other emerging types of cameras and digital sensors present new types of imaging and story possibilities. One such Wi-Fi technology captures wireless radio wave emissions (similar to sonar) reflected off the human body (or other objects) to see through walls. Dubbed Emerald by its inventors at the MIT computer science AI laboratory, the technology can detect and capture in real time a person's location (including distance off the floor), motion, and respiration rate (breathing and heart rate).[38] Such data could be used not only in medical situations but also to create new types of personal experiential news narratives. Yet the technology also raises potentially significant privacy considerations.

Research at the VR laboratory of Hannes Kaufmann at Technische Universität Wien, Austria, includes systems that capture volumetric 360-degree video and audio in real time and collect 3-D information that maps a physical space such as a venue where news is occurring, has recently occurred, or may soon occur.[39] Developed for fire fighters, such technology can render a space in precise 3-D immersive format. It could facilitate the production of six DOF VR news experiences for the user that are highly realistic, accurate, and generated in real time.

The mobility, ease of use, and relatively low cost of the current and emerging videographic technologies have made the production of experiential journalism an increasing possibility even for breaking news stories. Within a week of the Paris terrorist attacks in November 2015, for instance, the *New York Times* released a 360-degree video report on the vigils being held there to remember and honor the victims.[40] Of the report, the *Times* said

> As a reporting tool, virtual reality is still in its infancy; its power to create empathy is just beginning to be understood. Using this medium, we aimed to create a more textured experience—the streets of Paris distilled to voices and spaces. Although the technology is evolving, it is clear that this new frontier can soon become a crucial journalistic tool. . . . As journalists, we always seek to help readers understand what life feels like in the places we cover. Virtual reality allows us to do that in an entirely new way.

The topical domains that the *Times* is exploring through experiential reporting continue to expand as the flexibility and capacity of 360-degree video- and audio-capture technology continue to advance. In January 2016 the *Times* debuted its VR report, "Experiencing the Presidential Campaign: A Virtual Reality Film." Editors explain how the report was created: "The *Times* has produced a virtual reality film from footage taken over the last month capturing the candidates and perhaps the best part of their events: the crowds."[41] Similarly, the *Times* is experimenting with using the VR format to create immersive experiences of past events, such as the assassination of civil rights leader Malcolm X. "The civil rights leader Malcolm X was killed February 21, 1965, at a rally in New York City," recalls the *Times*. "Hear from a witness and visit the site of the assassination—in the past, present, and in 360-degree video."[42]

Citizen-reported experiential news may also be poised to increase in volume and scope. With the advent of inexpensive fish-eye lenses, omnidirectional cameras may enable citizen reporters to produce 360-degree photos and video for just a few hundred dollars' investment. These cameras may lack position tracking, thereby limiting user movement in the rendered 360-degree space,[43] yet these low-cost cameras can capture spherical images or high-definition 4K video at fifteen frames per second and support direct upload and sharing of the 360-degree content.

Also released onto the consumer market since 2017 are VR cameras that can attach to a smartphone. One camera attaches to an iPhone and enables the user to capture panoramic videos or photos and audio and to upload or share that content directly online or via social media.[44] These developments are creating an environment for relatively easy production and postproduction of 360-degree video and other experiential content. Even advanced user-generated AR and VR news content is likely in the near term. Tools include apps for creating spherical photographs.[45] Another app enables users to create and share interactive 3-D photos and videos generated via mobile device.[46] These often-free mobile apps may fuel the development of expanded volumes of citizen-reported experiential news.

REVENUES

Expected revenues are driving VR development both in terms of technology and content, including in journalism. Estimates are that total VR market revenues already top $120 billion worldwide.[47] Piper Jaffray investment bank says the VR content market is worth about $5.4 billion, but it is dwarfed by the VR hardware market, at well over $110 billion.

Central to the revenue economics of experiential content production is the growth of fee-based media. Media companies of all types are obtaining a shrinking portion of their funding from advertising and a growing portion from pay content, especially subscriptions. This trend is likely to continue for experiential news, with users facing not only an expensive set of options for the digital devices and bandwidth needed to access experiential content but also a high price tag for the content itself.[48]

Evidence suggests that citizens are increasingly willing to pay for content accessed through digital platform media, especially quality experiential content. The exact price that consumers are willing to pay for such content is still evolving. The *New York Times* reported that its digital-only subscribers, with subscriptions priced at twenty-five dollars per month, topped one million by year end 2015 and surpassed 2.7 million in 2017 and over 3 million in 2018.[49] The *Times'* chief executive says, "digital revenue can surpass that of print in five years, a key to the newspaper's long-term prospects."[50] At the *Washington Post*, another pioneer in experiential news reporting, digital subscribers also have surged, up 300 percent to more than one million in 2017.[51]

Smaller news organizations also are developing expanded goals regarding digital subscriptions and associated revenue models. One is the McClatchy group's *Sacramento Bee*, which has announced plans to reach sixty thousand paying digital subscribers, up from fifteen thousand in mid-2018, and to rely on those subscriptions as a primary revenue source.[52] The *Bee* has begun producing extensive 360-degree video reporting—users can experience the first day of the harvest of organic cantaloupes on the Del Bosque farm, an experiential report released June 26, 2018—a form of journalism that is available only in digital form and of potentially unique value to digital subscribers. Some news media are making their experiential content, often labeled immersive content, available even for non-subscribers, but that is apt to change as the market for such content matures.

It is hard to say what the total revenues are for digital subscriptions, such as at the *Post*. The *Post* company has not yet released figures, and the amount a subscriber pays depends on a number of factors. "The *Post* offers Amazon Prime subscribers free access for six months and then charges $3.99 per month; everyone else can pay $8.30 per month for a long-term commitment."[53] So with at least one million digital-only paying subscribers, annual digital-only subscriber revenues are at least $24 million, assuming all are Amazon Prime subscribers (one million subscribers with six months free, paying $3.99 a month for six months). Revenues could be much greater if Prime members make up a relatively small portion of total digital *Post* subscribers (up to about $96 million).

Revenues will likely jump substantially in 2018 and beyond, assuming there is not a mass fall-off in digital subscribers.

For the *New York Times*, the company's commitment to VR reporting has contributed to increasing revenues. The *Times* company reported in early 2016 that its digital revenue stream has grown substantially. "For the full year [2015], digital advertising revenue increased 8 percent compared with the previous year, to $197 million, and digital-only subscription revenue was $193 million last year, a roughly 14 percent increase from 2014." *Times* leadership attributes the growth directly to the launch of its VR story telling.[54] Despite falling revenues in the company's print business, the *New York Times* company reported fourth-quarter 2014 profits of $52 million.[55] These trends have continued, even accelerated, bringing total revenues from digital subscriptions to $1 billion for 2017.[56] In fact, the *New York Times* reported that the majority of its revenue (60 percent) is now from subscriptions (mostly digital) and that this helped total revenues reach $1.7 billion in 2017.[57]

Experiential media generally are proving vital to these developments. At the end of 2017, the *New York Times*, for example, provided data that illustrates the importance of its use of experiential media content, especially when it is packaged for social media access, to build audience.[58] Specifically, the Daily 360 was a yearlong joint *Times*-Samsung-sponsored project. Some two hundred *Times* journalists produced 360-degree video news reports from fifty-seven countries; the first was "The Displaced" published in November 2015, offering immersive narratives from three refugee camps. Over the year, the Daily 360 videos produced ninety-four million views on Facebook and two million views on YouTube. The *Times* has not publicly shared 360-degree-video viewing totals for its digital properties, but they would likely add substantially to the reported social network numbers, and they help to explain the substantial growth in the *Times'* digital-only subscriber base in 2017 and 2018.

INVESTMENT ACTIVITY

Anticipated revenues spur investment, including in experiential media platforms and news content. Industry observers report that investment in VR is substantial, with VR and AR revenues expected to reach $215 billion by 2021.[59] "Venture capital is pouring into virtual reality start-ups, as proponents of the technology extol its potential to transform entertainment, communications and work."[60] One industry report indicates that 2015 saw 120 VR-related deals for a combined $630 million.[61] Moreover, there was an estimated $4 billion invested in VR start-ups between 2010 and 2015.

Investment in the social networking side of VR is also growing. VR start-up WEVR has raised $25 million to launch Transport, which seeks to be the YouTube of VR.[62] Growth in social VR could stimulate demand for experiential news as users share their experiences.

Industry investment in the installed base of twenty-first-century experiential media technology, and the simultaneous development of immersive news content is reminiscent of the early twentieth-century development of radio, at least in the United States. One of the leaders of early commercial radio was David Sarnoff. In the first decades of the twentieth century, "Sarnoff became operator of the most powerful radio station in the world, established by John Wanamaker atop his Manhattan department store. There, on April 14, 1912, Sarnoff picked up the distress signal from the sinking Titanic; he remained at his instrument for 72 hours, receiving and passing on the news."[63] Based on his initial experience with the fledgling medium, Sarnoff obtained a position with the Marconi Company (founded by Italian radio inventor Guglielmo Marconi), and in 1916 he proposed a "radio music box," which would be the first commercially marketed radio receiver. By 1921 Sarnoff had joined the Radio Corporation of America (RCA), and on July 2 of that year RCA broadcast a heavyweight boxing championship match between Jack Dempsey and Georges Carpentier.[64] The broadcast marked a success for the new medium of radio. "The transmitter used was said to be the largest one ever built up to that time. It was built by General Electric and set up at the Lackawanna train terminal in Hoboken, from where the bout was transmitted to theaters, halls, and auditoriums in sixty-one other cities across the United States."[65] Moreover, "The fight became the first world title fight to be carried over on radio, ushering in an era of boxing radiocasts that lasted until televised boxing came along."[66] Consequently, by 1924 RCA had "sold more than $80,000,000 worth of receiving sets," and Sarnoff formed the National Broadcasting Corporation (NBC).[67]

The rise of the internet and a more participatory system of mediated communication has facilitated a new model for media platform and content investment. This investment model is online crowdfunding. There have long been venture capitalists and other large-scale investors who have at least occasionally invested in media enterprises and possible innovations. In contrast, investment from the general public generally has not been a significant option.

The emergence of new online investment models, especially crowdfunding, is reshaping the potential to create experiential media content forms, including in journalism. Crowdfunding in the digital era refers to entrepreneurs offering their proposed projects via an online platform such as Kickstarter or Indiegogo for support or investment from members of the public, usually in return for one of the early prototypes being developed.

A Pew study found that by early 2016, 658 journalism projects had been crowdfunded via Kickstarter.[68] Moreover, the amount funded has risen dramatically since 2009, when less than $50,000 in public support was invested in Kickstarter journalism projects. In 2015 some $1.7 million was raised for journalism projects on Kickstarter. Serious journalism projects capture the most support, Pew found.[69]

One successful Kickstarter project with substantial experiential journalism implications is that of the Oculus Rift. Oculus started as the brainchild of former journalism student Palmer Luckey, who had once been an intern for VR journalism pioneer Nonny de la Peña. In 2012 Luckey launched an effort to develop his VR platform as a $2.5 million Kickstarter project. After obtaining the sought-after funding, Luckey moved forward with the Oculus Rift prototype. Generating widespread interest in his innovative undertaking, he captured the attention of the social media giant Facebook. In 2014 Mark Zuckerberg's company acquired Oculus Rift for $3 billion dollars. The pioneering VR enterprise is now impacting the world of experiential news.[70] Facebook is also moving aggressively to develop AR technology and content, debuting its AR glasses prototype in April 2017.

Indiegogo has likewise seen the launch of crowdfunding projects to develop tools for experiential journalism. One that has raised more than $47,000 from 336 backers as of July 3, 2017, is the Wunder360 S1 camera.[71] It aims to be the first 3-D scanning, 360-degree camera employing AI for automatic image stitching, stabilizing the location tracking.

Technology companies such as Alphabet/Google, Apple, Facebook, Samsung, and Twitter have become increasingly dominant in the digital news distribution, production, and revenue-generating ecosystem. Alphabet (owner of Google and YouTube) had 2017 revenues in excess of $110 billion, up from $90 billion in 2016.[72] These revenues dwarf those of legacy news media operations by about fifty or one hundred to one. Founded in just 1998, Google's growth was fueled by heavy venture capital investment, including that of Amazon CEO Jeff Bezos. Return on investment has been a powerful force in the growth of the company, as Google transformed from a search engine to a global digital enterprise named Alphabet, whose principle revenue source is online advertising. Founded in 2004, Facebook has had a similar growth trajectory, seeing its revenues grow on an enormous scale, up to more than $40 billion in 2017. It has also come to be a dominant force in the distribution of news and information: virtually every U.S. journalism enterprise has its content available in at least some form on the social network, whose users access and widely share such news content, including the experiential (VR and 360-degree video). Facebook has a reported 2.2 billion active monthly users worldwide, many times that of even the largest U.S. news media organization.[73]

For the most part, technology behemoths are not focused on creating original news content, experiential or not. Rather, these companies essentially use content to build their audience or user base, which they then sell, largely through algorithms, to marketers, advertisers, or virtually anyone anywhere who wants to reach them. And this has been a factor in the increasing debate over so-called fake news and foreign influence in the U.S. 2016 elections. Moreover, these tech companies are also in the forefront of the production of technology used in creating experiential news. It is in their economic interest that news organizations adopt these tools as potential innovations, regardless of whether they make for better journalism. In many cases, effective use of these tools requires partnership between the technology companies and news organizations, creating a potential conflict of interest. To maintain editorial independence, newspapers of the twentieth century established strict divisions between their reporting and business units. News media of the twenty-first century should construct comparably impenetrable barriers between their experiential journalism units and their technology partners to ensure that editorial decisions are fully under the independent control of the journalists.

Although the economic dominance of the technology giants in the digital arena is well known, the implications for the use of experiential media in journalism are significant and less apparent. In an urgent effort to build audiences, legacy news media are investing heavily in innovative approaches to content production, design, and delivery. They are especially focused on an experiential media content strategy to encourage members of the public to become paying subscribers for unique content designed for an increasingly mobile yet connected public. This pressure to compete with technology behemoths is fueling widespread news industry experimentation with some of the very technology platforms that the digital giants are developing. But it is also encouraging a commitment in the news media to conduct original reporting, the foundation of quality journalism, using tools that support experiential media. It is also fostering a shift in the basic economics of news media away from predominant reliance on advertising and toward subscriber-based revenues.

Because of their high cost, the development of experiential media may increase political polarization and division. Those who can afford the high cost of experiential news may increasingly participate in a digital public news space where the less economically advantaged have decreasing access. The shift toward mostly digital subscriptions underscores the potential economics-driven divide between those who can afford quality experiential journalism and those who cannot, and this divide will likely grow. This trend may potentially further erode public trust in basic democratic institutions, at least among those for whom access is limited to the news content that swirls about in an often-unfiltered social networking environment.

More traditional or legacy news organizations such as the *New York Times* still play a fundamental role in the production and distribution of news (including experiential reporting) but the technology giants dominate the digital advertising landscape and therefore the lion's share of digital revenues. These tech giants serve as the primary conduit for news distribution for much of the U.S. and international public. Traditional news media are vital to the production of original journalism and news reporting and investigation, but they are in a powerful and highly contested race to reach the news public and do so via emerging experiential media. Recent developments and announcements, such as the *Times'* launch of its AR journalism initiative in February 2018, underscore this race.

This is a critical struggle between two sets of very different enterprises whose core missions diverge and sometimes even conflict but that coexist and oftentimes must collaborate in a digital world. One set comprises for-profit and not-for-profit news-producing organizations that rely on revenues to create quality news content but whose core mission is to serve the public good. The other set comprises the more intensely profit-oriented digital behemoths that distribute news to build a massive global user base and thereby huge advertising revenues and that serve primarily the interests of their shareholders. The outcome of this contest is uncertain, but what is at stake is the very shaping of democracy. How effectively experiential media, including AR and VR, are used in the production and delivery of quality journalism content may prove crucial to the outcome of this titanic struggle for the mindshare of the American and international news public.

OWNERSHIP PATTERNS

Who owns the media is also central to the development of new content forms, including the experiential. An international study released in 2015 looks at global media ownership, revealing some unexpected patterns. "Based on an extensive data collection effort from scholars around the world," Eli Noam and colleagues examined "thirteen media industries, including television, newspapers, book publishing, film, search engines, ISPs, wireless telecommunication and others, across a ten to twenty-five year period in thirty countries," from the United States to China, Egypt, and Russia.[74]

Somewhat surprisingly, the world's largest owner of media is not Rupert Murdoch, Google, or any other Western media mogul. Instead, the government of China is the world's most dominant media owner. In the realm of private media ownership, it is not well-known figures such as Italy's Silvio Berlusconi or telecommunications companies such as Comcast that are most dominant. Rather, it is a relatively little-known mix of hedge funds, such as Global Fund Media and Alden Global

Capital, that dominate the private ownership of media around the world.[75] The principal concern of these owners is profitability and obtaining large capital gains, often with a goal of greater than 10 percent annually. Whether hedge funds or other media investors invest in the development of quality experiential journalism will depend largely on expected financial returns.

SPEED, ACCURACY, AND HUMAN ATTENTION

Historically, Americans and their British counterparts are among the world's heaviest consumers of media, including books, magazines, newspapers, movies, radio, and television. In the twenty-first century media consumption increasingly means usage of screen-based media. In the early 2000s Americans and the British alike on average spent about two and a half hours (148 and 147 minutes respectively) per day using screen devices, mostly television sets and desktop computers. Today, screen devices have evolved considerably to include both digital TV sets as well as mobile devices, especially smartphones, laptops, and tablets, all of which are digital and network connected and constitute the primary means of engaging experiential news. By 2018 Americans had dramatically increased their screen time, up to a stunning eleven hours per day.[76] Brits spend almost as much time in front of, tapping on, plugged into, or talking with a screen device.[77] For both Americans and the British, much of this is via handheld devices, especially smartphones, and it is increasingly via wearable devices, from smart watches to HMDs.

Enabling or perhaps fueling much of the shift toward digital platform usage is the growth in the installed base of internet-connected smartphones and other networked mobile devices. Data shows that as of January 2017 almost all Americans (95 percent) own a cell phone and most (77 percent) own a smartphone.[78] One-third (32 percent) of American adults own an e-reader.[79] Almost half (42 percent) of American adults own a tablet computer. The impact on news consumption is especially pronounced among youths. API reports, "The average millennial (18–34) gets 74% of her news from online sources."

Brent Olson of AT&T reports that although TV is still a dominant platform in the United States and much of the world, mobile devices are the increasing platform of choice for video viewing, especially among the young who are cutting the cord from traditional TV delivery systems such as cable.[80] Olson reports that in 2015 more than 50 percent of video was viewed on various digital devices. This signals a likely key direction for the delivery of experiential news.

Americans are turning to their mobile devices to access news, Pew reports in "State of the News Media."[81] "Call it a mobile majority." Nearly three-fourths (72 percent) of Americans get news via a mobile device.[82] This is up from just over half (54 percent) in 2013. Data also shows that mobile news usage is age related, with mobile news users being an average of seventeen years younger than print readers. Mobile-only news users are growing rapidly, increasing by 83 percent between 2011 and 2012. ComScore reports that this trend is especially pronounced among millennials: "96% of millennial digital news readers get their news from mobile, and 36% of them only get their news from mobile."[83] Moreover, certain topical domains are particularly mobile oriented. Mobile consumption of political news, for instance, has grown to more than six times what it was in 2013. Millennials will likely rely on their mobile devices to access experiential news.

Americans still watch a great deal of television. Data indicates that Americans are among the heaviest viewers of television with the average American spending more than two hours a day watching TV programming. But viewership of local television news has been in steady decline for the past decade, Pew Research reports.[84] About one-quarter of Americans (twenty-three million) still watch evening local and network TV news at least once a week. Despite this overall high amount of TV viewership, the pattern is in decline whether morning, noon, or night, especially among the young. Experiential news delivered in UHD will face an uphill struggle in this climate of declining TV viewership unless it is available via online delivery platforms.

Nielsen data shows that American millennials have been disconnecting from their traditional TV sets and turning to online video sources instead. Since 2012, viewership of traditional TV had been dropping by about 4 percent per year. Likewise, the rate of cord cutting (those who discontinue their cable TV subscriptions) reached 3.4 percent in 2017, up from 2 percent in 2016.[85] In 2017, according to eMarketer, the total number of people in the United States who do not subscribe to pay TV—a combination of cord-cutters and cord-nevers (those who have never signed up for pay TV)—reached 56.6 million.[86] By 2021, eMarketer forecasts, more than eighty-one million people, more than one-quarter of U.S. households, will not pay for television through subscriptions to cable or satellite TV.

Millennials are engaging video content platforms via their mobile devices to access online programming producers and providers such as Netflix and YouTube. "The change in behavior is stunning. The use of streaming and smartphones just year-on-year is double-digit increases," Alan Wurtzel, NBC Universal's audience research chief, told the *Post*.[87] As Americans continue to cut the cord, the cable news and sports audience is shrinking.[88] Research shows that more cord-cutting millennials use streaming services than pay TV. "More than seven out of 10 (71%) of the 1,111 adult U.S. consumers in Clearleap's survey from earlier this year said they had used a streaming service, either currently or previously. Slightly more consumers (79%) said they currently subscribed to pay TV."[89] Mobile and online platforms are especially well suited for delivery of and access to experiential news content.

Usage of smart TV sets is also surging.[90] Smart TVs connect directly to the internet and give the user access to high-definition video, on-demand content, and potentially experiential news content. A Statista survey shows that almost one in five U.S. and UK adults (16 percent and 17 percent respectively) have used a smart TV.[91] An even greater portion, nearly one-quarter (23 percent) of adults in Spain have used a smart TV, a pattern similar throughout most of Europe. Further, usage of Apple TV, another digital platform, is surging.[92] TV Everywhere is the industry term for traditional TV content accessed through digital platforms. Adobe collected consumer video viewing data between the first quarters of 2014 and 2015 and "found that Apple TV represented 10 percent of TV Everywhere authentications in the first quarter, up from 5 percent in the final quarter of last year." Roku, another digital TV platform, "had an 8 percent share in the latest period, up one percentage point." Significantly, these various digital or smart TV platforms offer the consumer a possible pathway to access experiential news content.

While the combined consumption of online video and TV content surges, traditional broadcast radio usage reflects a pattern of long-term decline, much like that of traditional television. Nielsen data shows, for instance, that "the number of all-news radio stations declined slightly in

2014, to 31."[93] Online radio listenership, on the other hand, has increased substantially in recent years. Monthly online radio listenership, for instance, has more than doubled since 2007. As of 2015, more than half (51 percent) of Americans twelve years or older have listened to online radio, up from just about 20 percent in 2007.[94] In addition, Americans are increasingly using their mobile phones to access online radio while in their automobiles. Data shows that in 2015, more than one-third (35 percent) of Americans age twelve or older had used their mobile phones to access online radio while in a car. This is up from less than 30 percent in 2014 and only about 5 percent in 2010.[95]

Americans are also turning to digital platforms for audio content, downloading or streaming podcasts, news, and other content.[96] The Pew Research Center reports that fully one-third of U.S. adults have listened to a podcast.[97] This represents a threefold increase in the past decade. In 2006 just about one in eight (about 12 percent) had listened to a podcast. Reflecting this shift and potentially stimulating it even further is the December 2016 launch of Facebook Live Audio, the social media giant's podcasting initiative.[98] Digital audio, including that accessed via smart speakers such as the Amazon Echo, offers an intuitive and increasingly widely available platform for audio-based experiential news.

One of the consequences of the plethora of digital media platforms is increasing competition for limited and often-fragmented human attention, perhaps even information, entertainment, and news overload. The burgeoning digital media arena presents fundamental challenges to those seeking to create and fund quality media content, especially the expensive experiential. Traditional media have struggled to engage younger members of the public. Youths have turned increasingly to digital social media not only to communicate with each other but also to obtain news and information. Given millennials' interest in new digital media technologies, including wearable devices, experiential media might be an opportunity for journalism and other traditional content providers to heighten public engagement, especially among the young. Evidence to date indicates that about one in five (21 percent) Americans owns a wearable device. This includes not only HMDs but also a host of other wearable digital devices such as smart watches and wristbands such as the Fitbit.[99] "Who are these early adopters?" asks a 2014 report from PricewaterhouseCoopers (PwC) and its Health Research Institute.[100] The fact that this report is part of a health research institute also suggests that wearables may play a key role in collecting users' personal health data. "Our data show that current wearable users make up 21 percent of the population—a subset that is more affluent, more tech savvy and more educated than the general population at large," states the report.[101]

The PwC report further indicates that wearable ownership skews heavily toward younger users. "Millennials are 55 percent more likely to own wearable technology than adults 35 and over."[102] More than half (51 percent) of millennials say they are likely to buy a fitness band in the next year as compared to less than half (45 percent) of the total adult population. Similarly, more millennials (40 percent) said they are likely to buy a smart watch compared to the general population (35 percent).[103] These patterns suggest an opportunity for news media to develop experiential news (e.g., personalized health news) in formats designed for wearables such as smart watches and potentially engage a more youthful audience.

Industry analysts report that 7.5 million Apple Watch 2.0 devices had sold in the United States by year end 2015.[104] The newly introduced Apple Watch 3.0, with LTE wireless service, was selling even faster, with sales up 50 percent in 2018.[105] These devices enable a variety of functions, including access to news, including from the *New York Times*.[106] Also, users can play games, access Pandora (online personalized audio content including music and podcasts), and utilize a remote control to take photographs, including via an HD camera.[107] Future versions may support experiential news media engagement.

Public acceptance of wearable headsets may also be a key element in the development of immersive media content in the form of VR. Initial reactions to the early VR content experiences have been generally positive. One observer in 2015 offered a personal vantage point on his children's response to entering into a VR experience such as floating virtually down a computer-generated 3-D Garden of Eden, journeying through a photorealistic 3-D rendering of *Jurassic World*, or participating in Cirque du Soleil's *Kurios*, a 360-degree theatrical performance. Of his children's reaction he wrote, "They screamed and laughed like they were on a theme park ride." After letting them spend a few minutes with the VR experience, he explained, "I slowly, and firmly, separate the giddy kids from their magic VR glasses," adding, "It's time for dinner." Returning, he offered this further reflection: "I did this last year, during Hanukkah, with the original Gear VR Innovator Edition, showing my family virtual reality for the first time. I watched them explore virtual aquariums, imaginary movie theaters, giant solar systems. A year later, it's no less amazing."[108]

Another observer offered his reaction after experiencing VR systems demonstrated in early 2016: "Repairing robots, driving Rovers across Mars and zapping objects with a laser gun—but doing it all in virtual reality at the International CES in Las Vegas."[109] His conclusion: VR is here to stay because the content feels real.[110]

First-time users of VR smile and say things such as "you feel like you are in the video."[111] Watching video of first-time users of VR also demonstrates an interesting reaction not typically seen of users while engaged with other media, unless it involves music. People using VR move around a lot. They tilt their heads trying to see in a variety of directions. They react to what they see and move in response. This physical reaction to VR is potentially significant, as it contrasts with the largely passive audience engagement with traditional media. Journalists should incorporate this quality into experiential news, designing narratives that feature content (such as characters and graphics) positioned in various parts of the 3-D, 360-degree environment.

British science fiction writer and inventor Arthur C. Clarke once wrote, "Any sufficiently advanced technology is indistinguishable from magic."[112] Such might be an apt description of many users' reactions to their first encounters with VR, AR, or MR content.

Of course, not even the powerful reactions of users to their first forays into VR will ensure widespread public adoption of VR and experiential news. The shifting structure of the news ecosystem presents profound challenges to the quality of journalism, experiential or conventional. The decline of printed newspaper consumption and the corresponding drop in revenues to those legacy organizations pose long-term threats to the generation of original reporting, a cornerstone of quality journalism. The overall news system, particularly in the United States, for more than a century has relied especially on newspapers for original news reporting. Other media often recycle that content or repackage it for other formats, such as audio or video. Although TV, radio, and digital news media contribute some original reporting, it is often at a substantially lower rate than print media have provided historically. Moreover, it often has been largely the national networks that have been in the forefront of such original multimedia reporting. The role of generating original experiential news media content is currently largely from news organizations that are traditionally based in print, but the future is unsettled and potentially problematic, especially if little local experiential news content is produced.

Another potential concern is what impact on the news ecosystem the rise of citizen journalism will play in a globally connected media system where speed and multimedia are major drivers. Citizen reporting is flowing from a variety of sources, including not just formal citizen journalism endeavors such as the startup YouAnchor News Cast AR but also social media networks such as Facebook, Instagram, and Snapchat.[113] The dissemination of potentially disputed or fake news, mechanisms for vetting news, and the potential for crowd-based fact-checking are all topics of increasing relevance in a participatory media environment. These issues may be even more acute in an age of experiential media forms that can blur the line between the virtual and the real.

Serious and far-reaching adverse sociopolitical consequences will likely increase if accuracy, impartiality, and independence erode in an experiential news ecosystem in which content is exchanged via social networking. Stories distributed digitally from far-ranging sources might contain hidden bias or serve as a vehicle for propaganda. In experiential form, the apparent truthfulness of such content may require even higher levels of public sophistication and critical ability to recognize and filter out deception.

The hyperfrenetic, 24/7 nature of connected media will challenge the quality of public engagement in and attention to experiential journalism. Oregon journalism professor Peter Laufer has argued persuasively that "a slow news movement" may be the key to putting thoughtful reflection and critical understanding back into a central position in journalism and its public consumption.[114] The role of slow news is a topic that merits serious research investigation. Slow news, however, collides directly with the growing phenomenon of live-streaming audio and video, especially via citizens on social networks, and increasingly experiential media platforms.

Mobile and social networking media are also facilitating an ever-faster cycle of news delivery. Although sometimes speed is a compelling aspect of citizen reporting, as in an emergency situation such as a campus shooting, it can also adversely impact accuracy if fact-checking or real-world verification is sacrificed. Social (and mobile) media demand "that news be delivered ASAP," notes veteran journalist Gordon Deal.[115] "But journalists who choose speed over accuracy will find a quick path to unemployment and lack of credibility." Experiential news may heighten the speed-versus-accuracy tension.

LEGAL AND REGULATORY FRAMEWORKS

Beyond the issues of economics, the limits of human attention span, and the adoption of new technology, there is also a confluence of legal, regulatory, and policy forces shaping the evolution of experiential journalism. In some ways, these forces can either encourage innovative media content forms, including experiential news, or they can act as constraints upon its development. This is especially true in what is increasingly a global media system linked by various aspects of the world's digital telecommunications infrastructure, including the internet, satellite communications, and other various local and wide-area networks. Overlaid onto the world's telecommunications networks are several layers of law and regulation that can affect industry innovation in the development of new technologies that are relevant to experiential news. These layers include (1) intellectual property rights and competitive practices; (2) regulation to protect user rights, especially in the realm of privacy and control over user data; (3) anonymity, security, and encryption regulations; (4) liability; (5) network neutrality; and (6) cultural imperialism.

INTELLECTUAL PROPERTY CONSIDERATIONS AND COMPETITIVE PRACTICES

Intellectual property (IP) rights, including copyrights, patents, and royalties, have long played a key role in the development of new communication and media technologies.[116] The development of experiential media and the technologies they employ is no exception.

Apple and Samsung, two of the world's largest smartphone manufacturers, dueled in the international courts for years over allegations of IP infringement in the respective companies' mobile technology development, including in the design of the iPhone X. They finally settled the costly case in mid-2018, with the terms of the settlement not revealed.[117] Facebook was sued in a Texas court over allegedly stealing IP in the development of the Oculus Rift. In early 2017 a Dallas jury found Facebook guilty of IP theft in the design of its Oculus Rift headset, ordering the firm to pay $500 million in damages, an amount reduced by half on appeal.[118] Though that amount constitutes mere pocket change for a social networking giant whose third-quarter 2017 profits were $4.7 billion, the verdict precipitated the departure of Oculus founder Luckey from the company.[119] But resolving such IP cases can help to spur the development of experiential media by more widely and fairly distributing rights and royalties to those who have contributed to the underlying technologies and potentially fueling further investment in platforms that can enable experiential news.

A potentially significant IP issue regarding AR is who owns augments that are embedded in or accessed in public spaces such as a park or on a city street. In 2017 artists altered, or "vandalized," Snapchat augments that were overlaid on sculptures by artist Jeff Koons that had been placed in New York's Central Park.[120] One could argue that these modifications are derivative works or commentary and are allowed as fair use per the Lenz case discussed in chapter 1. This would likely pave the way for such user modification of or commentary on experiential news placed in public spaces.

Unfair competitive practices among major technology industry players have also been a key consideration, potentially affecting the development of experiential media, particularly in Europe. Regulators have issued fines and orders to reshape industry practices and foster a more level playing field in online communications. European regulators, for example, fined Google $2.7 billion for search practices that treated competitors such as Microsoft Bing unfairly.[121] Encouraging more fair practices in the digital space could help nurture the development of experiential journalism by opening up more unfettered access to news and information.

USER RIGHTS

Regulatory and legal structures can act as means to protect and serve the public interest, which was once a foundational principle in American communication law. The 1934 Communications Act established this principle in the United States while simultaneously advancing the commercial and nonprofit use of the limited public airwaves. But this public service mandate was reduced in the 1996 Telecommunications Act rewrite in favor of fostering competition and innovation in a digital age. Policy makers had concluded that the scarcity of the airwaves was no longer an overriding concern. Priorities have continued to evolve in the twenty-first century, and a balance has yet to be struck among the competing interests of freedom of speech and press, user rights, and corporate innovation and profit taking.

A growing consideration in the legal and regulatory arena involves the collection and use of user data by media and communication enterprises. Digital media enterprises have been especially adept at exploiting user data to generate revenues. Protecting user privacy has been an increasingly significant concern, especially in Europe and to a lesser degree in the United States.

Since the mid-1800s, newspapers—and throughout most of the twentieth century, radio and television—have sold advertising based on a promise to deliver audiences to companies that seek to sell products and services to those consumers. In the twenty-first century, digital enterprises are increasingly able to utilize the addressability of digital media to sell individually targeted advertising in an efficient fashion. In fact, the addressability notion has evolved into the selling of users' personal information, including their online behaviors, demographic characteristics, and media and consumer patterns. Who owns personal data has become a major regulatory question. Columbia University CITI scholar Benjamin Compaine has asked, "Who owns information?"[122] In the digital age this issue has become a central and contentious one. Do individual users own their data, whether in the form of personal background information, video, audio, or other experiential content? In 2017 President Trump signed legislation allowing internet service providers (ISPs) to sell users' mobile and internet browsing data (including use of experiential news) without the users' permission.

Google routinely collects a broad spectrum of data about its users via algorithms. The *Washington Post* provided a useful examination of the types of information the search giant collects about individual users and makes publicly available.[123] When logged in to Google, users can access the "About Me" page and see what information is being made publicly available. I did that on March 6, 2018, and here is some of what I found: my photograph, my employment status and employer, and my gender. Various other bits of information about me are locked and not available publicly, but Google records them. This locked information includes my birthdate. Users can also access the Google "Privacy Checkup" page to lock various pieces of personal data. Google sells users' personal information to advertisers so that they can more efficiently target advertising messages. Users can change the settings on the privacy checkup page to block this advertising. It is not a simple operation, but users who are concerned about their privacy may want to follow the advice offered in the *Post*: "The last section focuses on advertising. You'll actually have to click off to a separate page to manage those settings, but from there you can opt-out of being served ads that are based on the online activities that Google tracks."[124] Other digital enterprises also collect and utilize such personal information. Facebook tracks extensive user online behaviors and characteristics, including users' photographs and video, and uses facial recognition algorithms to automatically track users and their online friends. Soon, if not already, these digital enterprises may track and sell data about users' engagement with experiential news, for instance, how much time users spent engaged in AR or 360-degree video news about the U.S. migrant crisis and whether they liked or shared stories about the Trump administration's zero-tolerance policy.

Protecting privacy versus exploiting personal data for the sake of generating revenues has been a major source of tension in public policy and regulation in Europe and to a lesser extent in the United States. Digital enterprises such as Google and various social media platforms have advanced algorithm-based systems for monitoring the public's digital media behaviors and targeting users with advertising. Yet these systems have sometimes struggled with the complexities of automatic message placement. In 2017 mishaps in the automatic placement of ads resulted in the positioning of commercial messages next to highly objectionable content such as extremist messages on YouTube.[125] As a result, several major advertisers pulled their commercials from the social network. Traditional journalism and media enterprises have been less aggressive in implementing automated ad sales and placement. How such automated tools will develop in an experiential journalism environment is an unsettled issue.

In May 2018 European regulators issued new privacy rules called the General Data Privacy Regulations (GDPR).[126] All online content providers, social networks, and digital companies are required to comply with the new rules, which go much further to protect user privacy than most laws in the United States. If U.S. news media are to operate in Europe, then they now need to indicate to users how data is being collected and for what purpose, including the use of cookies (which collect data on users' online actions when they visit a site, including a news site) and how they will be shared with advertisers. Users must be given the option to decline to allow their data to be collected. When the new GDPR rules went into effect, the result was that many U.S. news sites essentially went dark or became unavailable in Europe until the sites or mobile apps could be made fully compliant. Any new content or apps, including AR, VR, or any other form of experiential news will need to fully adhere to the GDPR requirements, or the news organization will be subject to fines or other penalties by the EU. In effect, the GDPR may become the global standard for online privacy, including for experiential news, as it will be a potentially ponderous, digitally complex, and limiting business strategy to try to implement different sets of data rules for a news operation country by country. Some U.S. states have passed similar strong online privacy protection laws such as California in 2018.

The issue of exploiting user data is apparent not only in the realm of online search and media activity. IPTV and so-called smart TV technology, which can display experiential news, also raise the issue. For example, a ProPublica investigation reveals how the Vizio smart TV takes tracking to a new level. ProPublica reports that Vizio smart TVs are automatically tracking users' "viewing behavior and sharing it with third parties—along with your IP address."[127] Other reports indicate that smart TVs can even track where a viewer's eyes are looking on the screen.[128]

Internet-connected devices also raise a combination of privacy concerns, law enforcement capabilities, and news-gathering potential for experiential journalism. In early 2017 a massive WikiLeaks document dump revealed that the CIA had developed plans to eavesdrop via a wide swath of digitally connected devices, including smart TVs, smartphones, and other types of internet-connected devices such as audio-based digital assistants, all of which may be public gateways to experiential news.[129]

Amazon received a subpoena in a murder investigation in which investigators believed an Echo Alexa digital assistant might have audio evidence pertinent to the killing, which took place in the homeowner's hot tub. Amazon at first resisted a request for the data, claiming that the First Amendment protects Alexa, but later relented after receiving the subpoena. Audio recordings from internet-connected, always-on audio-interface digital devices might play a role in future experiential news stories as a source of geo-located spatial audio.

Even the U.S. Department of Transportation has developed plans to require new cars to feature vehicle-to-vehicle communication, or "car talk." For consumers, this safety enhancement may make road travel safer and increase the cost of cars by about $100. The feature also raises potential privacy concerns as future criminal investigations involving private vehicles may lead to subpoenas of the data. This data may also become a potential source in experiential news stories related to those investigations.

ANONYMITY, SECURITY, AND ENCRYPTION

A privacy-related dimension concerns whether devices and applications should provide the means to enable user-controlled anonymity on digital platforms, including via encryption. Anonymity has long been a vital part of public media communication. Since American Revolution leader Thomas Paine's anonymous publication of "Common Sense" in 1776, anonymity has played an occasionally important role in free and open democratic societies.[130] Whistleblowers often need to protect their identities to prevent retribution, and many of the same principles of protecting journalists' sources when relying on anonymous sources apply, ethical questions notwithstanding. But in an age of terrorists operating in secrecy online or teenagers who sext in secret, there is increasing concern about the role of anonymous and encrypted mediated communication.

Online anonymity and encryption could become key issues in experiential journalism in a variety of circumstances. Undercover stories or investigations, for example, that involve allegations of corruption in government or criminal activity might necessitate protecting the identities of sources or whistleblowers. The urgency to protect a source could be heightened if sources provide digitally watermarked, first-person video that establishes the veracity of the content. Governmental and law enforcement officials have often sought to prosecute people who are suspected of leaking classified information to journalists. Prosecution may become particularly vigorous in an era of experiential eyewitness accounts. Strong encryption of the leaked information may be the only secure way to a hide the identity of a vulnerable source.

Security and anonymous communication are also considerations in networked multiplayer gaming. Multiplayer game platforms can provide users a communication haven beyond the eyes of government or other surveillance. Sony's PlayStation console is a popular networked gaming platform that is reportedly sometimes used by criminals and terrorists to evade surveillance.[131] Teams form and disappear quickly online and communicate via the game platform regarding game strategies. As a result, people seeking to evade surveillance reportedly use the platform in almost total secrecy. Such possibilities may increase as these networks grow in experiential formats that enable users to exchange even more powerful communications. Journalists developing experiential news may find the domain of multiplayer games relevant when reporting on terrorism or other security-related stories. Laws and regulations that affect access to or use of such games may limit their role in the development of experiential journalism.

LIABILITY

Liability represents another important legal or regulatory issue that is pertinent to experiential journalism. Wearables, robotics, and drones are among the technologies in which liability, or legal responsibility, for possible harm to person or property can occur for news media. As experiential media develop, news media must consider the potential health consequences for users. For example, a person wearing an HMD might be injured while engaging in an AR or VR news experience, potentially making the news organization liable for medical costs and subject to lawsuits. Liability may expand exponentially with the rise of socially networked experiential news.

NETWORK NEUTRALITY

Network neutrality (that is, equal access to online bandwidth regardless of source) represents another unsettled legal and regulatory consideration central to the development of experiential news. A regulatory mandate of network neutrality was key to the development of widespread high-speed distribution networks in the United States. But the future of network neutrality in the United States is in doubt. Trump-appointed FCC chair Ajit Pai directed the agency to end the net neutrality rule in the spring of 2018. Officials in states from New York to Washington have vowed to protect the rule, but it is unclear whether they will succeed on a matter that transcends state borders. Ending net neutrality could give substantial marketplace advantages to ISPs such as AT&T, Verizon, and Comcast, especially with regard to high-bandwidth content services such as VR, AR, and MR. This could inhibit consumer access to experiential news, especially from enterprises that are not owned by the ISPs. Unfettered bandwidth access will also prove crucial in the development of experiential news in an international context.

CULTURAL IMPERIALISM

Also potentially significant are concerns about the possible cross-cultural influence of experiential news. Historically, some European countries and many developing nations have been concerned about media-related globalization, especially in the form of cultural imperialism (the sometimes-dominant flow of media, entertainment, or news, from West to East around the globe). Experiential journalism produced in the West may confront this same concern. The development of experiential news globally may depend on the extent to which a sustainable system of international laws and regulations can balance the competing interests of security, innovation, user privacy, and free and independent journalism.

ROBUST NETWORK INFRASTRUCTURE

Experiential news is bandwidth intensive, and its distribution requires a high-capacity network. Fiber-optic networks are increasingly able to deliver high-bandwidth experiential news content at relatively low cost. Likewise, as advanced wireless networks deploy, mobile user access to quality on-demand VR, AR, and MR news content also may accelerate, although possibly at an increasing cost.[132]

But the need for improved network infrastructure to distribute experiential news content continues to grow. This continual need is highlighted by the efforts of industry leaders to advance new video formats and capabilities.[133] Japanese public broadcaster NHK provides a useful example. NHK has a long and well-established history of innovation in video technology. In the twentieth century NHK helped lead the creation of HDTV, and in the twenty-first century NHK has helped develop ultra-high-definition TV (UHD TV).

UHD TV not only brings visual advantages. It also brings substantial bandwidth requirements for the distribution network. An 8K UHD video features pixel resolution that is substantially higher than previous generations of video technology at 7,680 pixels horizontally by 4,320 vertically, which is equivalent to an Imax film. In fact, Imax has introduced VR movies in several of its immersive cinema venues.[134] In 8K UHD videos, there are thirty-three million pixels in each individual frame.[135] This translates into extraordinary bandwidth requirements to transmit uncompressed UHD video. "At 120 frames per second, a raw 7680×4320 video feed clocks in at 48 gigabits per second (Gbps)," reports one analyst.[136] In 2018 many bandwidth providers boast internet speeds at about one hundred megabits per second (Mbps), a tiny fraction (far less than 1 percent) of the delivery requirements of uncompressed 8K UHD TV. Moreover, UHD TV also features substantially higher sound quality, with 22.2 audio channels, which translates into transmission requirements of about 50 Mbps. Even with new, advanced compression technologies, analysts estimate that the bandwidth requirements to deliver UHD TV (3-D or not) in real time will likely top 500 Mbps, about fifty times the requirements of HDTV. These bandwidth requirements pose a potentially serious impediment to the development of experiential news unless network capacity can be dramatically increased.

A new generation of commercial wireless network technology for mobile devices such as smartphones is also poised to enter and possibly transform the marketplace. By 2020 so-called 5G (fifth-generation) networks are expected to play a significant role in the United States and many international wireless markets. It is possible that 5G could deliver enough bandwidth to support mobile UHD TV and other ultrabroadband content services, including experiential news.[137] Industry forecasts predict that the 5G wireless network will provide bandwidth ten times that of the current 4G network, or 10 Gbps versus 1 Gbps.[138]

Other innovative efforts are also underway to improve network capacity. One example is Li-Fi—light-based wireless broadband technology that uses light-emitting diodes (LED) as the transmission means—developed by Harald Haas from the University of Edinburgh, which is now in wider-scale experimentation. As LED technology grows in the marketplace, it offers a platform for delivering low-cost high-speed wireless internet connectivity.[139]

Cloud computing is also relevant to efficient utilization of bandwidth capacity. Cloud computing enables decentralized storage, processing, and production of media content including experiential news. In a high-bandwidth environment, distributed computing systems can facilitate the user experience by putting some of the required system intelligence into the network but close to the end user. These same capabilities also raise potential security questions by distributing more potential nodes for cyberattacks or hacks.

It is still unclear how long or at what cost the higher-speed fiber or wireless networks will take in development. But with Moore's Law still in apparent operation, it is likely to occur in the next decade, providing the technical infrastructure needed for experiential journalism.

Overarching all these developments is a network parameter known as Metcalfe's Law, which "states that the value of a telecommunications network is proportional to the square of the number of connected users of the system (n^2)."[140] A simple way to understand Metcalfe's Law is for the reader to imagine being the only person in the world with a telephone. Such a phone would have limited value even if it were mobile and multifunctional. Adding a second person to the phone network increases the value of the network. Using the n^2 formula, a one-person network has a value of $1 \times 1 = 1$. A two-person network has a value of $2 \times 2 = 4$. So it has quadruple the value of a single-person network. The value of the network increases exponentially as users are added to the network. In the age of the Internet of Things, it is not only people but also devices connected to the network that increase its value. Metcalfe's Law is generally credited to internet coinventor Robert Metcalfe.[141] Though it is not without detractors, Metcalfe's Law perhaps best explains why digital behemoths such as Google and Facebook launched their internet delivery initiatives such as Project Loon—Google's initiative to deliver free wireless internet via weather balloons—to provide free wireless internet access in sub-Saharan Africa and other underserved regions around the globe. Such global connectivity is more than a public service. It adds to the overall value of the network. It also will enable worldwide experiential news engagement.

Metcalf's Law is also relevant, at least as a metaphor, for the simultaneous dual role of content and technological development. Great experiential journalism, without a platform for its distribution or user access, is of very little value. Likewise, an advanced content distribution system, or installed base of UHD TV receivers or VR headsets, has little value without quality experiential news and user engagement. The combination, however, could be transformative. For news industry leaders, planning strategically for the business opportunities afforded by Metcalfe's Law may prove pivotal in any future fiscal viability for experiential journalism in the twenty-first century and beyond.

CHAPTER EIGHT

An Experiential News Parable

O wonder!
How many godly creatures are there here!
How beauteous mankind is! O brave new world,
That has such people in't.

—WILLIAM SHAKESPEARE, *THE TEMPEST*

This chapter presents a parable of future experiential journalism and media. As an allegorical story, this cautionary narrative is meant to illustrate or reveal a set of fundamental truths, principles, or moral lessons for life in a news environment transformed by virtual reality and other experiential media.[1]

BRAVE NEW MEDIA WORLD

In the spirit of Aldous Huxley's twentieth-century parable *Brave New World*, I outline below the nature and potential consequences of a transformed media landscape.[2] I posit that in a not-too-distant future, experiential news will engage the user in journalism and media environments that at times may be almost indistinguishable from reality.[3]

The year is 2032, one century since the publication of Huxley's landmark novel. AI has infused journalism and media. Multisensory and synthetic media environments are omnipresent and on demand for purchase or wish fulfillment. Volumetric displays project apparently real, interactive 3-D objects and acoustics throughout a wide range of social settings. Ubiquitous sensors provide a continuous feed of

data into the algorithm-guided media network. The fusion of con-
tent and real-world objects manifests itself as tangible media avail-
able from inexpensive and automated 3-D and 4-D printers (some
are available at public kiosks or vending machines) that can shift
form and function depending on environmental factors such as
temperature, humidity, lighting, acoustics, or other objects in that
space. Haptic technologies infuse media experiences with touch and
force feedback to make virtual contact seem real, even with artifi-
cial objects or across vast distances or time. Such tangible media con-
tinue in popularity, echoing the demand in 2018 for vinyl records.[4]
Public demand for tangible media is not surprising or inconsistent
with wider trends. Tangible media give users a sense of authenticity
and comfort that is widely sought after in an increasingly congested,
networked, and digital public environment often marked by anomie,
anxiety, and frenetic change.

Tiered economics has produced a highly stratified media plat-
form where those individuals of extreme wealth are able to obtain
richly reported and fact-checked real-time information to support
actions that further the growth and accumulation of wealth. At the
top of this tiered media pyramid, experiential news content is highly
customizable and virtually indistinguishable from reality when so
desired.

Experiential news provides a modality-rich environment aided
by expert systems to facilitate language learning or other educa-
tional outcomes. Such experiential news plays a vital role not only
in entertainment and journalism but also in training and even ther-
apy. Medical researchers at Emory University, for instance, have
since 1995 been using VR approaches to help treat those suffering
from posttraumatic stress disorder (PTSD) as a result of sexual
assault in the military.[5] *Professional and college football teams use*
VR technology for player training with reduced exposure to possible
injury.[6] *A Johns Hopkins University project uses VR via the Oculus*
to teach young doctors in geriatric care.[7] *"We Are Alfred" is a VR*
experience that simulates what life is like for a seventy-four-year-
old, roughly fifty years older than most of the medical students in
training. Preliminary studies indicate that VR therapy could be a
tool to effectively treat depression and autism.[8]

But experiential content also finds a receptive marketplace in pornography and in the dark net, where pedophiles and terrorists exploit the immersive and tangible nature of the new media form.[9] Anonymity is a key factor in this dark net, where encryption, block-chain, and crypto-currency enable many users to evade government surveillance and operate under an online cloak of invisibility. Government forces and others seek to use the experiential nature of networked news to manipulate public opinion at home and abroad by flooding the social media environment with false but apparently real news experiences in VR, AR, and MR format.

Industry analysts have identified VR pornography as a major future economic arena: "Piper Jaffray, an investment bank, reckons the industry activity will pay off." By 2020 VR porn had become a $1 billion-a-year business, "making it the third-largest VR segment after gaming and sports."[10]

At the other end of the spectrum, a "free" tier gives users access to highly commoditized news and entertainment experiential media content. In exchange for users' personal data, experiential content of limited value and timeliness is available. Homogenous newsfeeds, general entertainment, and marketing information complement a media space dominated by user-generated content shared on social networking platforms, where individuals rarely stray beyond their personal filter bubble. Quality experiential journalism is available but generally as premium content once was in 2018. Users must pay a premium for news and information that has been vetted for reliability and accuracy. More often, experiential content is available as a form of product placement where marketing is algorithmically synthesized directly into a personalized media narrative.

Wearable, even implantable technologies are a natural and increasingly ubiquitous reality in much the same way that handheld mobile devices were in 2018. It has been nearly a half century since Steve Mann invented the wearable computer in 1987. Parents' earlier concerns about the potential harmful effects of cell phone radiation on their children seem almost quaint in an environment where human senses are increasingly fusing with digital media and creating twenty-four-hour-connected human-digital cyborgs. McLuhan's 1964 suggestion that media act as extensions of human senses was a prescient foreshadowing of the experiential convergence of the AI-dominated digital singularity of 2032.

In 2012 the Pew Research Internet Project showed that in that year nearly two-thirds (61 percent) of people ages eighteen to twenty-four slept with their smartphones next to their heads. This was almost triple the rate for those sixty-five and older (22 percent). In 2032 a growing portion of the world's population welcomes digital embeds, which enable easy, continuous communication and news flow, especially during the increasingly frequent times of crisis sweeping across the planet. In retrospect, it is easy to see how analysts vastly underestimated the advance of wearables when in 2015 they forecast that five hundred million wearable devices would be sold worldwide by 2018, including twenty-one million pairs of AR and VR goggles.

The rapid diffusion of wearables has led to a tipping point in which not having continuous access to real-time news experiences is a serious detriment both economically and in terms of social capital. More than that, embedded digital media have become a critical experiential news lifeline. For some, wearables are embedded in clothing and other fashion accessories, but for others, digital media are implanted under the skin. Parents implant chips in their children as a means of ensuring safety from abduction and also for continuous location tracking and automatically generated personal experiential news that helps parents stay engaged in their children's lives. For immigrants, implanted technology is a condition of admission in order to guarantee continuous tracking data for government security agencies. These implants serve as a crucial IoT source of data for experiential news to keep concerned citizens fully engaged in border-control issues. Implantable digital devices are a natural extension of the extensive body modifications that were often performed for a variety of reasons in earlier times, some medical such as birth control implants and some cosmetic such as tattoos. VR and other immersive media have profound influence on a wide swath of society from medicine to education to media and news experience.[11]

Robots with sophisticated artificial general intelligence have become capable of reading human thoughts. They do not rely on a sixth sense; instead, they use advanced computer vision to read and

analyze micro facial movements and other biomarkers and respira-
tory patterns as well as embedded chips to assess the emotions and
estimate the thoughts of humans. Hackers try to put such capacities
to nefarious use to access even the most secret thoughts of any indi-
vidual, including passwords or more. Speaking at the 2016 World
Economic Forum in Davos, Switzerland, Nita Farahany, professor
of law and philosophy at Duke University, warned that within a gen-
eration, brain function could be used to unlock secure electronic
devices.[12]

Drones, sensors, and other IoT digital surveillance technologies
are ubiquitous. They track individuals and collect multisensory data
continuously. Using ultra-high-resolution cameras and advanced
acoustical recording technologies, privacy has become impossible
except for the ultrarich who can pay the large fees necessary to stay
off the grid or to remain anonymous when so desired.

Experiential news deeply engages users emotionally and intel-
lectually. It transcends time, place, and individual and fosters
extraordinary social, political, and cultural dynamics including
triggering rapid behavioral responses (much as earlier generations
saw online social movements emerge quickly and sometimes globally
in response to news reports). The consequences and implications of
such profound experiential news engagement are far reaching and
raise reasons for optimism as well as cause for serious concern. With-
out substantial, independent, reliable, and ethical experiential
journalism, there is little hope for anything but a dysfunctional, frag-
mented, and polarized political system and dystopian future.

REFLECTIONS ON THE FUTURE OF
EXPERIENTIAL MEDIA

This parable has explored four dimensions of the future of experiential
media and journalism. First are the economic, legal, and regulatory
frameworks that undergird the media system and its evolving experiential form. These frameworks shape and limit the potential for vibrant
journalism in the years ahead. Second is the coming fusion of wearables
and humans, possibly even in the form of miniature embedded digital
technologies. This fusion may signal an almost inseparable bond between

users and the media as well as the end of privacy. Third is the ubiquity of internet-connected devices. The IoT generates enormous flows of experiential news but also enables ubiquitous surveillance. Fourth is the potential of experiential media to eclipse reality or at least simulate real-world experiences in such a convincing, multisensory fashion so as to make experiential news and reality virtually indistinguishable.

Many elements of this cautionary forecast are already in place. Fake-App, for example, is a software tool released in 2018 for creating photo-realistic "face-swap" videos.[13] Propagandists might use such a tool to produce highly realistic but false immersive video of a president declaring war or admitting collusion. Even the most robust journalism may be unable to effectively or promptly fact-check such artificial realities.

The Media Insight Project has determined that the majority of Americans now pay for their news. A survey of 2,199 American adults conducted between February 16 and March 20, 2017, shows that "slightly more than half (53 percent) of all U.S. adults subscribe to news in some form—and roughly half of those to a newspaper."[14] These numbers include those who subscribe to newspapers or magazines, pay for news apps, or donate to public media. It excludes those who pay for cable TV bundles, which could include news channels. Consequently, paying for news in some form is an increasing norm for Americans, and it is a pattern likely to grow in the years ahead as advertising dollars continue to flow toward digital companies such as Google and as news providers increasingly require paid subscriptions or other forms of user payment to access the news. Moreover, the implication is that those who cannot afford to pay for news will have less access to quality news, especially expensive experiential news, and their views may be less salient to decisions that news executives make about future news directions in coverage and format.

Similar evidence of tiered media access can be found in the growing paywall being erected around quality journalism. An increasing number of the best news media have installed paywalls to block access to their digital journalism content for people without paid subscriptions. Among the most notable examples are the *New York Times* and the *Washington Post*. These organizations are among the most highly regarded for the quality of their journalistic content, having won dozens of Pulitzer Prizes and other awards for excellence. Each is known for its innovative approach to digital, experiential journalism. The *Times* produces extensive VR story telling. The *Post*, purchased by Amazon's Jeff Bezos with the promise of expanding the organization's use of innovative approaches in journalism, is advancing an AR journalism initiative. Both the *Times* and the *Post* give readers free access to a few (about ten) stories per month online or via mobile. After that, readers must subscribe. During the 2015 terrorist attacks on Paris, the *Times* used its digital platform to give nonsubscribers access at no cost to its coverage of the Paris attacks, as it did with Election Day coverage in November 2016. Producing quality journalism is expensive, and experiential forms even more so. Substantial revenues are needed to sustain such quality journalism and immersive stories. The consequences for democracy are uncertain. The increasingly expensive nature of quality journalism in the digital age harkens back to the early days of the American colonies when the colonial press was expensive and only the wealthy could afford to buy the newspapers of the day.

Some readers may accept the idea of a tiered media economic system as a fiscal necessity. But they may view with much more incredulity the idea that people would ever accept the idea of a computer chip being implanted in humans. Yet such microchip implantation in humans has been a reality in the United States since at least 2004.[15] In that year the Food and Drug Administration (FDA) approved medical applications of microchips that involve the implantation of a rice-size chip into a patient's arm. The device captures and transmits to medical providers, including hospitals, various data such as blood pressure, heart rate, and medical history. It takes less than twenty minutes to implant the chip. Advances in the technology in the past decade have been considerable. Implanting digital technology in humans is more a matter of where, why, and for whom than when. Congress has considered legislation that would involve the creation of a medical device registry including implantables.[16] Legendary for having developed the internet, the U.S. military's Defense Advanced Research Agency (DARPA) is conducting research designed to develop implantable technology to interface between the human brain and the digital world.[17]

In Sweden, Epicenter is an initiative to advance bio-hacking. Bio-hacker Hannes Sjoblot has implanted a rice-size chip into his left hand to experiment with the fusion of humans and digital technology.[18] The chip features wireless technology known as radio-frequency identification (RFID). It enables Sjoblot to unlock his office door, access his computer, and interact with a variety of digital technologies simply by bringing his hand near various RFID sensors. He considers it an "upgrade" to the human body. Initiatives such as Epicenter are not alone. Biohack.me is another such project where proponents get "chipped."[19] A Wisconsin company in 2017 chipped some fifty of its employees, enabling various capabilities via an RFID reader, such as passing one's hand past a chip reader to make food purchases in the company snack room at work.[20] In development is an AR-enabled lens that is surgically implanted in the human eye. By mid-2017, Omega Opthalmics had already conducted a small-scale trial in Europe and is awaiting FDA approval to begin a trial in the United States.[21]

Some oppose the idea of implantable technology, but others consider it inevitable. In either case, such implants are likely to lead to inescapable twenty-four-hour surveillance and communication. Implanted chips may one day deliver new forms of experiential news that are felt (like a text alert on a current smartphone set on vibrate mode) rather than seen or heard.

Wearables and implantables are interrelated and growing phenomena. Combined, they constituted a $3.4 billion industry in 2016. Participants in "maker" culture are developing a swath of related devices such as a next-generation micro wireless camera embedded in a realistic synthetic human eye. Such technology could help the visually impaired and may go much further than Google Glass to one day transform documentary making and experiencing. Users with AR contact lenses or even implanted AR lenses could live continuously in an AR-enabled news and media world.

Perhaps even more remarkable are advances in a field known as brain-computer interfaces (BCI). BCI enables humans to control a digital device purely through thought. "Until recently, the dream of being able to control one's environment through thoughts had been in the realm of science fiction," Mayo Clinic researchers report in their investigations of BCI. "However, the advance of technology has brought a new reality: Today, humans can use the electrical signals from brain activity to interact with, influence, or change their environments."[22]

Elon Musk has launched Neuralink, a company developing implantable BMI technology.[23] Neurable is a start-up whose technology uses BCI as a VR game interface.[24] Some call this growing field neuroreality.[25] Today's BCI requires a wired connection between human and computer. Tomorrow's may function without the tether. An HTC Vive prototype allows VR game play via brain wave.[26] Experiential journalism could utilize neuroreality as an experiential news interface. Such an experiential news platform for people with disabilities could prove highly effective and pave the way for broader applications.

Pioneering neuroscientist David Eagleman points out that developments in the arena of the human-machine interface trace their roots to the 1970s with the invention of a single miniature technology: the cochlear implant.[27] It is an electronic device that enables the deaf to hear.[28] Largely enabled by Moore's Law, implantable devices such as the cochlear are now dramatically smaller, more powerful, and cheaper. Eagleman notes that nearly a quarter million people around the world can hear because of these implants. Soon such implants are likely to be much more widespread as prices fall and performance continues to improve. Eagleman adds that his research demonstrates that there is no reason to think implants would be limited to repairing disabilities. They could also give the brain new capacities to enhance our senses. In fact, he explains, in theory there is almost no limit to what would be possible. He offers an example of enabling people to plug directly into the financial markets and obtain a real-time intuitive sense of market trends in a truly unprecedented form of multisensory experiential news engagement.

People could begin to shape their own sensory experiences. Eagleman's research also demonstrates how in 2016 people suffering from paralysis could use implantable technology to control networked real-world physical objects, such as a robotic arm. Readers might ponder how experiential media content could evolve in an environment where the user might control or interact with digital content such as the news through thought alone. Research suggests that implantable technology may soon provide a viable medium for the generation and experience of unique musical content.[29] Some are calling this new implantable audio form "dynamically generated music."[30] Dynamically generated experiential news could follow suit. For example, dynamically generated news could automatically interpret the qualities of one's environment—whether outdoors in nature or indoors at home or in the office—and represent the data in a continuous flow of customized hyperlocal news and information.

Increasingly evident are ubiquitous cameras and other networked data-collection sensors. Many of these digital devices are combined with AI or at least sophisticated algorithms and machine vision. Illustrative is the "ring of steel" installed in 2011 in lower Manhattan, New York.[31] As a mechanism for advanced law enforcement, authorities in New York City installed in lower Manhattan some three thousand cameras, at least one hundred of which are license-plate readers. In November 2015, Freeport, Long Island, followed New York City's lead and installed its own "ring of steel" perimeter surrounding its borders.[32] The license plate of every vehicle entering or exiting the community is automatically scanned and correlated with a state and federal database containing information on drivers and vehicles such as traffic violations or status as known or wanted felons. Such intelligent, automated camera systems are installed in dozens of cities around the world in dozens of countries, including Australia, France, Saudi Arabia, Sweden, Ukraine, and the United Kingdom.[33] Many of these automated surveillance systems are not only capable of reading license plates but also of capturing and storing photographs and video of the drivers. Facial recognition technology such as that developed by Amazon can automatically scan and identify any individual passing within sight of what could be a 360-degree camera.[34] The implications are significant for the generation of multimedia content including in news reporting on crime or terrorism. This content could take an experiential form, produced in interactive documentaries and the like.

Mark G. Frank of the University of Buffalo has conducted research on machine vision and its various communication-related applications, including security, facial recognition, and emotion analysis. Frank and colleagues' research indicates that people often attempt to mask pain or other emotions.[35] They find that, "Machine vision may, however, be able to distinguish deceptive from genuine facial signals by identifying the subtle differences between pyramidally and extrapyramidally driven movements." The team's research shows "that human observers could not discriminate real from faked expressions of pain better than chance, and after training, improved accuracy to a modest 55%. However a computer vision system that automatically measures facial movements and performs pattern recognition on those movements attained 85% accuracy." Such a system might have powerful implications for experiential news reporting, enabling an AI-aided interviewer to instantly and accurately detect the true emotional reactions of those being interviewed (and perhaps trying to disguise a lie).

Critics wisely point to the possibility of errors and inaccuracies in these automated surveillance systems and their potential threat to privacy. But with rising concern about terrorism around the globe, there is powerful momentum to not only keep these systems in place but also to expand their presence and usage. Their potential for experiential journalism, including their use in news reporting, is equally substantial.

These largely fixed-location surveillance sensors are in complement to the estimated five billion networked mobile cameras operated by citizens around the globe. Body-worn cameras constitute a major subset of these mobile cameras. Increasingly worn by police and other law enforcement officials, they are in addition to dashboard cameras on police and private citizens' vehicles. Police are not the only law enforcement agencies in the United States or elsewhere using body-worn cameras: "The United States border patrol is launching a test of body cameras for its 21,000 agents."[36] Such cameras are a major source of video in crime reporting and will likely prove to be a substantial source of news coverage in an experiential media environment. As next-generation UHD body cams enter the marketplace, their potential role in experiential news reporting will grow.

Dark net applications of experiential media content and functionality are also apparent. U.S. intelligence analysts have described how terrorist leaders as early as in 2008 were developing avatars and other online VR applications to recruit and train virtual jihadists.[37] In 2011 the Silk Road emerged as an online black market for a wide range of illegal activities.[38]

Sexually explicit content is also likely to play a role in the evolution of experiential media, just as it has played a role in the development of earlier media technologies. In the 1980s, for example, the videocassette recorder gave interested parties the ability to watch explicit materials in the privacy of their homes.[39] The dramatic surge in online access to pornography conversely contributed to the decision by executives of Playboy Enterprises to cease publishing nude photos on its website. Pornography had become so widely available online that it made business sense for Playboy to expand its nonexplicit content offerings. Christie

A. Hefner, chair and chief executive officer of Playboy Enterprises, reported in 2017 that as "new content has been added to Playboy.com, traffic to the site has increased 38%. Playboy.com began expanding its content offerings in early May. Page views increased to 65.5 million in June, up from 47.6 million in April."[40]

On the immersive media front, a firm specializing in adult content has developed a VR application for users interested in virtual sexual encounters. According to the *New York Post*, "CamSoda, a mobile-first adult site that specializes in live webcasts of porn stars, is launching a virtual-reality show that promises to plunge viewers into entire roomfuls of naked models and sex scenes in real time."[41] The advance of highly realistic, haptic, humanoid robots designed for sexual activity with humans is also merging within the realm of experiential media engagement.[42] Sexual harassment and assault in VR have become significant concerns. Experiential journalism that engages these issues interactively could find a significant level of user demand.

Negative consequences of media immersion represent an important dimension of experiential news, including possible health effects, threats to user privacy and security, and beyond. There are at least three levels at which these effects might occur: the individual (e.g., psychological effects), the relational (e.g., social media), and the societal or institutional (e.g., policy).

At the individual level, experiential news media may generate a sense of psychological immersion in the narrative. Potentially such immersion might lead to beneficial effects, such as greater empathy. But it may also foster user addiction or other harmful side effects on individual mental or physical well-being, especially among young users.[43] Research by psychologists Robert Kubey and Mihaly Csikszentmihalyi has shown that viewing television can be an addiction.[44]

There is little reason to think that users of digital, electronic, and immersive media such as VR might not have the same or even greater potential to form addictions to enveloping experiences. This might be especially likely for young users, whose overall behavior patterns, habits, and even brains are still in formative stages of development. Moreover, the more compelling a VR-based narrative, the more addictive it might be. This might constitute a dilemma for those creating VR-based news narratives; quality experiential journalism might increase understanding but also possible user addiction.

The consequences of participating in a story or piece of content may be far reaching and little understood. Experiential news may heighten public engagement, empathy, tolerance, and compassion. Or an internet echo chamber may become an inescapable digital house of horrors. Ultimately the most important implications for society may be the unanticipated consequences of a transformed experiential news environment. Users may fail to differentiate between direct and mediated experience, regardless of the source or construction of the experiential journalism. Academic investigators are conducting research to help advance understanding of the nature and impact of user engagement with experiential forms of journalism and media content.

Other health effects of experiential content are of concern as well. One of the problems associated with HMDs is that users have often experienced feelings of nausea or motion sickness when immersed in virtual environments for more than a brief time. Labeled "virtual reality sickness," this may be solved by the latest generation of wearables.[45] One of the factors is the resolution of the VR displays. Systems such as the Oculus and HTC deliver about 1.2 megapixels per eye, significantly less than the resolution a human eye perceives when observing reality directly. For the user, this can result in what is known as sensory conflict, where visual input is incongruent with the user's usual experience or expectations. Finnish company Varjo has developed a headset that delivers seventy megapixels per eye.[46] Currently available only to the professional marketplace and with the price tag of 6,995 euros plus a license fee of 995 euros (a total of more than $8,500 US), the VR-1 HMD provides users the resolution of 20/20 human vision and delivers a VR experience very close to visual reality.

Eyestrain is also an important area meriting research attention. This may be especially relevant for users of HMDs when experiencing video that was not originally designed for an immersive experience, including documentaries. Netflix, for instance, offers an app that enables viewers to watch in a VR format any video otherwise available for streaming or download. "This sounds thoughtful in theory," notes one observer, "but watching an episode of 'Futurama' made my eyes feel as if I had been staring at a light bulb for an hour; it also is not comfortable to lie in bed with a headset strapped to your face."[47] This same observer added, "In my testing of the device [Gear VR] over a week, the video strained my eyes and the extra weight on my head made my neck sore."[48] Even the manufacturers of VR headsets acknowledge the potential physical difficulties of the technology. "Virtual reality is a new experience for many, and there is a natural acclimation process."[49] Adding, "As you use VR more, it becomes more comfortable for longer periods of time." Samsung recommends using its HMD only while seated or standing still; VR experiences such as standing on the edge of a cliff can seem so real that the user can easily become disoriented and fall over in the real world and potentially suffer significant physical injury. It is possible that concerns such as these may relegate VR content experiences, at least in its wearable form, to the realm of game play and only a secondary news media niche.

Research on screen use also suggests a health problem labeled "inattentional deafness."[50] Studies indicate that while using a screen device, users are sometimes unable to hear external sounds, including human voices. Users are so absorbed in the screen activity that they become deaf to the surrounding environment. Experiential journalism, with potentially profoundly immersive qualities, may exacerbate the problem of inattentional deafness.

At the relational level, research should examine how digital media content, especially that which engages multiple users (such as multiplayer games) or affects social networks and interrelationships. Research might look at how experiential digital narratives intersect with other forms of user communication or interaction with individuals who are not as digitally connected. As new social-VR environments enter the marketplace, research on the implications for social interaction will be increasingly important, including regarding journalistic applications such as news discussion forums carried out in virtual worlds or virtual reality.

Relational research might also examine the nature and impact of derivative work in experiential journalism. As the father of hypertext, Ted Nelson, originally proposed in 1963, linking between works online would be an ideal means to build on previous work. He argued that links could help to credit previous work accurately and facilitate compensation for the reuse of copyrighted expression.[51] Research might examine the nature of derivative work in the content and contextualization of experiential journalism in an industry where derivative work has long been a widespread practice.

At the societal or institutional level, research could examine the role that experiential journalism can play in the well-being of the larger social system, including the political process and the formation of public opinion. Journalism has long played a central role in democratic society, providing an independent source of news and information that the citizenry can rely upon for matters of public importance such as elections. Adapted from an eighteenth-century notion, contemporary observers sometimes describe journalism as the Fourth Estate or branch of government that serves as a check on the other three more formal branches, the legislative (e.g., Congress), the judicial (e.g., the courts), and the executive (e.g., the president). How this role may be evolving with the rise of experiential content and the potential for highly convincing fake experiential news, especially in a participatory system, is an essential research question for the twenty-first century. It is quite possible that algorithm- and data-driven experiential fake news could have potentially dangerous consequences (intended or not) in a connected global media system where a false experiential news message or rumor shared online could influence public opinion, trigger a mass panic, or worse, perhaps affect an election outcome or ignite a late-night presidential tweet-storm that produces an international crisis.

Regardless of the emerging experiential possibilities, the system of media and communication and the forces that shape it are so complex and multidimensional that any forecast is apt to lose precision over time. Readers might consider the fact that the first television sets were being sold to consumers in 1928.[52] But for a variety of reasons, including the advent of World War II, TV did not develop into a mass medium until some two decades later. The likelihood of the developments outlined in this chapter's parable and the contours of their shape may well depend on policy makers and the decisions they make regarding the relevant economic, regulatory, and legal infrastructure in the United States and around the world.

As experiential journalism becomes an increasing reality, considering both the good and bad possibilities will prove essential to making informed and wise choices. For context, it may be useful to recall the poetic observations of one nineteenth-century newspaper editor on an earlier technologically driven shift in media content.

Reflecting on the story-telling potential of the newly invented daguerreotype, the precursor to modern photography, this sage observer wrote, "In whatever direction you turn your peering gaze, you see naught but human faces! There they stretch, from floor to ceiling—hundreds of them. Ah! what tales might those pictures tell if their mute lips had the power of speech! How romance then, would be infinitely outdone by fact."[53]

Published in 1846 in the *Brooklyn Daily Eagle* newspaper, these words foreshadowed the twentieth-century invention of television and even the rise of experiential journalism in the twenty-first century. The writer of these prescient words was Walt Whitman, American poet and former editor of the *Brooklyn Daily Eagle.* Whitman's contemporary, Samuel Morse, saw the daguerreotype as a new tool for journalism, encouraging his newspaper publisher brothers to adopt the technology as a visual reporting tool.

There are also lessons to be learned about the power of images in the nineteenth-century experiences of Frederick Douglass. Formerly enslaved, Douglass rose to prominence in the nineteenth century as an abolitionist, orator, and journalist. As reported by Harvard scholar John Stauffer and colleagues, Douglass was also the most photographed American of the nineteenth century.[54] "Frederick Douglass was in love with photography," according to historians.[55] Douglass believed that photography could help end slavery. He was convinced that even in the hands of an avowed racist, photographs could still tell the truth. Consequently, Douglass actively sought to have his photograph taken and shared widely so others could see that African Americans were human beings worthy of freedom. Douglass was convinced that photographs could tell an irrefutable truth. By removing the photographic frame and immersing the viewer in 360-degree photographs or video, journalists might amplify telling that truth by letting the individual examine the wider context of a visual story.

PILLARS OF EXCELLENCE IN EXPERIENTIAL JOURNALISM

This book has presented evidence that news media are evolving toward an immersive, interactive, and multisensory future. Users, or members of the public, will increasingly encounter experiential journalism and become active participants in the news rather than simply passive recipients of it. On a theoretical level, experiential stories are apt to engage the public emotionally or intellectually and also transcend the moment, the place, or the individual. Research suggests this may increase the user's recall of news-related information and empathy for people featured in the news.

When crafted skillfully, experiential news stories will rest on three pillars of excellence. First is a strong foundation of fundamental elements, including extensive research, quality writing or presentation, and effective design or structure. Second is the adroit use of the features of the digital media environment, including multiple modalities, immersion, and interaction with the public. Blending these capabilities will make news experiences powerful and compelling. Third, and perhaps most important, is the accurate presentation of messages of substance, with relevance to society and life and death on Earth and beyond. It is critical here to avoid mixing fact and opinion in story experiences. Users may become confused, and trust in experiential news will erode and potentially disintegrate completely. Combined, these qualities of experiential news can thereby help advance public understanding of the truth on matters of public interest and importance.

These pillars of quality news content are particularly germane to the challenge of capturing the attention of today's mobile, participatory, and multitasking citizenry. Effectively integrated, an array of digital elements can enable an experiential story to heighten the engagement of the citizen, whether in news narratives, nonfiction, or even fiction-based media stories. Public engagement has always been a central goal of journalism, and it is increasingly relevant for nonfiction and fiction-based narratives regardless of form or delivery medium. Public engagement is vital to the healthy functioning of journalism and other forms of mediated stories in a democracy. But engagement has often been difficult to achieve. Many citizens, at least in the United States, have often detached from traditional media and become increasingly alienated or disconnected from the political process, which patterns of falling voter turnout evident since 1960 suggest.[56] Moreover, media systems are increasingly fragmented, and user attention is harder to capture and maintain. Early research suggests that experiential media have the potential to engage audiences on multiple levels and to build empathy or create a sense of awe for the user.

Experiential journalism may also play a key role in fostering experiential learning. Experiential learning is an ancient concept, articulated by Aristotle.[57] More recently, scholars such as John Dewey and Jean Piaget have developed a theoretical framework for understanding how learning by doing can facilitate understanding, comprehension, and memory among other learning outcomes.[58] A substantial body of research has confirmed the relevance of experiential learning theory to media, especially the role of multiple modalities, interactivity, and narrative structures on cognitive outcomes.[59] The dual-coding hypothesis indicates that visual-verbal representations facilitate learning better than single-media portrayals.[60] The effect might be heightened with fully immersive and multisensory news experiences.

Research also suggests that children respond positively to using immersive tools to create their own stories.[61] In a project called Kidstory, researchers from Sweden, the UK, and the United States studied how children ages five to seven years could collaboratively create stories: "The final set-up allowed children to dynamically produce story content, to create basic narrative structures and to retell their stories in a collaborative and adaptable physical space." Extending this capacity into the realm of kid-created experiential news could help foster a generation of engaged and well-informed citizens and future experiential journalists.

Beyond user engagement, the success of experiential journalism may depend on the scope and inclusivity of the stories told. Throughout the history of media, there have been important gaps in the narratives presented. In early radio, diversity was a notable programming weakness, with little programming about sexual orientation or the realities of mental illness. Mainstream newspapers and television news often have underreported about rural America, the nation's inner cities, and life in Native American communities.

Gaps in the experiential stories of tomorrow's news media are also likely. Will the sweep of stories include those of marginalized groups? How will experiential content reflect the experiences and narratives of indigenous people? What role will issues such as gender, race, social class, disability, sexual orientation, and identity play in the experiential news media environment?

If content flows increasingly from the ranks of those who participate in the digital and networked ecosystem, then we should expect their stories to reflect their realities, experiences, or concerns. Even if their numbers are five billion, there will still be more than two billion people worldwide who are excluded from this experiential news story space. Whose voices will not be heard? What story experiences will be excluded? Will the digital media system be inclusive of even those voices that are not amenable to the commercial or funding priorities of media industry or otherwise at odds with the prevailing power structure?

Demand for media-delivered content, especially original narratives, continues to be strong and manifests on many levels. Raw material for original stories is particularly intense in the video environment. Although broadcast and cable television have seen their role decline, video as a story platform has morphed digitally into online, mobile, and social networking platforms. As such, the digital video industry rivals that of cinema and video games. This is evident in the United States' TV and video industries' combined multiplatform annual revenues ($66 billion in 2014 for broadcast and cable TV, $43 billion for online) as well as the amount of time most Americans spend watching TV and video programming in various digital formats.[62] Signs point to continued high demand for experiential stories including news, especially those that reflect a diversity of users, perspectives, and subject matter.

Tuna Amobi, director and senior equity analyst of Standard & Poor's Capital IQ, reports, "Never before have we seen investment in content development as we have today."[63] Investors are pouring billions of dollars into content production, Amobi explains. Their objective is to exploit the emerging opportunities in the digital video marketplace, especially in the nonlinear, experiential arena. Gordon Goldstein, managing director and head of external affairs of Silver Lake, adds that Netflix spent "$6 billion in content development in 2016," roughly double what it spent in 2015.[64] At least a portion of this is likely to be in the realm of nonfiction content and increasingly long-form experiential news and interactive documentaries.

If past is prologue, there is certainly likely to be demand for more stories about Martians and other extraterrestrial forms. From H. G. Wells's *War of the Worlds* to Ray Bradbury's *The Martian Chronicles*, media and the public have long been enamored with tales of Earth's closest planetary neighbor. Radio, film, and digital television and cinema have produced multiple versions of these and other fiction and nonfiction tales of the red planet. Released in 2015, *The Martian* offers a key lesson for related experiential media stories in the twenty-first century: emphasize authenticity.[65] As noted in a *CBS Evening News* report, NASA has acknowledged this production for accurately portraying the science of deep-space exploration. This faithfulness to the truth may explain the popularity of the movie and its ability to engage viewers. CBS News's Jim Axelrod said in his report about *The Martian*, Hollywood is "not letting facts get in the way of a good story but using them to construct one instead."[66] Time Inc. launched its VR brand, Life VR, with a "photorealistic journey to Mars with astronaut Buzz Aldrin," who flew on NASA's Apollo 11 mission.[67] NASA has created *Mars 2030*, its own nonfiction VR experience of the red planet, which is free for public download.[68] On April 30, 2018, the *New York Times* launched a factual AR Mars experience based on NASA's latest mission to the planet.

Stories that come from every corner of the Earth (or beyond) may bring new insight and understanding and potentially great benefit. Cross-cultural understanding may reach new heights. But such enlightenment is not an automatic outcome from the media system, digital, experiential, or otherwise.

Interactive content and public participation or engagement in digital, experiential content, whether journalism or other forms of nonfiction, or even fiction and entertainment stories more widely, may enrich the marketplace of ideas across the nation and around the globe, or they may fuel further cross-cultural tensions and polarization.

Facebook founder and CEO Mark Zuckerberg told the United Nations General Assembly that universal internet access is a right and that achieving it should be a UN priority.[69] Global connectivity could have profound implications for digital stories, and its prospects should be an essential part of an experiential journalism future. Research might fruitfully explore the influence of diverse, international stories, with or without explicit local connections, in a globally connected, participatory (e.g., social media), and experiential media network.

Like much scholarship, this book may have raised more questions than it has answered. The domain of experiential news is an increasingly extensive and dynamic realm. It merits not only citizen involvement but also further academic research investigation and professional journalism consideration and development. Acclaimed twentieth-century journalist Edward R. Murrow once told senior television and radio news executives that the then-increasingly important story-telling medium of television "can teach, it can illuminate; yes, and it can even inspire."[70] Reflecting an aversion to technological determinism, Murrow admonished the assembled journalists that it was up to humans to determine whether TV would be more than simply "wires and lights in a box."

In the twenty-first century, Murrow's admonition might extend to experiential journalism. It is up to all story creators, not just journalists and media professionals, but all digitally connected persons, to strive for excellence in the experiential content they create, consume, and share. As the Internet of Things becomes increasingly dominant, we might add that this imperative applies to story creators both human and algorithmic, and to those who design the algorithms. Experiential journalism can play a central role not only in helping entertain but also in advancing understanding in an increasingly diverse, global, and networked age. Creating quality experiential journalism will hinge on a new generation of digital media story creators who can skillfully and ethically produce, share, and engage immersive, interactive, and multisensory content of depth, breadth, and social relevance.

Pointing the way are quality experiential journalism reports from the *New York Times* and elsewhere. The *Times*'s "Antarctic Series" enables users to experience climate change research presented in 360-degree format, while "The Fight For Fallujah" gives users a first-person experience of war-torn Iraq.[71] ARTE's "Paintings in Chauvet Cave" invites users on an immersive journey to the South of France to explore and learn about some of the world's oldest known paintings (32,000 years BP) and the role of technology in their study and preservation.[72] "Hekeng Tulou Cluster," another 360-degree report from the *Times*, enables users to enter an ancient "Tulou home in Fujian, China, where multiple families live together in a circular structure. These houses have been designated World Heritage sites."[73] Although forty-six Tulou homes have been so designated, the remaining three thousand lack heritage status and are under threat of abandonment and destruction.[74]

Or users can experience the richly reported immersive story, "We Who Remain." A coproduction of the *New York Times*, the Emblematic

Group, and Nuba Reports, "We Who Remain" introduces a character-driven narrative approach to 360-degree video journalism.[75] Some sixteen people collaborated on the fourteen-minute production, which includes immersive video reporting, postproduction stitching, motion graphics, and sound design.

In the experiential report, the user journeys to the Nuba Mountains of Sudan and experiences life in a conflict zone. A student, a mother, a journalist, and a rebel soldier offer their perspectives on the nature of the conflict and its impact on their lives. Ambient natural and spatial sound envelops the user. A mixed-reality map situates the story in proximity to historic Khartoum.

Such experiential journalism holds the potential to take news users on a series of immersive, interactive, and multisensory journeys that can enlighten and engage a divided twenty-first-century public. Experiential stories can generate for the news user a sense of presence within the story and ultimately foster greater empathy and understanding.

In a digitally connected age where data flows from billions of sources in a constant global stream, it is essential that journalists adhere to the highest ethical standards in creating experiential news. Some elected officials and others may seek to undermine press freedom, credibility, and independence. By sticking to the facts, delivering the news responsibly, and producing experiential news that engages the public, journalism can help guide society on a collaborative course in pursuit of the truth. In the twenty-first century, the viability of democracy itself will depend upon it.

Notes

INTRODUCTION

1. James Carey, "A Cultural Approach to Communication," in *Communication as Culture: Essays on Media and Society* (Boston: Unwin Hyman, 1989), 15.
2. "Newspaper Fact Sheet," Pew Research Center, June 13, 2018, http://www.journalism.org/fact-sheet/newspapers/.
3. "Newspapers Deliver Across the Ages," Nielsen Scarborough, December 15, 2016, retrieved August 13, 2017, http://www.nielsen.com/us/en/insights/news/2016/newspapers-deliver-across-the-ages.html?cid=socSprinklr-Nielsen.

1. EXPERIENTIAL STORIES

1. Wilbur Schramm, *The Story of Human Communication: Cave Painting to Microchip* (New York: Harper & Row, 1988).
2. Cory Blair, "'Experiential Journalism': How Virtual Reality Could Depict News in 3D," *American Journalism Review*, December 10, 2014, retrieved March 23, 2017, http://ajr.org/2014/12/10/experiential-journalism-virtual-reality-depict-news-3d/.
3. T. Kim and F. Biocca, "Telepresence via Television: Two Dimensions of Telepresence May Have Different Connections to Memory and Persuasion," *Journal of Computer-Mediated Communication* 2 (September 1997).
4. Samuel Gibbs, "The 10 Most Influential Wearable Devices," *Guardian*, March 3, 2017, retrieved March 23, 2017, http://flip.it/rWiiPj.

5. Steve Mann, Department of Electrical and Computer Engineering, University of Toronto, retrieved March 25, 2017, http://www.eecg.toronto.edu/~mann/.

6. Gibbs, "The 10 Most Influential Wearable Devices."

7. Los Angeles Times, "Anti-Google Glass Attack in San Francisco," video, You-Tube, February 26, 2014, retrieved April 6, 2018, https://youtu.be/m8coAu WZL2o.

8. Chuck Todd, "Kellyanne Conway Gave Alternative Facts," *Meet the Press*, NBC News, January 22, 2017, retrieved May 25, 2018, https://www.nbcnews.com/meet -the-press/video/conway-press-secretary-gave-alternative-facts-860142147643.

9. Pippa Norris, Montague Kern, and Marion Just, *Framing Terrorism* (Cambridge, MA: Harvard University Press, 2003).

10. Chip Scanlan, "Birth of the Inverted Pyramid: A Child of Technology, Commerce and History," Poynter, June 20, 2003, retrieved March 23, 2017, https:// www.poynter.org/reporting-editing/2003/birth-of-the-inverted-pyramid-a -child-of-technology-commerce-and-history/.

11. Sabrina Rubin Erdely, "A Rape on Campus," *Rolling Stone*, November 19, 2014, retrieved November 20, 2014; this story has since been retracted and removed from the site, but an archived copy can be accessed at https://archive.is/2014 1119163531/http%3A%2F%2Fwww.rollingstone.com%2Fculture%2Ffeatures %2Fa-rape-on-campus-20141119.

12. Sheila Coronel, Steve Coll, and Derk Kravitz, "*Rolling Stone* and UVA: The Columbia University Graduate School of Journalism Report," *Rolling Stone*, April 5, 2015, retrieved August 13, 2017, http://www.rollingstone.com/culture /features/a-rape-on-campus-what-went-wrong-20150405.

13. Ben Sisario, Hawes Spenser, and Sydney Ember, "*Rolling Stone* Loses Defamation Case over Rape Story," *New York Times*, November 4, 2016, retrieved August 13, 2017, https://nyti.ms/2em32tJ.

14. Oxford Reference, s.v. "Instantaneous Field of View," retrieved March 13, 2017, http://www.oxfordreference.com/view/10.1093/oi/authority.201108031000 05771.

15. Michael Schudson, "The Objectivity Norm in American Journalism*," *Journalism* 2, no. 2 (August 2001): 149–70, retrieved March 23, 2017, https://doi.org/10 .1177/146488490100200201; Bren Cunningham, "Re-thinking Objectivity," *Columbia Journalism Review* (July/August 2003), retrieved March 23, 2017, http://www.cjr.org/feature/rethinking_objectivity.php?page=all.

16. Teju Cole, "Against Neutrality," *New York Times*, January 17, 2016, retrieved March 23, 2017, https://nyti.ms/1N9aZvU.

17. Michel Foucault, "Truth and Power," in *Power/Knowledge: Selected Interviews and Other Writings, 1972–1977*, ed. Colin Gordon (New York: Pantheon, 1980): 230–31.

18. Nicholas Lehmann, "Can Journalists Be Objective," video, Big Think, February 6, 2008, retrieved March 23, 2017, http://bigthink.com/videos/nicholas-lemann-can-journalists-be-objective.

19. Nikki Usher, *Making News at the New York Times* (Ann Arbor: University of Michigan Press, 2014), locs. 259, 261, Kindle.

20. Adrienne Russell, *Journalism as Activism: Recoding Media Power* (New York: Wiley, 2016).

21. Eli Pariser, *The Filter Bubble: How the New Personalized Web Is Changing What We Read and How We Think* (London: Penguin, 2011).

22. John V. Pavlik, *Journalism and New Media* (New York: Columbia University Press, 2004), 27.

23. Frederick Fico, Stephen Lacy, Steven S. Wildman, Thomas Baldwin, Daniel Bergan, and Paul Zube, "Citizen Journalism Sites as Information Substitutes and Complements for United States Newspaper Coverage of Local Governments," *Digital Journalism* 1, no. 1 (2013): 152–68.

24. Susan Sarandon, "The Crossing," HuffPost, retrieved March 23, 2017, http://test kitchen.huffingtonpost.com/thecrossing/.

25. Nicolle A. Mode, Michele K. Evans, and Alan B. Zonderman, "HYPERLINK "https://www.ncbi.nlm.nih.gov/pmc/articles/PMC4865101/" Race, Neighborhood Economic Status, Income Inequality and Mortality," *PLoS One* 11, no. 5 (2016): e0154535, retrieved February 22, 2019, https://doi.org/10.1371/journal.pone.0154535.

26. Josh Stearns, "The Rise of Hands-On Journalism," Local News Lab, September 16, 2014, retrieved April 2, 2017, https://localnewslab.org/2014/09/16/the-rise-of-hands-on-journalism/.

27. Pablo J. Boczkowski, *News at Work: Imitation in an Age of Information Abundance* (Chicago: University of Chicago Press, 2010), 6.

28. John V. Pavlik, "The Future of Online Journalism: Bonanza or Black Hole?," *Columbia Journalism Review* (July/August 1997): 30–34, 36.

29. Hedrick Smith, "Pentagon Papers: Study Reports Kennedy Made 'Gamble' into a Broad Commitment," *New York Times*, July 1, 1971, retrieved May 21, 2018, https://nyti.ms/2Gfzr3L.

30. *POV*, "The Pentagon Papers, Daniel Ellsberg and the Times," PBS, October 5, 2010, retrieved May 21, 2018, http://www.pbs.org/video/pov-the-pentagon-papers-daniel-ellsberg-and-the-times/.

31. Ben Sisario, "YouTube 'Dancing Baby' Copyright Ruling Sets Fair Use Guideline," *New York Times*, September 16, 2015, https://nyti.ms/1QBocSi.

32. "The Digital Millennium Copyright Act of 1998: U.S. Copyright Office Summary," U.S. Copyright Office, December 1998, retrieved March 25, 2017, https://www.copyright.gov/legislation/dmca.pdf.

33. Michelle Kim and Jazz Monroe, "Watch Beyoncé's Coachella 2018 Weekend 2 Set: Destiny's Child, Jay-Z, More," Pitchfork, April 22, 2018, retrieved May 21, 2018, https://pitchfork.com/news/watch-beyonces-coachella-2018-weekend-2 -set-destinys-child-jay-z-more/.

34. Dave Jamieson, "The Supreme Court Just Made It a Lot Harder for You to Sue Your Employer," HuffPost, May 21, 2018, retrieved May 21, 2018, https://www .huffingtonpost.com/entry/supreme-court-sue-your-employer_us_5afb2b cde4b09a94524ca8f3.

35. Meribah Knight, "Reinvigorating the *Chicago Defender*, a Historic Print Voice," *New York Times*, May 2, 2015, retrieved August 31, 2015, https://nyti.ms /1zDs6X9.

36. Knight.

37. Kai El' Zabar, "Wake Up: There's No Justice for Black Men," *Chicago Defender*, November 26–December 2, 2014, http://content.yudu.com/Library/A389xp /ChicagoDefender1126/resources/1.htm.

38. Jack Hitt and Chenjerai Kumanyika, "Uncivil: The Raid—77th Annual Peabody Award Acceptance Speech," video, Peabody, 2018, retrieved June 15, 2018, http://peabodyawards.com/award-profile/uncivil-the-raid.

2. DIGITAL DESIGN IN EXPERIENTIAL NEWS

1. Heather Chaplin, "Guide to Journalism and Design," *Columbia Journalism Review*, July 13, 2016, https://www.cjr.org/tow_center_reports/guide_to_jour nalism_and_design.php/.

2. Roger Fidler, interview, Riptide, March 4, 2013, retrieved June 16, 2018, https:// www.digitalriptide.org/person/roger-fidler/.

3. Kil-Soo Suha and Sunhye Chang, "User Interfaces and Consumer Perceptions of Online Stores: The Role of Telepresence," *Behavior & Information Technology* 25, no. 1 (2006): 99–113, https://doi.org/10.1080/01449290500330398.

4. Sally J. McMillan and Jang-Sun Hwang, "Measures of Perceived Interactivity: An Exploration of the Role of Direction of Communication, User Control, and Time in Shaping Perceptions of Interactivity," *Journal of Advertising* 31, no. 3 (2002): 29–42, https://doi.org/10.1080/00913367.2002.10673674.

5. Célia Maria Magalhães, "A Critical Discourse Analysis Approach to News Discourses and Social Practices on Race in Brazil," *DELTA* 22, no. 2 (2006), retrieved May 22. 2018, http://dx.doi.org/10.1590/S0102-44502006000200003.

6. Nick Newman, "Digital News Report: Overview and Key Findings of the 2018 Report," Reuters Institute for the Study of Journalism, retrieved June 16, 2018, http://www.digitalnewsreport.org/survey/2018/overview-key-findings-2018/.

7. Snapchat, retrieved March 23, 2017, www.snapchat.com.

8. "Campus Stories," Snapchat, retrieved March 23, 2017, https://support.snapchat.com/a/campus-story.

9. Carmel DeAmicis, "Snapchat's 'Our Stories' Are Generating Tens of Millions of Views," Gigaom, February 24, 2015, retrieved June 16, 2015, https://gigaom.com/2015/02/24/snapchats-our-stories-are-generating-tens-of-millions-of-views/.

10. DeAmicis.

11. Arielle Pardes, "Why Snap Needs Its Spectacles," *Wired*, April 27, 2018, retrieved June 16, 2018, https://www.wired.com/story/why-snap-needs-its-spectacles/.

12. Reggie Ugwu, "At Snapchat, Redrawing the Bounds of Reality," *New York Times*, June 14, 2018, retrieved June 15, 2018, https://nyti.ms/2Moy3iM.

13. Steller, retrieved June 16, 2018, https://steller.co/.

14. Karin Huising (karinbrigitta), "Santorini," Steller, retrieved June 16, 2018, https://steller.co/s/8JgwRjeNXW7.

15. Daisuke Wakabayashi and Sheera Frenkel, "Instagram Allows Longer Videos in Challenge to YouTube," *New York Times*, June 19, 2018, retrieved June 19, 2018, https://nyti.ms/2K6Bv09.

16. Tobias Höllerer, Steven Feiner, and John Pavlik, "Situated Documentaries," retrieved May 22, 2018, http://graphics.cs.columbia.edu/projects/mars/mjwSd.html.

17. Höllerer, Feiner, and Pavlik.

18. Ellen Wallwork, "Women's Aid Interactive Billboard Dares You to Face Domestic Violence Without Flinching," HuffPost, May 3, 2015, retrieved March 23, 2017, http://www.huffingtonpost.co.uk/2015/03/05/womens-aid-domestic-violence-interactive-billboard_n_6800450.html.

19. Pardis Mahdavi, "How #MeToo Became a Global Movement," *Foreign Affairs*, March 6, 2018, retrieved June 16, 2018, https://www.foreignaffairs.com/articles/2018-03-06/how-metoo-became-global-movement.

20. Lorne Manly, "A Virtual Reality Revolution, Coming to a Headset Near You," *New York Times*, November 19, 2015, https://nyti.ms/1IozCtI.

21. Charlie Hall, "Watch VR's First Oscar-Nominated Short Film," Polygon, January 24, 2017, retrieved March 23, 2017, http://www.polygon.com/2017/1/24/14370892/virtual-reality-first-oscar-nominated-short-film-pearl.

22. KeepSafe, "The Future of Cinematic Virtual Reality by Jaunt TV—KeepSafe Tech Talk," video, YouTube, September 19, 2014, https://youtu.be/4nr1aMt1GlM.

23. KeepSafe.

24. KeepSafe.

25. "Google Presents Inside Abbey Road," Abbey Road Studios, retrieved March 23, 2017, https://www.abbeyroad.com/news/take-a-virtual-step-into-abbey-road-studios-with-google-cardboard-2097.

26. "Google Presents Inside Abbey Road."

27. Angela Watercutter, "How a Pixar Vet Is Shaping the Future of VR Storytelling," *Wired*, September 23, 2015, retrieved March 23, 2017, http://www.wired.com/2015/09/pixar-vet-writing-grammar-virtual-reality-stories.

28. "Our Films," Oculus Story Studio, retrieved March 23, 2017, https://www.oculus.com/story-studio/films/.

29. Will Mason, "Golden State Warriors Owner Peter Guber Makes a Big Bet into Virtual Reality with NextVR," Upload, May 13, 2015, retrieved March 25, 2017, https://uploadvr.com/golden-state-warriors-owner-peter-gruber-makes-a-big-bet-into-virtual-reality-with-nextvr/.

30. Mason.

31. Mark Joyella, "CBS This Morning to Air Live Virtual Reality Stream Friday," TV Newser, May 12, 2016, retrieved March 23, 2017, http://www.adweek.com/tvnewser/cbs-this-morning-to-air-live-virtual-reality-stream-friday/293379.

32. Michal Addady, "You Can Now Practice with the Patriots in Virtual Reality," *Fortune*, June 12, 2015, retrieved March 23, 2017, http://fortune.com/2015/12/06/patriots-virtual-reality/.

33. Art Molella, "How a Refugee from the Nazis Became the Father of Video Games," *Jewish Journal*, December 7, 2015, retrieved March 23, 2017, http://jewishjournal.com/culture/180182/.

34. Emma Carter, "Samsung Gear VR Is Preparing a Thriller Game 'Gone,'" *Utah People's Post*, December 5, 2015, retrieved March 23, 2017, http://www.utahpeoplespost.com/2015/12/samsung-gear-vr-is-preparing-a-thriller-game-gone/.

35. Carter.

36. Nonny de la Peña, Peggy Weil, Joan Llobera, Elias Giannopoulos Ausiàs Pomés, and Bernhard Spanlang, "Immersive Journalism: Immersive Virtual Reality for the First-Person Experience of News," *Presence: Teleoperators & Virtual Environments* 19, no. 4 (2010): 291–301, https://doi.org/10.1162/PRES_a_00005.

37. Steven Rosenbaum, "Virtual Reality and Journalism—Can They Get Along?," *Forbes*, February 9, 2016, retrieved March 23, 2017, https://www.forbes.com/sites/stevenrosenbaum/2016/02/09/virtual-reality-and-journalism-can-they-get-along/#76c66df93240.

38. Manly, "A Virtual Reality Revolution."

39. Jean Yves Chaimon, "Immersive Journalism in Your Newsroom," Global Editors Network, November 12, 2015, http://www.globaleditorsnetwork.org/press-room/news/2015/11/how-to-implement-immersive-journalism-in-your-newsroom/?utm_source=Company+Newsletter&utm_campaign=4aade79562-NL%3A+12-Nov-2015&utm_medium=email&utm_term=0_68e99b1866-4aade79562-119565641.

40. Chaimon.

41. "Sallie Gardner at a Gallop," Wikipedia, retrieved March 23, 2017, https://en.wikipedia.org/wiki/Sallie_Gardner_at_a_Gallop.

42. John Maxwell Hamilton, *Journalism's Roving Eye: A History of American Foreign Reporting* (Baton Rouge: Louisiana State University Press, 2011).

43. "Cinerama Crews Shooting New Movie at Eglin AFB," *Okaloosa News-Journal*, November 1, 1956, 1.

44. Sree Sreenivasan, "3 Years @MetMuseum: Digital, Mobile, Social Lessons," slides (presentation at the Metropolitan Museum of Art, New York, September 30, 2015), bit.ly/sree2yrs.

45. Sam Earp, "Maldives VR 360—4K," video, YouTube, November 1, 2016, retrieved May 22, 2018, https://youtu.be/MgJITGvVfRo.

46. Robert Pepper, remarks, "Infrastructure and Technology" panel, Columbia Institute for Tele-Information Annual Conference on the State of Telecom, Columbia University, New York, October 19, 2015, retrieved February 22, 2019, http://broadbandbreakfast.com/2015/10/columbia-institute-for-tele-information/.

47. Alisa Valudes Whyte, "The Future of the Internet of Things Is Amazing, If We Don't Muck It Up," HuffPost, November 25, 2015, retrieved March 23, 2017, https://www.huffingtonpost.com/alisa-valudes-whyte-/the-internet-of-things-future_b_8640360.html.

48. Pepper, remarks.

49. Mark Hachman, "Intel Embraces Internet of Things, Puts Sensors on Everything," PC World, January 6, 2016, retrieved March 23, 2017, http://www.pcworld.com/article/3019557/Internet-of-things/intel-embraces-Internet-of-things-puts-sensors-on-everything.html.

50. Francesco Marconi, "Making the Internet of Things Work for Journalism?," AP Insights, July 14, 2016, retrieved February 22, 2019, https://insights.ap.org/industry-trends/making-the-internet-of-things-work-for-journalism.

51. Xiao Xiao, "Andante," Xiao Xiao Portfolio, retrieved March 23, 2017, http://portfolio.xiaosquared.com/Andante.

52. "Tangible Media," MIT Media Lab, retrieved March 23, 2017, https://www.media.mit.edu/research/groups/tangible-media.

53. FireEye, retrieved February 22, 2019, https://www.fireeye.com/cyber-map/threat-map.html.

54. Roy Greenslade, "News Media Websites 'Vulnerable to Cyber-Attacks'—Research," *Guardian*, October 23, 2015, retrieved March 23, 2017, http://www.theguardian.com/media/greenslade/2015/oct/23/news-media-websites-vulnerable-to-cyber-attacks-research.

55. Mark Scott, "BBC Websites Said to Be Target of Online Attack," *New York Times*, December 31, 2015, https://nyti.ms/1RbnFIK.

56. Eli Blumenthal and Elizabeth Weise, "Hacked Home Devices Caused Massive Internet Outage," *USA Today*, October 21, 2016, retrieved March 24, 2017, http://www.usatoday.com/story/tech/2016/10/21/cyber-attack-takes-down-east-coast-netflix-spotify-twitter/92507806/.

57. Mike Isaac, "Facebook Mounts Effort to Limit Tide of Fake News," *New York Times*, December 15, 2016, retrieved August 13, 2017, https://nyti.ms/2hKDeO2.

58. Ashley Carman, "VR Sense Is an Arcade Machine That Lets You Feel Snow in Your Face and Bugs at Your Feet," Verge, February 6, 2017, retrieved March 23, 2017, http://www.theverge.com/circuitbreaker/2017/2/6/14523014/vr-sense-arcade-machine-launch-japan.

59. Peter B. Seel, "Telepresence and Immersion with Ultra-High-Definition Digital Displays," in *Digital Technology and the Future of Broadcasting: Global Perspectives*, ed. John V. Pavlik (New York: Routledge, 2016), 94–106.

60. Bob G. Witmer and Michael J. Singer, "Measuring Presence in Virtual Environments: A Presence Questionnaire," *Presence: Teleoperators and Virtual Environments* 7, no. 3 (June 1998): 225–40; Pavel Zahoric and Rick L. Jenison, "Presence as Being-in-the-World," *Presence: Teleoperators and Virtual Environments* 7, no. 1 (February 1998): 78–89.

61. Taeyong Kim and Frank Biocca, "Telepresence via Television: Two Dimensions of Telepresence May Have Different Connections to Memory and Persuasion," *Journal of Computer-Mediated Communication* 3, no. 2 (September 1997).

62. Jonathan Steuer, "Defining Virtual Reality: Dimensions Determining Telepresence," *Journal of Communication* 42, no. 4 (December 1992): 73–93.

63. David Westerman, Patric R. Spence, and Kenneth A. Lachlan, "Telepresence and the Exemplification Effects of Disaster News," *Communication Studies* 60, no. 5 (2009): 542–57, https://doi.org/10.1080/10510970903260376.

64. James Covert, "LG Unveils TV That's Thin Enough to Fit in Your Wallet," *New York Post*, January 5, 2016, retrieved March 23, 2017, http://nypost.com/2016/01/05/lg-unveils-tv-thats-thin-enough-to-fit-in-your-wallet/.

65. David Katzmaier, "LG Rolls Up OLED TV, Smokes My Mind (Hands-On)," CNET, January 7, 2016, retrieved March 23, 2017, https://cnet.co/2grTILe.

66. Shree Nayar, "What Is a Computational Camera?," CAVE, 2006–2011, http://www1.cs.columbia.edu/CAVE/projects/what_is/.

67. Joe Cox, "Winter Olympics to Showcase First 8K HDR Broadcasts," WhatHiFi, February 8, 2018, retrieved May 22, 2018, https://www.whathifi.com/news/winter-olympics-to-showcase-first-8k-hdr-broadcasts.

68. Will Huntsberry, "Nature's Ready for Her Close-Up: 'Planet Earth II' Returns in Ultra High-Def," NPR, February 17, 2017, retrieved March 23, 2017, http://www.npr.org/2017/02/17/515461598/natures-ready-for-her-close-up-planet-earth-ii-returns-in-ultra-high-def.

69. "Planet Earth II in 360," BBC One, retrieved May 22, 2018, http://www.bbc.co.uk /programmes/articles/365zWpz7HypS4MxYmdosS36/planet-earth-ii-in-360.

70. Eli Noam, "Coming Soon: Mobile, Immersive, Interactive Entertainment," Columbia Business School: Media and Technology Program, July 17, 2009, https:// www8.gsb.columbia.edu/media/newsn/1223/eli-noam-coming-soon-mobile -immersive-interactive-entertainment-the-financial-times-online.

71. Chris Forrester, "Homes Equipped with UHD Screens to Reach 335M by 2020," IBC, April 18, 2017, retrieved May 22, 2018, https://www.ibc.org/consumption /uhd-the-race-for-adoption-/1890.article.

72. "Apple TV Now Plays 360-Degree Video," video, ABC News, December 24, 2016, retrieved March 23, 2017, http://abcnews.go.com/Technology/video/apple-tv -now-plays-360-degree-video-35938951.

73. Jefferson Graham, "More 4K TV Programming Finally Here in 2016," ABC News, January 1, 2016, retrieved March 23, 2017, http://usat.ly/1Oxq8YL.

74. Robert LaRose, "The Problem of Media Habits." *Communication Theory* 20, no. 2 (May 2010): 194–222, retrieved June 17, 2018, https://doi.org/10.1111/j.1468 -2885.2010.01360.x.

75. Wai Ho Lo and Benjamin Ka Lun Cheng, "The Use of Melodramatic Anima-tion in News, Presence and News Credibility," *Journalism Studies* 18, no. 6 (2017): 787–805, https://doi.org/10.1080/1461670X.2015.1087814.

76. GoogleDoodles, "Nellie Bly's 151st Birthday," video, YouTube, May 4, 2015, retrieved May 22, 2018, https://youtu.be/BrrgeZKvFE0.

77. Dan Reynolds, "Immersive Journalism: Using Transmedia, VR, Comics and Animation to Boost Engagement" (Society for News Design, "SNDDC: The Future of News and Design," Washington, DC, April 9–11, 2015), retrieved March 4, 2018, https://www.snd.org/dc2015/immersive-journalism-using -transmedia-vr-comics-and-animation-to-boost-engagement/.

78. Vice News, "Animations on Vice News Tonight," video playlist, YouTube, updated December 7, 2018, https://www.youtube.com/playlist?list=PLw613 M860505crIvrGu-00Aiyq7xkagYM.

79. Vice News, "The Tech That Powers Bitcoin Could Tackle Corruption (HBO)," video, YouTube, November 9, 2017, retrieved May 22, 2018, https://youtu.be /862rBp7P_f8.

80. Adam C. Powell III, interviewed by the author, September 22, 2015.

81. Drew Olanoff, "Google Cardboard's SDK Gets Spatial Audio Support," Tech Crunch, January 13, 2016, retrieved March 23, 2017, http://techcrunch.com/2016 /01/13/google-cardboards-sdk-gets-spatial-audio-support/.

82. Manly, "A Virtual Reality Revolution."

83. Rachel Grozanick, "Voxhop Will Help Mediamakers Record Location-Based Audio VR," VoxHop, July 31, 2017, retrieved August 13, 2017, http://www

.storybench.org/voxhop-will-help-mediamakers-record-location-based
-audio-vr/.

84. Alison MacAdam via NPR Storytelling, "Building a Neighborhood Scene," Tumblr, retrieved August 8, 2017, http://nprstorytelling.tumblr.com/post /128033217738/building-a-neighborhood-scene.

85. MacAdam.

86. MacAdam.

87. "Tomlinson Holman," LinkedIn, retrieved March 23, 2017, https://www .linkedin.com/pub/tomlinson-holman/5/938/154; "Tom Holman, TMH President," TMH, retrieved March 23, 2017, http://www.tmhlabs.com/research /research.html.

88. Powell interview, September 22, 2015; T. de Broucker, "Synaesthesia, an Augmented Sensory World: Phenomenology and Literature Review," *Revue Neurologique* (in French) 169, no. 4 (April 2013): 328–34. https://doi.org/10.1016/j .neurol.2012.09.016.

89. "CBS News Sunday Morning," Wikipedia, retrieved March 23, 2017, https://en .wikipedia.org/wiki/CBS_News_Sunday_Morning.

90. Powell interview, September 22, 2015.

91. Adam Clayton Powell III, email to the author, January 13, 2017.

92. NPR, "Inauguration 360," video, Facebook, January 22, 2017, https://www .facebook.com/NPR/videos/10155217559116756/; NPR "Women's March 360," video, Facebook, January 22, 2017, https://www.facebook.com/NPR/videos /10155217564866756/; Kassie Bracken, Niko Koppel, Kaitlyn Mullin, and Chang W. Lee, "A Divided Nation at Inauguration," video, *New York Times*, https://nyti.ms/2jQFT8t.

93. PonoMusic, retrieved April 8, 2017, https://www.ponomusic.com/.

94. Matt Pharr, Wenzel Jakob, and Greg Humphreys, *Physically Based Rendering: From Theory to Implementation*, 3rd ed. (Amsterdam: Morgan Kaufmann, 2017).

95. Charles Arthur, "Pono: Only a Man Pays for Music Quality That He Can't Hear," *Guardian*, April 5, 2014, https://www.theguardian.com/technology/2014/apr/05 /pono-neil-young-24bit-192khz-review.

96. "Pono (digital music service)," Wikipedia, https://en.wikipedia.org/wiki /Pono_(digital_music_service).

97. Mel Slater, John McCarthy, Francesco Maringelli, "The Influence of Body Movement on Subjective Presence in Virtual Environments," *Human Factors* 40, no. 3 (September 1998): 469–77, https://doi.org/10.1518/001872098779591368.

98. Oculus Rift, retrieved March 23, 2017, https://www.oculus.com/en-us/rift/.

99. Katie Kindelan, "7 Apps to Support Your Mental Health and Mindfulness," ABC News, June 15, 2018, retrieved June 16, 2018, https://abcnews.go.com/GMA /Wellness/apps-support-mental-health-mindfulness/story?id=55890971.

100. Kieth Stuart, "The Climb—The Most Head-Spinning Virtual Reality Experience Yet," *Guardian*, December 24, 2015, http://www.theguardian.com/technology/2015/dec/24/the-climb-virtual-reality-oculus-rift-crytex.

101. Nicholas St. Fleur, "Aztec Turquoise Tiles May Solve a Mesoamerican Mystery." *New York Times*, June 13, 2018, retrieved June 16, 2018, https://nyti.ms/2JMUxIM.

102. Francesco Marconi, "Report: How Virtual Reality Will Impact Journalism," AP, September 26, 2017, retrieved March 8, 2018, https://insights.ap.org/industry-trends/report-how-virtual-reality-will-impact-journalism?utm_source=francesco&utm_medium=francesco-share&utm_campaign=3-d-report.

103. Josh Stearns, "The Rise of Hands-On Journalism," Medium, September 16, 2014, retrieved May 22, 2018, https://medium.com/the-local-news-lab/the-rise-of-hands-on-journalism-17806112caf8.

104. Youngho Lee, Sejin Oh, Youngmin Park, Beom-Chan Lee, Jeung-Chul Park, Yoo Rhee Oh, Seokhee Lee, Han Oh, Jeha Ryu, Kwan H Lee, Hong Kook Kim, Yong-Gu Lee, JongWon Kim, Yo-Sung Ho, and Woontack Woo, "Responsive Multimedia System for Virtual Storytelling," *Advances in Multimedia Information Processing—PCM 2005* (Berlin: Springer, 2005), 361–72; Nonny de la Peña, Peggy Weil, Joan Llobera, Elias Giannopoulos, Ausiàs Pomés, Bernhard Spanlang, Doron Friedman, Maria V. Sanchez-Vives, and Mel Slater, "Immersive Journalism: Immersive Virtual Reality for the First Person Experience of News," *Presence: Teleoperators and Virtual Environments* 19, no. 4 (2010): 291–301, https://doi.org/10.1007/11581772_32; Gary M. Hardee, "Immersive Journalism in VR: Four Theoretical Domains for Researching a Narrative Design Framework," *VAMR 2016: Virtual, Augmented and Mixed Reality* (Cham: Springer, 2016), 679–90, https://doi.org/10.1007/978-3-319-39907-2_65; Raney Aronson-Rath, James Milward, Taylor Owen, and Fergus Pitt, "Virtual Reality Journalism," *Columbia Journalism Review*, Tow Center for Digital Journalism, November 11, 2015, https://www.cjr.org/tow_center_reports/virtual_reality_journalism.php/.

105. "Leid Stories," Podbean, retrieved March 23, 2017, http://leidstories.podbean.com/.

106. Joan D. Firestone. "The Moth Radio Hour Wins Peabody Award," *Moth*, April 12, 2011, retrieved August 9, 2017, http://themoth.org/posts/the-moth-radiohour-wins-peabody-award.

107. James Cridland, email interview with the author, September 07, 2015.

108. Molly Ringwald, "Mothering in Captivity," *Moth*, 2015, retrieved February 22, 2019, http://themoth.org/http://themoth.org/posts/storytellers/molly-ringwald.

109. Nicola Smith, "International Journalists Depart for North Korea's Nuclear Test Site, as Experts Warn Demolition Could Destroy Valuable Evidence," *Telegraph*, May 23, 2018, retrieved May 23, 2018, https://www.telegraph.co.uk/news/2018/05/23/international-journalists-depart-north-koreas-nuclear-test-site/.

110. Jonathan Kruk, interview with author, September 15, 2015.

111. Brian Reed and Julie Snyder, podcast, *S-Town*, retrieved March 31, 2017, https://stownpodcast.org/.

112. Brian Reed, "Chapter 1," podcast, *S-Town*, retrieved March 14, 2018, https://stownpodcast.org/chapter/1.

113. Cjross, "Marooned in the Mojave," *Snap Judgment*, retrieved August 13, 2017, http://snapjudgment.org/marooned-mojave.

114. "Pitching a Story to Snap," *Snap Judgment*, http://snapjudgment.org/pitches.

115. Anita Sthankiya, "There's a Lack of Diversity in News Media," Medium, December 21, 2017, retrieved May 23, 2018, https://medium.com/@dnnmedia/theres-a-lack-of-diversity-in-news-media-but-where-does-it-stem-from-3c72406d18d9.

116. Laurence Butet-Roch, "The 4 Best Virtual Reality Experiences at the Tribeca Film Festival," *Time*, April 27, 2017, retrieved May 23, 2018, http://time.com/4757532/virtual-reality-tribeca/.

117. Kelly Anderson, "My Brooklyn," video, Vimeo, June 23, 2014, retrieved August 9, 2017, https://vimeo.com/ondemand/mybrooklyn/46006398.

118. Isobel Hamilton, "David Attenborough's VR Project 'Hold the World' Is Absolutely Astonishing," Mashable, May 24, 2018, retrieved May 25, 2018, https://mashable.com/2018/05/24/david-attenborough-hold-the-world-vr/?utm_campaign=Mash-BD-Synd-Flipboard-Watercooler-Full&utm_cid=Mash-BD-Synd-Flipboard-Watercooler-Full.

119. Elizabeth Howell, "AstroReality's Earth Augmented Reality Project Blows Past Fundraising Goal," Space, May 25, 2018, retrieved May 25, 2018, https://www.space.com/40702-augmented-reality-earth-app-fundraising-goal.html.

120. *Rashomon*, dir. Akira Kurosawa (Japan: Daiei Film, 1950).

121. Melena Ryzik and the Culture, Design and Graphics Teams of the *New York Times*, "Augmented Reality: David Bowie in Three Dimensions," *New York Times*, March 20, 2018, retrieved May 24, 2018, https://www.nytimes.com/interactive/2018/03/20/arts/design/bowie-costumes-ar-3d-ul.html.

122. Evangeline Morphos, "The Future of Telecommunications" (Columbia Institute for Tele-Information conference, Columbia University, New York, October 19, 2015).

123. Everette E. Dennis, "Seminar on Experiential Media" (Northwestern University–Qatar, Doha, Qatar, January 10, 2017).

124. Clyde Bentley, "The End of the Beginning: Viar and Virtual Reality May Change the Order in Which a Story Is Told," Reynolds Journalism Institute, March 22, 2017, retrieved March 27, 2017, https://www.rjionline.org/stories/the-end-of-the-beginning-viar-and-virtual-reality-may-change-the-order-in-w.

125. Dejan Gajsek, "(Video 360 in VR) Tekme Maribora in njenega zakulisja tako še niste videli," Večer, July 20, 2017, retrieved May 24, 2018, https://www.vecer.com

/video-360-in-vr-tekme-maribora-in-njenega-zakulisja-tako-se-niste-videli
-6282250.

126. T. Höllerer, S. Feiner, and J. Pavlik, "Situated Documentaries: Embedding Multimedia Presentations in the Real World" (Third International Symposium on Wearable Computers, San Francisco, CA, October 18–19, 1999), 79–86.

127. Höllerer, Feiner, and Pavlik.

128. J. Pavlik, R. Avrahami, and A. Pineda, "Video as Input: Exploring the Implications of *Natural Control* for Storytelling in Journalism and Education" (white paper, Intel Corp., 1999).

129. Melanie Pinola, "Speech Recognition Through the Decades: How We Ended Up with Siri," *PCWorld*, November 2, 2011, https://www.pcworld.com/article /243060/speech_recognition_through_the_decades_how_we_ended_up_with _siri.html.

130. Sarah Perez, "47.3 Million US Adults Have Access to a Smart Speaker, Report Says," TechCrunch, March 7, 2018, retrieved March 7, 2018, https://techcrunch .com/2018/03/07/47-3-million-u-s-adults-have-access-to-a-smart-speaker -report-says/; Dieter Bohn, "Amazon Says 100 Million Alexa Devices Have Been Sold—What's Next?," Verge, January 4, 2018, retrieved February 25, 2019, https:// www.theverge.com/2019/1/4/18168565/amazon-alexa-devices-how-many-sold -number-100-million-dave-limp.

131. Andy Orin, "Google Home Now Supports Multiple Users and Can Recognize Your Voice," Life Hacker, April 20, 2017, retrieved April 21, 2017, from http:// lifehacker.com/google-home-now-supports-multiple-users-and-can-recogni -1794497912.

132. Lucinda Southern, "How MTV, the *Telegraph* and *Evening Standard* are using Amazon Echo Show," Digiday, November 22, 2017, retrieved May 24, 2018, https:// digiday.com/media/mtv-telegraph-evening-standard-using-amazon-echo -show/.

133. Garette Sloane, "Scripps, Time Inc. Among Media Companies Starting Shows on Amazon's Echo," Ad Age, May 28, 2017, retrieved May 24, 2018, http://adage .com/article/digital/media-partners-advantage-amazon-s-echo-show-screen /309613/.

134. "Listen to Your Music," Amazon, https://www.amazon.com/gp/help/customer /display.html?nodeId=201601830.

135. NoHold, http://www.nohold.com/.

3. THE NEWS USER EXPERIENCE

1. Ike Picone, "Conceptualizing Media Users Across Media," *Convergence* 23, no. 4 (August 2017): 378–90.

2. Melvin Mencher and John V. Pavlik, "News Reporting Simulation: A Fire Scenario," Columbia Interactive E-Seminars, 2001, retrieved March 23, 2017, http://ci.columbia.edu/ci/eseminars/0802_detail.html.

3. Sandra Gaudenzi, "The Living Documentary: From Representing Reality to Co-creating Reality in Digital Interactive Documentary" (PhD thesis, Goldsmiths, University of London, 2013), http://research.gold.ac.uk/7997/.

4. Coral Davenport, "E.P.A. Blocks Obama-Era Clean Water Rule," *New York Times*, January 31, 2018, retrieved June 18, 2018, https://nyti.ms/2FxQNIn.

5. "Who Coined the Term 'Virtual Reality'?" Virtual Reality Society, retrieved March 23, 2017, http://www.vrs.org.uk/virtual-reality/who-coined -the-term.html.

6. "Ivan Sutherland," A. M. Turing Awards, ACM Awards, retrieved March 23, 2017, http://amturing.acm.org/award_winners/sutherland_3467412.cfm.

7. "Inventor in the Field of Virtual Reality," Morton Heilig, retrieved March 23, 2017, http://www.mortonheilig.com/InventorVR.html.

8. "Who Coined the Term 'Virtual Reality'?"

9. "The History of Stereo Photography," RPI, retrieved March 23, 2017, http://www .arts.rpi.edu/~ruiz/stereo_history/text/historystereog.html.

10. Ray Bradbury, "The Veldt," Mr. Jost's Internet Classroom, retrieved March 23, 2017, http://mrjost.weebly.com/uploads/1/2/8/8/1288468o/the_veldt.pdf.

11. Google Dictionary, s.v. "virtual reality," retrieved March 23, 2017, https://www .google.com/search?q=Dictionary#dobs=virtual%20reality.

12. Robert V. Kenyon, "'The Cave' Automatic Virtual Environment: Characteristics and Applications," NASA Technical Reports Server, 1995, retrieved June18, 2018, https://ntrs.nasa.gov/archive/nasa/casi.ntrs.nasa.gov/19960026 482.pdf.

13. L. Frank Baum, *The Master Key: An Electrical Fairy Tale, Founded Upon the Mysteries of Electricity and the Optimism of its Devotees* (Indianapolis, IN: Bowen-Merrill, 1901), 94, retrieved June 18, 2018, https://books.google.com /books?id=uucQAAAAYAAJ&dq=%22the%20master%20key%22%20baum &pg=PP1#v=onepage&q=%22the%20master%20key%22%20baum&f=false.

14. Tango, 2016, retrieved March 23, 2017, https://get.google.com/tango/, website has been removed.

15. Andrew West, "RFK Assassinated," June 5, 1968, audio recording, University of Maryland Library of American Broadcasting, archived from the original, April 26, 2012, retrieved June 18, 2018, https://web.archive.org/web/201204 26042140/http://jclass.umd.edu/archive/hearitnow/1968.htm.

16. Taylor Kerns, "'Pokémon Go' Developer Niantic Shows Off AR Tech That Lets Pikachu Hide Behind Real-World Objects," Android Police, June 28, 2018,

https://www.androidpolice.com/2018/06/28/pokemon-go-developer-niantic-shows-off-ar-tech-lets-pikachu-hide-behind-real-world-objects/.

17. John V. Pavlik and Franklin Bridges, "The Emergence of Augmented Reality (AR) as a Storytelling Medium in Journalism," *Journalism and Communication Monographs* 15, no. 1, (March 2013): 4–59.

18. Bryan Carter, interviewed by author, September 15, 2015.

19. Carter interview.

20. Carter interview.

21. Michael Bove, "Narratarium—Environmental Displays," video, MIT Industrial Liason Program, May 14, 2013, retrieved March 23, 2017, http://ilp.mit.edu/videodetail.jsp?id=816.

22. "NBA's Sterling Brown Arrest Video Released, Shows NBA Player Getting Tased," TMZ Sports, May 28, 2018, http://www.tmz.com/2018/05/23/sterling-brown-arrest-video-nba-milwaukee-bucks/.

23. Rachel Metz, "Augmented Reality Study Projects Life-Sized People into Other Rooms," MIT Technology Review, January 19, 2016, retrieved March 23, 2017, http://www.technologyreview.com/news/545466/can-augmented-reality-make-remote-communication-feel-more-intimate/.

24. ListenTree, MIT Media Lab, retrieved March 23, 2017, http://listentree.media.mit.edu/.

25. ListenTree.

26. Rahawa Haile, "'Forest Bathing': How Microdosing on Nature Can Help with Stress," *Atlantic*, June 30, 2017, retrieved June 18, 2018, https://www.theatlantic.com/health/archive/2017/06/forest-bathing/532068/.

27. Zach Epstein, "Virtual Reality Just Got Real: New Tech Lets Users Feel VR," BGR, November 11, 2015, retrieved March 23, 2017, http://bgr.com/2015/11/11/virtual-reality-games-accessory-impacto/.

28. "Ultrahaptics—A Sense of Touch in Virtual Reality," Nanalyze, July 31, 2017, retrieved August 13, 2017, http://www.nanalyze.com/2017/07/ultrahaptics-sense-touch-virtual-reality/.

29. Tim McKeough, "How Microbatch Textiles Became Cool," *New York Times*, March 1, 2017, retrieved June 18, 2018, https://nyti.ms/2lzrAEo.

30. Detlef la Grand, "Immersive Storytelling with Virtual Reality," VRmaster, May 4, 2015, retrieved March 23, 2017, http://www.vrmaster.co/immersive-storytelling-with-virtual-reality/.

31. Gretchen Parker, "Nonny de la Peña Introduces Immersive Journalism with Paper in MIT Journal," USC Annenberg, May 13, 2015, retrieved March 23, 2017, https://annenberg.usc.edu/nonny-de-la-pe%C3%B1a-introduces-immersive-journalism-paper-mit-journal.

32. Taylor Owen, Fergus Pitt, Raney Aronson-Rath and James Milward, "New Report: Virtual Reality Journalism," Tow Center for Digital Journalism, November 11, 2015, retrieved February 24, 2019, https://www.cjr.org/tow_center _reports/virtual_reality_journalism.php/.

33. John V. Pavlik, Everette E. Dennis, Rachel Davis Mersey, and Justin Gengler, *Mobile Disruptions in the Middle East* (New York: Routledge, 2018).

34. S. Shyam Sundar, Jin Kang, and Danielle Oprean, "Being There in the Midst of the Story: How Immersive Journalism Affects Our Perceptions and Cognitions," *Cyberpsychology, Behavior, and Social Networking* 20, no. 11 (November 2017).

35. Matt Swayne, "Virtual Reality Makes Journalism Immersive, Realism Makes It Credible," Penn State University, December 5, 2017, retrieved March 5, 2018, http://news.psu.edu/story/496395/2017/12/05/research/virtual-reality-makes -journalism-immersive-realism-makes-it.

36. Swayne.

37. Dan Archer and Katharina Finger, "Walking in Another's Virtual Shoes," *Columbia Journalism Review*, March 15, 2018, retrieved March 16, 2018, https:// www.cjr.org/tow_center_reports/virtual-reality-news-empathy.php.

38. Frank Rose, *The Art of Immersion* (New York: Norton, 2011).

39. M. Csikszentmihalyi, *Flow: The Psychology of Optimal Experience* (New York: Harper & Row, 1980).

40. Michael Rubinstine, "See Invisible Motion, Hear Silent Sounds," TEDxBeacon-Street, video, TED, December 2014, retrieved March 23, 2017, https://www.ted .com/talks/michael_rubinstein_see_invisible_motion_hear_silent_sounds _cool_creepy_we_can_t_decide/transcript?language=en.

41. Nina Strochlic, "Scientists Are Turning Your Body into Holograms," *National Geographic* (June 2017), retrieved May 24, 2018, https://www.nationalgeographic .com/magazine/2017/06/explore-teaching-anaotmy-with-hololens/.

42. Pavlik and Bridges, "The Emergence of Augmented Reality (AR) as a Storytell-ing Medium in Journalism."

43. Tim Pool, "Tim Pool Live Streaming from Istanbul," Vice, June 13, 2013, retrieved October 1, 2014, https://www.vice.com/en_us/article/7begxg/tim-pool-live -streaming-from-istanbul.

44. "Livestream Your World with Google Glass App," Bloomberg, April 14, 2014, retrieved April 16, 2014, https://www.telegraph.co.uk/technology/google /10765608/LiveStream-your-world-with-Google-Glass-app.html.

45. Ken Yeung, "Facebook Opens Up Live Broadcasting and Its Mentions App to Verified Profiles," Venture Beat, September 10, 2015, http://venturebeat.com /2015/09/10/facebook-opens-up-live-broadcasting-and-its-mentions-app-to -verified-profiles/.

46. Paul Milgram, H. Takemura, A. Utsumi, and F. Kishino, "Augmented Reality: A Class of Displays on the Reality-Virtuality Continuum," *Proceedings of Telemanipulator and Telepresence Technologies* 2351 "Telemanipulator and Telepresence Technologies" (December 21, 1995): 34, https://doi.org/10.1117/12.197321.

47. John Branch, "Augmented Reality: Four of the Best Olympians, as You've Never Seen Them," *New York Times*, February 5, 2018, https://www.nytimes.com/interactive/2018/02/05/sports/olympics/ar-augmented-reality-olympic-athletes-ul.html.

48. Max Rettig, "New York Times AR Gives Readers New Look at Olympic Athletes," Sport Techie, February 7, 2018, retrieved May 24, 2018, https://www.sporttechie.com/new-york-times-augmented-reality-readers-new-look-olympic-athletes/.

49. "Total Solar Eclipse Path," *CBS This Morning*, August 18, 2017, retrieved August 18, 2017, https://www.cbsnews.com/videos/total-solar-eclipse-path-what-to-expect/.

50. Damon Kiesow, "The Readers We Ignore and the News They Want," Kiesow 9.0, June 29, 2015, http://kiesow.net/2015/06/29/the-readers-we-ignore-and-the-news-they-want/.

51. "How Millennials Get News: Inside the Habits of America's First Digital Generation," American Press Institute, March 16, 2015, retrieved June 28, 2018, http://www.americanpressinstitute.org/publications/reports/survey-research/millennials-news/.

52. "How Millennials Get News."

53. Matt Mansfield, "Social Media Statistics 2016," Small Business Trends, November 27, 2016, retrieved March 23, 2017, https://smallbiztrends.com/2016/11/social-media-statistics-2016.html.

54. "Newspaper Fact Sheet," Pew Research Center, June 13, 2018, http://www.journalism.org/fact-sheet/newspapers/.

55. "Newspaper Fact Sheet."

56. Tanya Dua, "No Brand Favorites: 360-Degree Videos Are Popular on Both YouTube and Facebook," Digiday, June 29, 2016, retrieved May 24, 2018, https://digiday.com/marketing/no-brand-favorites-360-degree-videos-popular-youtube-facebook/.

57. Dua.

58. "NewsKid: Startups for News—Eighth Battle," Global Editors Network, 2017, retrieved March 23, 2017, http://www.globaleditorsnetwork.org/programmes/startups-for-news/newskid/.

59. Eva Dominguez, interviewed by the author, September 18, 2015.

60. Dominguez interview.

61. Dominguez interview.

62. Shree Nayar, "Omnicamera," Columbia University, 2000, retrieved March 1, 2017, http://www.columbia.edu/cu/record/23/20a/omnicamera.html.

63. Patrick Doyle, Mitch Gelman, and Sam Gill, "State of VR in Journalism," Gannett, March 2016, retrieved March 23, 2017, http://storynext.gannett.com/state-of-vr.pdf, page has been removed.

64. Jarrard Cole, "Virtual Reality: Behind the Scenes with a Ballerina at Lincoln Center," *Wall Street Journal*, November 4, 2015, retrieved March 23, 2017, http://www.wsj.com/articles/behind-the-scenes-with-a-ballerina-at-lincoln-center-1446646806.

65. "Japan Is Changing How We'll Grow Old," *Wall Street Journal*, November 29, 2015, retrieved March 23, 2017, http://www.wsj.com/articles/virtual-reality-video-japan-is-changing-how-well-grow-old-1448809232.

66. Alejandro Alba, "New York Times Launches VR App, Delivers 1 Million Google Cardboards to Print Subscribers," *New York Daily News*, October 22, 2015, retrieved March 23, 2017, http://www.nydailynews.com/news/national/ny-times-launches-vr-app-ships-1-million-google-cardboards-article-1.2407586.

67. Luca Locatelli, "Pilgrimage: A 21st-Century Journey to Mecca and Medina," *New York Times*, July 21, 2016, retrieved March 23, 2017, https://nyti.ms/2abst1X.

68. Locatelli.

69. Ravi Somaiya, "The Times Partners with Google on Virtual Reality Project," *New York Times*, October 21, 2015, retrieved March 27, 2017, https://nyti.ms/1RTJ5c7.

70. "The Daily 360," *New York Times*, retrieved August 9, 2017, https://www.nytimes.com/video/the-daily-360.

71. "The Daily 360."

72. "NYTVR," *New York Times*, retrieved August 26, 2017, http://www.nytimes.com/marketing/nytvr/?mcubz=1.

73. 2020 Group, "Journalism That Stands Apart," *New York Times*, retrieved March 23, 2017, https://www.nytimes.com/projects/2020-report/.

74. *CBS This Morning*, March 3, 2016, http://www.cbsnews.com/cbs-this-morning/.

75. Mark Binelli, "10 Shots Across the Border," *New York Times*, March 3, 2016, https://nyti.ms/1QNMvu9.

76. Jake Silverstein, "Editor's Letter: Take Flight with Virtual Reality," *New York Times*, December 10, 2015, retrieved March 23, 2017, https://nyti.ms/1QxEM72.

77. Univision PR Team, "Univision News Launches Virtual Reality Documentary Series—'In Danger of Deportation,'" Univision, February 3, 2017, retrieved March 23, 2017, https://corporate.univision.com/press/2017/02/03/univision

-news-launches-virtual-reality-documentary-series-in-danger-of-deportation; Kurt Schlosser, "Watch This Striking Virtual Reality Footage Chronicling Seattle's Homeless Crisis," Geek Wire, January 20, 2017, retrieved March 23, 2017, http://www.geekwire.com/2017/seattles-king5-uses-striking-vr-footage-short-documentary-chronicle-homeless-problem/.

78. Daniel Terdiman, "Virtual Reality Journalism Is Coming to the Associated Press," Fast Company, November 5, 2015, retrieved March 23, 2017, http://www.fastcompany.com/3053219/fast-feed/virtual-reality-journalism-is-coming-to-the-associated-press.

79. Terdiman.

80. Jake Kreinberg, "Behind the Scenes on Our First Animated VR Experience," Associated Press, November 4, 2016, retrieved August 9, 2017, https://insights.ap.org/whats-new/behind-the-scenes-on-our-first-animated-vr-experience.

81. John Gaudiosi, "Why the AP Just Launched a Virtual Reality News Channel," Fortune, February 17, 2016, retrieved March 23, 2017, http://fortune.com/2016/02/17/associated-press-launches-vr-news-channel/.

82. AP-VR360, "Nimrud's Riches: The Islamic State's Efforts to Erase History," video, YouTube, December 23, 2016, retrieved May 25, 2018, https://youtu.be/ZOTlGlWXB5g.

83. "CNN Will Live Stream Democratic Debate in Virtual Reality," CNN, September 24, 2015, retrieved March 23, 2017, http://cnnpressroom.blogs.cnn.com/2015/09/24/cnn-will-live-stream-democratic-debate-in-virtual-reality/.

84. Lucas Matney, "CNN Launches Dedicated Virtual Reality Journalism Unit," Tech Crunch, March 7, 2017, retrieved March 23, 2017, https://techcrunch.com/2017/03/07/cnn-launches-dedicated-virtual-reality-journalism-unit/.

85. "CNN VR," CNN, retrieved May 23, 2017, https://www.cnn.com/vr.

86. Patrick Doyle, Mitch Gelman, and Sam Gill, "State of VR in Journalism," Gannett, March 2016, retrieved March 23, 2017, http://storynext.gannett.com/state-of-vr.pdf.

87. "USA Today Wants VR-Storytelling for Daily News," WAN-IFRA, June 6, 2016, retrieved March 23, 2017, http://blog.wan-ifra.org/2016/06/06/usa-today-wants-vr-storytelling-for-daily-news.

88. "New Frontier Lab," Sundance Institute, retrieved March 23, 2017, http://www.sundance.org/programs/new-frontier.

89. S. D. Byard, G. Cleary, V. Subryan, and J. A. Bell, "Ocular Evolution and Development of the Human Eye," Investigative Ophthalmology and Visual Science 47, no. 13 (May 2006), retrieved May 25, 2018, https://iovs.arvojournals.org/article.aspx?articleid=2392972.

90. Oscar Raby, "Assent: An Immersive VR Documentary," 2014, retrieved February 24, 2019, https://oscarraby.net/assent/.

91. Drew DeSilver, "Q&A: Telling the Difference Between Factual and Opinion Statements in the News," Pew Research Center, June 18, 2018, retrieved June 18, 2018, http://www.pewresearch.org/fact-tank/2018/06/18/qa-telling-the-difference-between-factual-and-opinion-statements-in-the-news/.

92. "How We Created a Virtual Crime Scene to Investigate Syria's Chemical Attack," *New York Times*, June 24, 2018, retrieved June 25, 2018, https://nyti.ms/2MYXdVE.

93. Kalin Kalinov, "Transmedia Narratives: Definition and Social Transformations in the Consumption of Media Content in the Globalized World," *Postmodernism Problems* 7 (2017): 60–68.

94. WashPostPR, "The Washington Post Releases Augmented Reality View of Freddie Gray's Case," *Washington Post*, May 10, 2016, retrieved July 2, 2018, https://www.washingtonpost.com/pr/wp/2016/05/10/the-washington-post-releases-augmented-reality-view-of-freddie-grays-case/?noredirect=on&utm_term=.7a054f8cb27d.

95. Lucia Moses, "The Washington Post Preps Its Augmented Reality Push," Digiday, March 16, 2017, retrieved March 23, 2017, http://digiday.com/media/washington-post-preps-augmentedreality-push/.

96. Nausicaa Renner, "The Media Today: The Rise of Virtual Reality Journalism," *Columbia Journalism Review*, October 4, 2017, retrieved May 25, 2018, https://www.cjr.org/tow_center/virtual-reality-journalism-media-today.php.

97. Kenneth Chang, "In a Dome in Hawaii, a Mission to Mars," *New York Times*, October 20, 2014, retrieved May 25, 2018, https://nyti.ms/1puEyh6.

98. Dominguez interview, September 18, 2015.

99. "Degrees of Freedom," XinReality, retrieved March 4, 2018, https://xinreality.com/wiki/Degrees_of_freedom.

100. Gabe Cary, "Oculus Rift Creator Proves the Headset Does Work on a 'Room-Scale,'" Digital Tends, December 15, 2015, retrieved March 23, 2017, http://www.digitaltrends.com/computing/oculus-rift-works-room-scale/.

101. Adi Robertson, "The Second HTC Vive Development Kit Has a Built-In Camera and New Controllers," Verge, January 5, 2016, retrieved August 9, 2017, http://www.theverge.com/2016/1/5/10714522/htc-valve-vive-pre-v2-development-kit-ces-2016.

102. "How a Virtual Reality Journalist Takes Viewers Inside Stories," video, *Wired*, November 2017, retrieved March 5, 2018, https://www.wired.com/video/2017/11/how-a-virtual-reality-journalist-take-viewers-inside-stories/.

103. "A Virtual Reality Experience About Accessing Abortion in America," Across the Line, retrieved March 5, 2018, http://www.acrossthelinevr.com/#accessing-abortion-in-america.

104. Avegant, retrieved March 28, 2018, https://www.avegant.com/.

105. Richard Lawler, "'Light Field' 3D Maps Take VR Broadcasting to the Next Level," Engadget, March 2, 2015, retrieved March 23, 2017, https://www.engadget.com /2015/03/02/nextvr-light-field/.

106. Lawler.

107. Alan Sullivan, "DepthCube Solid-State 3D Volumetric Display" (SPIE Proceedings 5291, Stereoscopic Displays and Virtual Reality Systems XI, Electronic Imaging, San Jose, CA, 2004), https://doi.org/10.1117/12.527543.

108. Sullivan.

109. "Looking Glass Offers a Volumetric Display for the Consumer," Display Daily, September 29, 2016, retrieved August 9, 2017, https://www.displaydaily.com /paid-news/ldm/ldm-technology/looking-glass-offers-a-volumetric-display -for-the-consumer.

110. Lightform, retrieved April 5, 2017, https://lightform.com/.

111. Object-Based Media Group, MIT Media Lab, retrieved August 9, 2017, http:// obm.media.mit.edu/.

4. ENCODED CONTENT

1. "Geofilters," Snapchat, retrieved March 23, 2017, https://www.snapchat.com /geofilters/.

2. "Safetycheck," Facebook, retrieved March 23, 2017, https://www.facebook.com /about/safetycheck/.

3. "Code Barre," NFB, retrieved August 9, 2017, http://codebarre.tv/en/#/en.

4. A. Schmitz Weiss, "Location-Based News in Mobile News Apps: Broadcast Leads in Geolocated News Content, Newspapers Lag Behind," *Newspaper Research Journal* 39, no. 1 (March 2018): 42–54.

5. Erin Petenko, "Every N. J. Gun Death Reported in 2015 on a Single Map," NJ Advance Media, NJ.com, April 19, 2017, retrieved August 9, 2017, http://s.nj.com /GdRyTXV.

6. Laura M. Holson, "Fishing or Stories via Instagram," *New York Times*, April 18, 2018, retrieved May 25, 2018, https://nyti.ms/2JWRRso.

7. "Open Journalism," GitHub, retrieved July 2, 2018, https://github.com/show cases/open-journalism; "Surround360," GitHub, https://github.com/facebook /Surround360.

8. Justin Wolfers, David Leonhardt, and Kevin Quealy, "1.5 Million Missing Black Men," *New York Times*, April 20, 2015, https://nyti.ms/2jSwAoL.

9. Bryan Carter, interviewed by author, September 15, 2015.

10. "A Sunday on La Grande Jatte—1884," Art Institute Chicago, retrieved March 27, 2017, http://www.artic.edu/aic/collections/artwork/27992.

11. Adam Satariano, "U.S. News Outlets Block European Readers over New Privacy Rules," *New York Times*, May 25, 2018, retrieved May 25, 2018, https://nyti.ms/2xbNhUD.

12. Object-Based Media Group, MIT Media Lab, retrieved March 23, 2017, http://obm.media.mit.edu/.

13. Russell Brandom, "Uber's New Tool Gives Cities a Mind-Bogglingly Detailed View of Traffic Patterns," Verge, January 8, 2017, retrieved May 25, 2018, https://www.theverge.com/2017/1/8/14193548/uber-movement-traffic-pattern-analysis-travel-time.

14. "Movement Cities," Uber Movement, retrieved May 25, 2018, https://movement.uber.com/cities?lang=en-US.

15. Tom Kent, "An Ethical Reality Check for Virtual Reality Journalism," Medium, August 31, 2015, retrieved March 23, 2017, https://medium.com/@tjrkent/an-ethical-reality-check-for-virtual-reality-journalism-8e5230673507#.8cp2coafg.

16. Benjamin Mullin, "Virtual Reality: A New Frontier in Journalism Ethics," Poynter, January 6, 2016, retrieved March 23, 2017, http://www.poynter.org/2016/virtual-reality-the-next-frontier-in-journalism-ethics/390280/.

17. Don Heider, "Pressing Issues in Digital Ethics" (panel, Association for Education in Journalism and Mass Communication, Chicago, August 9–12, 2017).

18. Thomas H. Cormen and Charles E. Leiserson, *Introduction to Algorithms*, 3rd ed. (Cambridge, MA: MIT Press, 2009).

19. FiveThirtyEight, retrieved March 27, 2017, https://fivethirtyeight.com/.

20. Nate Silver, "How the FiveThirtyEight Senate Forecast Model Works," FiveThirtyEight, September 17, 2014, retrieved July 7, 2015, http://fivethirtyeight.com/features/how-the-fivethirtyeight-senate-forecast-model-works/.

21. Sarah Bolesworth, Barry Neild, Peter Beaumont, Paul Lewis, and Sandra Laville, "Tottenham in Flames as Riot Follows Protest," *Guardian*, August 6, 2011, retrieved July 7, 2015, http://www.theguardian.com/uk/2011/aug/06/tottenham-riots-protesters-police.

22. Bolesworth et al.

23. "Google Fusion Tables," Google, retrieved June 18, 2018, https://support.google.com/fusiontables/#topic=1652595, site has been removed.

24. Simon Rogers, "Data Journalism Reading the Riots: What We Know. And What We Don't," *Guardian*, December 9, 2011, retrieved May 25, 2018, https://www.theguardian.com/news/datablog/2011/dec/09/data-journalism-reading-riots.

25. Corinna Underwood, "Automated Journalism—AI Applications at *New York Times*, Reuters, and Other Media Giants," Emerj, January 17, 2018, retrieved May 25, 2018, https://emerj.com/ai-sector-overviews/automated-journalism-applications/.

26. Clare Llewellyn, Claire Grover, and Jon Oberlander, "Summarizing Newspaper Comments" (Proceedings of the Eighth International Association for the Advancement of Artificial Intelligence Conference, 2014), retrieved May 25, 2018, http://homepages.inf.ed.ac.uk/grover/papers/8098-37715-1-PB.pdf.

27. Thomas N. Friemel, and Mareike Dötsch, "Online Reader Comments as Indicator for Perceived Public Opinion," in *Kommunikationspolitik für die digitale Gesellschaft*, ed. Martin Emmer and Christian Strippel (Berlin: Digital Communication Research, 2015), https://doi.org/10.17174/dcr.v1.8.

28. V. Michael Bove, "Object-Based Media," MIT Media Lab, https://www.media .mit.edu/research/groups/object-based-media.

29. Don Dahler, "Robot Submarine Finds 'Holy Grail of Shipwrecks' with up to $17 Billion in Treasure," CBS News, May 23, 2018, retrieved May 25, 2018, https:// www.cbsnews.com/news/robot-submarine-finds-shipwreck-san-jose-carrying -17-billion-treasure/.

30. Shelley Podolny, "If an Algorithm Wrote This, How Would You Even Know?," *New York Times*, March 7, 2015, retrieved August 9, 2017, https://nyti.ms /1FrObpk.

31. Larry Birnbaum, Narrative Science, retrieved August 9, 2017, http://www .narrativescience.com/larry-birnbaum, page has been removed.

32. Narrative Science, "Xerox Profit Expected to Slip," *Forbes*, July 22, 2015, retrieved March 23, 2017, http://www.forbes.com/sites/narrativescience/2015/07/22/xerox -profit-expected-to-slip/.

33. Will Oremus, "The First News Report on the L.A. Earthquake Was Written by a Robot," Slate, March 17, 2014, retrieved August 9, 2017, http://www.slate.com /blogs/future_tense/2014/03/17/quakebot_los_angeles_times_robot_journal ist_writes_article_on_la_earthquake.html.

34. "The Homicide Report," *LA Times*, retrieved February 3, 2017, http://homicide .latimes.com/.

35. "Wordsmith," Automated Insights, retrieved February 3, 2017, http://automate dinsights.com/wordsmith/.

36. "Trends in Newsrooms 2015," World Association of Newspapers and News Publishers (WAN-IFRA), http://www.wan-ifra.org/showcases/trends-in-newsrooms -2015, page has been removed.

37. Joseph Lichterman, "The AP Wants to Use Machine Learning to Automate Turning Print Stories into Broadcast Ones," NiemanLab, October 31, 2016, retrieved May 25, 2018, http://www.niemanlab.org/2016/10/the-ap-wants-to-use -machine-learning-to-automate-turning-print-stories-into-broadcast-ones/.

38. Noah Kulwin, "Tribune Publishing Chairman: We Want to Start Publishing 2,000 Videos a Day with Artificial Intelligence," Recode, June 6, 2016, retrieved

March 23, 2017, http://www.recode.net/2016/6/6/11871908/tribune-publishing
-artificial-intelligence-videos.

39. Alexander Fanta, "Putting Europe's Robots on the Map: Automated Journalism in News Agencies," Reuters Institute for the Study of Journalism, University of Oxford, 2017, retrieved May 25, 2018, https://reutersinstitute.politics.ox.ac.uk /sites/default/files/2017-09/Fanta%2C%20Putting%20Europe's%20Robots%20 on%20the%20Map.pdf.

40. Emergent, retrieved July 7, 2015, http://www.emergent.info/.

41. Mark McCormick, Paddy Allen, and Alastair Dant, "Afghanistan War Logs: IED Attacks on Civilians, Coalition and Afghan Troops," *Guardian*, July 26, 2010, retrieved June 18, 2018, https://www.theguardian.com/world/datablog/interac tive/2010/jul/26/ied-afghanistan-war-logs.

42. Nick Penzenstadler, "'Surgeon Scorecard' Measures Docs by Complications," *USA Today*, July 14, 2015, retrieved February 3, 2017, http://www.usatoday.com /story/news/2015/07/14/surgeons-scored--new-online-tool/30083213/.

43. "Dollars for Docs," ProPublica, retrieved March 23, 2017, https://projects .propublica.org/docdollars/company.

44. Stephanie Knoll, "Algorithms, Journalistic Investigations and Holding Digital Power Accountable," Journalist's Resource, June 25, 2015, retrieved March 23, 2017, http://journalistsresource.org/studies/society/news-media/algorithms -journalistic-investigations-holding-digital-power-accountable.

45. Knoll.

46. Magda Abu-Fadil, "Today's Newsrooms = Robo-Journalism, Games, Apps, Gen-der Equality," HuffPost, December 6, 2017, https://www.huffingtonpost.com /magda-abufadil/todays-newsrooms-robo-journalism_b_7502798.html.

47. Abu-Fadil.

48. E. T. Meyer, "The Expert and the Machine," *Convergence* 21, no. 3 (2015):306–13, https://doi.org/10.1177/1354856515579840.

49. Art Swift, "Americans' Trust in Mass Media Sinks to New Low," Gallup, Sep-tember 14, 2016, retrieved March 23, 2017, http://www.gallup.com/poll/195542 /americans-trust-mass-media-sinks-new-low.aspx.

50. Sydney Ember, "New York Times Co.'s Decline in Print Advertising Tempered by Digital Gains," *New York Times*, February 2, 2017, retrieved March 23, 2017, https://nyti.ms/2k3r2YB.

51. Paul Bedard, "'Trump Bump' Boosts News Industry, NYT Adds 500,000, WSJ 200,000," *Washington Examiner*, March 7, 2018, retrieved May 31, 2018, https:// www.washingtonexaminer.com/trump-bump-boosts-news-industry-nyt -adds-500-000-wsj-200-000.

52. Claire Atkinson, "The Washington Post Still Plays Catch-Up, but is Gaining on the Times," NBC News, December 28, 2017, retrieved June 22, 2018, https://www

.nbcnews.com/news/us-news/washington-post-still-plays-catch-gaining
-times-n833236.

53. Atkinson.

54. A. J. Katz, "Feb. 2018 Ratings: CNN Has Second-Best February in 10 Years," TV Newser, February 27, 2018, retrieved May 31, 2018, https://www.adweek.com /tvnewser/feb-2018-ratings-cnn-has-second-best-february-in-10-years/358288.

55. "Voltair Overview," Telos Alliance, retrieved March 23, 2017, http://www .telosalliance.com/25-Seven/Voltair.

56. Caitlin Petre, (lecture, Rutgers University, New Brunswick, NJ, March 1, .2017).

57. James Cridland, "Radio Is Going Multi-Platform" (speech, Global Communication Association conference, "Digital Transformation—Media Management, Digital Education, Media Convergence, and Globalization," Berlin, 2015).

58. Nikki Usher, *Making News at the New York Times* (Ann Arbor: University of Michigan Press, 2014).

59. "Alexa Prize," Amazon, retrieved February 3, 2017, https://developer.amazon .com/alexaprize.

60. Tacotron, retrieved March 18, 2018, https://google.github.io/tacotron/publica tions/tacotron2/index.html.

61. Freia Nahser, "How the BBC, *Financial Times* and Bayerischer Rundfunk Are Experimenting with Voice Interfaces," Medium, March 1, 2018, retrieved March 28, 2018, https://medium.com/global-editors-network/how-the-bbc -financial-times-and-bayerischer-rundfunk-are-experimenting-with-voice -interfaces-c7588a430ed1.

62. John Vibes, "MIT Professor Wants to Build Robots to Free You from Your Robot Overlords," True Activist, October 23, 2014, retrieved August 9, 2017, http:// www.trueactivist.com/mit-professor-wants-to-build-robots-to-free-you-from -your-robot-overlords/.

63. Timothy Williams, "Can 30,000 Cameras Help Solve Chicago's Crime Problem?" *New York Times*, May 26, 2018, retrieved May 26, 2018, https://nyti.ms /2xePa39.

64. Mikael Priks, "The Effects of Surveillance Cameras on Crime: Evidence from the Stockholm Subway," *Economic Journal*, November 17, 2015, retrieved June 19, 2018, http://www.ne.su.se/polopoly_fs/1.153803.1429170587!/menu/standard/file /EJMpriks.pdf.

65. Jane Wakefield, "Robo-Reporter Goes to War," BBC News, March 28, 2002, retrieved March 23, 2017, http://news.bbc.co.uk/2/hi/science/nature/1898525 .stm.

66. Adam Schlosser, "You May Have Heard Data Is the New Oil. It's Not," World Economic Forum, January 10, 2018, retrieved June 13, 2018, https://www .weforum.org/agenda/2018/01/data-is-not-the-new-oil/.

67. Martin Ford, *The Rise of the Robots* (New York: Basic, 2015).

68. Joe Keohane, "What News-Writing Bots Mean for the Future of Journalism," *Wired*, February 16, 2017, retrieved June 13, 2018, https://www.wired.com/2017/02/robots-wrote-this-story/.

69. John Pavlik, "Cognitive Computing and Journalism," presentation, Second International Meeting on Technology, Communication and Cognitive Science, Methodist University of São Paulo, Campo Grande, Brazil, December 3–4, 2015.

70. "Cognitive Computing," Wikipedia, retrieved August 9, 2017, https://en.wikipedia.org/wiki/Cognitive_computing.

71. "Benjamin Fletcher," LinkedIn, retrieved February 3, 2017, https://www.linkedin.com/pub/benjamin-fletcher/4/333/bb7.

72. IBM Cognitive Insight, "Inside the 'Brain' of IBM Watson: How 'Cognitive Computing' Is Poised to Change Your Life," *Wired*, August 26, 2016, retrieved June 13, 2016, http://www.wired.co.uk/article/watson-in-the-world-experiencing-ibm-watson.

73. Pablo Martín Fernández, "Getting Automated Fact-Checking from Science Fiction to Reality," Poynter, February 10, 2017, retrieved March 23, 2017, http://www.poynter.org/2017/getting-automated-fact-checking-from-science-fiction-to-reality/448016/.

74. Mark Bergen, "Google Is Training Machines to Predict When a Patient Will Die," Bloomberg, June 18, 2018, retrieved June 18, 2018, https://www.bloomberg.com/news/articles/2018-06-18/google-is-training-machines-to-predict-when-a-patient-will-die.

75. Glenn Kessler, "Trump's False Assertion That Canada Claims to 'Make' $100 Billion in Trade with the U.S," *Washington Post*, June 12, 2018, retrieved June 13, 2018, https://www.washingtonpost.com/news/fact-checker/wp/2018/06/12/trumps-false-claim-that-the-u-s-has-a-100-billion-trade-deficit-with-canada/?noredirect=on&utm_term=.eb07cbc9f850.

76. John Markoff, "Artificial-Intelligence Research Center Is Founded by Silicon Valley Investors," *New York Times*, December 11, 2015, retrieved March 23, 2017, https://nyti.ms/1Y35I4E.

77. Jason Murdock, "Elon Musk Goes to War with the Media, Promotes Site with Alleged Sex Cult Ties," *Newsweek*, May 27, 2018, retrieved June 13, 2018, http://www.newsweek.com/elon-musk-goes-war-media-promotes-website-alleged-sex-cult-ties-946022.

78. Laura Hazard Owen, "How 7 News Organizations Are Using Slack to Work Better and Differently," NiemanLab, July 3, 2015, retrieved June 13, 2018, http://www.niemanlab.org/2015/07/how-7-news-organizations-are-using-slack-to-work-better-and-differently/.

79. Shoko Oda, "This Media Startup Is Beating the Competition with a Newsroom Run by Robots," Bloomberg, May 27, 2018, retrieved June 13, 2018, https://www .bloomberg.com/news/articles/2018-05-27/the-airline-geek-trying-to-build-a -media-giant-with-no-reporters.

80. Oda.

81. "Trending Review Guidelines," Facebook, May 2016, retrieved February 3, 2017, https://fbnewsroomus.files.wordpress.com/2016/05/full-trending-review -guidelines.pdf.

82. Jessica Guynn, "Facebook Begins Flagging 'Disputed' (Fake) News," *USA Today*, March 6, 2017, retrieved March 23, 2017, http://www.usatoday.com/story/tech /news/2017/03/06/facebook-begins-flagging-disputed-fake-news/98804948/.

83. Gerald J. Baldasty, *E. W. Scripps and the Business of Newspapers* (Urbana: University of Illinois Press, 1999).

5. INTERACTIVE DOCUMENTARIES

1. Interactive Narratives, retrieved January 3, 2017, http://www.interactivenarra tives.org/.

2. Robert Knoth and Antoinette de Jong, "Poppy Interactive," Submarine, retrieved June 13, 2018, https://poppy.submarinechannel.com/start.

3. John Branch, "Snow Fall," *New York Times*, retrieved August 13, 2017, http:// www.nytimes.com/projects/2012/snow-fall/#/?part=tunnel-creek.

4. Christine Haughney, "*Times* Wins Four Pulitzers; Brooklyn Nonprofit Is Awarded a Reporting Prize," *New York Times*, April 15, 2013, retrieved August 13, 2017, https://nyti.ms/XCJPsj.

5. Daniel Duane, "The Heart-Stopping Climbs of Alex Honnold," *New York Times*, March 12, 2015, retrieved August 13, 2017, https://nyti.ms/1AoqHgx.

6. "Crime in Chicago: Explore Your Community," *Chicago Tribune*, January 9, 2018, http://crime.chicagotribune.com/.

7. "Firestorm," *Guardian*, retrieved March 23, 2017, http://www.theguardian .com/world/interactive/2013/may/26/firestorm-bushfire-dunalley-holmes -family.

8. Nikki Usher, *Making News at the New York Times* (Ann Arbor: University of Michigan Press, 2014); Usher, "Interactive Journalism," (lecture, Rutgers University, New Brunswick, NJ, October 8, 2015).

9. Joseph Lichterman, "Culture Change Is Hard: What Nikki Usher Learned in Five Months Embedded in the *New York Times* Newsroom," Nieman Lab, May 12, 2014, retrieved June 13, 2018, http://www.niemanlab.org/2014/05 /culture-change-is-hard-what-nikki-usher-learned-in-five-months-embedded -in-the-new-york-times-newsroom/.

10. Nikki Usher, *Interactive Journalism: Hackers, Data, and Code* (Urbana: University of Illinois Press, 2016), i.

11. Usher, 48.

12. Usher.

13. "Inside Raqqa, the Capital of ISIS," *New York Times*, retrieved March 23, 2017, http://nyti.ms/1PFQKwP.

14. David Poyer, "Crafting the Braided Narrative," retrieved August 13, 2017, http://www.esva.net/~davidpoyer/braid.htm, page has been removed but a similar source is available at http://cimsec.org/a-conversation-with-naval-fiction-writer-david-poyer-author-of-deep-war/39120; Whitney Dow, "Mutable Narrative and Interactive Storytelling," IMA-MFA, retrieved August 13, 2017, http://ima-mfa.hunter.cuny.edu/?ima-course=mutable-narrative-interactive-storytelling.

15. "How to Not (Accidentally) Raise a Racist," Longest Shortest Time, March 8, 2017, retrieved March 31, 2017, http://longestshortesttime.com/episode-116-how-to-not-accidentally-raise-a-racist/.

16. Miquel Francés, "El documental interactivo en la estrategia de la multidifusión digital," Telos, no. 96 (October 2013–January 2014), https://telos.fundacionte lefonica.com/archivo/numero0096/el-documental-en-la-multidifusion-digital/.

17. *Le Mystere de Grimouville*, FranceBleu, retrieved August 9, 2017, http://grimou ville.francebleu.fr/#/.

18. *Hollow*, retrieved August 13, 2017, http://hollowdocumentary.com/; "Hollow," Peabody, 2013, http://www.peabodyawards.com/award-profile/hollow-www .hollowdocumentary.com.

19. *Fort McMoney*, retrieved August 13, 2017, http://www.fortmcmoney.com /#/fortmcmoney.

20. *Inside Disaster*, retrieved August 13, 2017, http://insidedisaster.com/haiti/.

21. *A Journey to the End of Coal in China*, retrieved August 13, 2017, http://www .honkytonk.fr/index.php/webdoc/.

22. Simon Cox, *The Reykyavik Confessions*, BBC News, May 2014, retrieved August 13, 2017, http://www.bbc.co.uk/news/special/2014/newsspec_7617/index.html.

23. *Harvest of Change*, Des Moines Register, retrieved August 9, 2017, http://www .desmoinesregister.com/pages/interactives/harvest-of-change/; "Register Wins Murrow Award for Innovative Video Project," *Des Moines Register*, June 24, 2015, http://www.desmoinesregister.com/story/news/2015/06/24/edward-r -murrow-journalism-award-harvest—change/29219905/.

24. *Gaza Confidential*, France24, http://webdoc.france24.com/Gaza-Confiden tial/index.html#home. Interactive docs include *Gaza Confidential, Jazz, Xcuse my French.* "Klynt Interactive Workshop Review," Crossover, http://www.xolabs .co.uk/2014/08/22/klynt-interactive-workshop-review/.

25. *Losing Ground: Louisiana Erosion*, ProPublica/the Lens, retrieved August 13, 2017, http://projects.propublica.org/louisiana/; Steve Beatty, "Lens, ProPublica Win Award for Innovation and Watchdog Journalism for 'Losing Ground,'" Lens, April 3, 2015, http://thelensnola.org/2015/04/03/lens-propublica-win-award-for-innovation-in-watchdog-journalism-for-losing-ground/.

26. *Fukushima, POV*, PBS, 2014, retrieved August 13, 2017, http://www.pbs.org/pov/shorts/#fukushima; "POV Interactive Documentaries Nominated for a 2015 Webby Award!," POV's Documentary Blog, April 7, 2015, http://www.pbs.org/pov/blog/povdocs/2015/04/pov-interactive-documentaries-nominated-for-a-2015-webby-award/.

27. John V. Pavlik and Jackie O. Pavlik "Understanding Quality in Digital Storytelling: A Theoretically Based Analysis of the Interactive Documentary," in *Digital Transformation in Journalism and News Media*, ed. Mike Friedrichsen and Yahya Kamalipour (Berlin: Springer, 2017).

28. "Academy Announces Canadian Screen Awards' Winner," *Broadcaster Magazine*, February 25, 2015.

29. Gigapan, retrieved January 1, 2017, http://www.gigapan.com/.

30. "Fort McMoney," Wikipedia, retrieved January 1, 2017, https://en.wikipedia.org/wiki/Fort_McMoney.

31. T. Sean Herbert (comments on panel, "Quality Journalism in the Digital Age," Media + the Public Interest Initiative conference, Rutgers University, New Brunswick, NJ, April 10, 2015), http://mpii.rutgers.edu/quality-journalism-in-the-digital-age; Phil Napoli, "Quality Journalism in the Digital Age" (Media + the Public Interest Initiative conference, April 10, 2015), http://mpii.rutgers.edu/quality-journalism-in-the-digital-age.

32. Oliver Sacks, *Musicophilia: Tales of Music and the Brain* (New York: Vintage, 2008).

33. *CBS This Morning*, March 30, 2018.

34. Mark Henry Phillips and Nick Thorburn, "Music from Season Three," *Serial* Podcast, 2015, retrieved August 9, 2017, http://serialpodcast.org/music.

35. Joyce Barnathan, "Why *Serial* Is Important for Journalism: Transparency Is Key," *Columbia Journalism Review*, November 25, 2014, retrieved August 9, 2017, http://www.cjr.org/the_kicker/serial_sarah_koenig_journalism.php.

36. Margaret Hartmann, "Upcoming Season of 'Serial' Will Focus on Sergeant Bowe Bergdahl," *New York*, September 23, 2015, http://nymag.com/daily/intelligencer/2015/09/upcoming-season-of-serial-covers-bowe-bergdahl.html.

37. Ben Sisario, "Pandora to Stream 'Serial' Podcast," *New York Times*, November 2, 2015, https://nyti.ms/1kmyn2r.

38. John V. Pavlik, *Journalism and New Media* (New York: Columbia University Press, June 2001), 3.

39. Pavlik, 3.

40. "Can You Spot the Threats," NBC News, retrieved January 1, 2017, http://www.nbcnews.com/id/34623505/ns/us_news-security/t/can-you-spot-threats/.

41. "Cutthroat Capitalism: The Game," *Wired*, July 20, 2009, retrieved January 1, 2017, http://archive.wired.com/special_multimedia/2009/cutthroatCapitalism TheGame.

42. Jon Huang, Jeremy White, and Karen Yourish, "Roots of the Recent Violence Between Israelis and Palestinians," *New York Times*, February 14, 2016, retrieved January 1, 2017, https://www.nytimes.com/interactive/2016/02/14/world/middle east/east-jerusalem-map.html.

43. Storming Juno, retrieved January 1, 2017, http://www.stormingjuno.com/, page has been removed.

44. Last Hijack, retrieved January 1, 2017, http://lasthijack.com/.

45. Door into the Dark, retrieved January 1, 2017, http://doorintothedark.com/, page has been removed.

46. Shaun Gladwell, "Orbital Vanitas," *New York Times*, January 25, 2017, retrieved March 1, 2017, https://nyti.ms/2ku7TMY.

6. DRONE MEDIA AND BEYOND

1. Robert Graves, "92—Daedalus and Talus," in *The Greek Myths* (New York: Penguin, 1992).

2. Eric Hynes, "Finding Meaning in Virtual Reality," Sundance Institute, January 24, 2015, retrieved January 2, 2017, http://www.sundance.org/blogs/news /finding-meaning-in-virtual-reality--a-closer-look-at-new-frontier.

3. Bob Pool, "Obituary: John D. Silva, 92; TV Engineer Devised the World's First News Helicopter," *Washington Post*, December 11, 2012, B6.

4. "News Aircraft Accidents," Wikipedia, retrieved August 9, 2017, http://en .wikipedia.org/wiki/List_of_news_aircraft_accidents_and_incidents.

5. Jennifer Preston, "TV News Helicopter Crashes in Seattle, Killing at Least Two," *New York Times*, March 18, 2014, retrieved August 9, 2017, http://thelede.blogs .nytimes.com/2014/03/18/tv-news-helicopter-crashes-in-seattle-killing-at -least-two/?_php=true&_type=blogs&hpw&rref=us&action=click&module =Search&region=searchResults%230&version=&url=http%3A%2F%2Fquery. nytimes.com%2Fsearch%2Fsitesearch%2F%3Faction%3Dclick%26region%3DM asthead%26pgtype%3DHomepage%26module%3DSearchSubmit%26contentC ollection%3DHomepage%26t%3Dqry570%23%2Fhelicopter%2Bcrash%2Bseattl e%2F&_r=0.

6. Martin E. Dempsey, "'Eyes of the Army': U.S. Army Roadmap for Unmanned Aircraft Systems, 2010–2035," Homeland Security Digital Library, https://www.hsdl.org/?abstract&did=705357.

7. Dempsey.

8. Jaime Lopez, "BBC Documentary Teaches About Dolphin Megapods in Costa Rica," *Costa Rica Star*, January 6, 2014, retrieved August 9, 2017, http://news.co.cr/bbc-documentary-teaches-about-dolphin-megapods-in-costa-rica/31250/.

9. Parrot AR.Drone 2.0 Elite Edition, retrieved August 9, 2017, https://www.parrot.com/us/drones/parrot-ardrone-20-elite-edition.

10. Nick Bilton, "With Purchase of Drone Maker, Google Sees a Fleet of Satellites," *New York Times*, April 14, 2014, retrieved August 9, 2017, http://bits.blogs.nytimes.com/2014/04/14/google-buys-high-altitude-drone-maker/?ref=technology.

11. Farhad Manjoo, "The Autonomous Selfie Drone Is Here. Is Society Ready for It?," *New York Times*, March 13, 2018, retrieved March 8, 2018, https://nyti.ms/2BW57MZ.

12. John V. Pavlik, "Quadricopters and Geo-Located Video: Implications of Drones for the Broadcasting, Media and Film Industry" (presentation, International Conference on Broadcasting Media & Film Industry, Baltimore, MD, October 14, 2014), https://doi.org/10.4172/2165-7912.S1.001.

13. Justin Peters, "And Now Drones Can Take Pictures at Night," Slate, December 11, 2015, retrieved March 23, 2017, http://www.slate.com/blogs/future_tense/2015/12/11/drones_can_take_pictures_at_night_with_dji_s_zenmuse_xt_camera.html.

14. "Drone Video Captures Melting Ice Sheets," *USA Today*, November 30, 2015, retrieved August 9, 2017, http://www.usatoday.com/videos/news/nation/2015/11/30/76563106/.

15. Conde Nast Traveler, "10 Magnificent Drone Photos That Capture the World Like You've Never Seen It," HuffPost, December 11, 2015, retrieved March 23, 2017, http://www.huffingtonpost.com/conde-nast-traveler/10-insane-drone-photos-of_b_8751300.html.

16. Conde Nast Traveler.

17. "Drone Captures Views of Long-Forbidden Island," video, CNN, October 22, 2015, retrieved March 23, 2017, http://www.cnn.com/videos/world/2015/10/22/cuba-travel-destinations-tips-drone-footage-orig.cnn.

18. Brian Wilson, "Drone Captures E-Harlem Explosion Scene," *New York Daily News*, March 12, 2014, retrieved August 9, 2017, http://www.nydailynews.com/new-york/uptown/drone-captures-e-harlem-explosion-scene-video-article-1.1719988.

19. Nick Visser, "Syrian City Shown Utterly Destroyed After 5 Years of War," Huff-Post, February 2, 2016, retrieved March 23, 2017, http://www.huffingtonpost .com/2016/02/02/homs-syria-drone-video_n_9146110.html.

20. Carter Evans, "GoPro CEO Reveals New POV Action Camera," video, HuffPost, September 29, 2014, retrieved March 23, 2017, https://www.huffingtonpost.com /entry/homs-syria-drone-video_us_56b15c7de4b08069c7a57a47.

21. "Drones, Virtual Reality GoPro Cam Among Top Gadgets at CES 2016," video, CBS News, February 6, 2016, retrieved March 23, 2017, http://www.cbsnews.com /videos/drones-virtual-reality-gopro-cam-among-top-gadgets-at-ces-2016/.

22. Christine Hauser, "In Thailand, a Drone's Eye View of Protests," *New York Times*, December 2, 2013, retrieved August 9, 2017, http://thelede.blogs.nytimes.com /2013/12/02/in-thailand-a-drones-eye-view-of-protests/.

23. Newley Purnell, "Bangkok's Unlikely Embrace of Drone Journalism Shows the Extent of the Government's Problems," Quartz, November 25, 2013, retrieved August 9, 2017, http://qz.com/150668/bangkoks-unlikely-embrace-of-drone -journalism-shows-the-extent-of-the-governments-problems/.

24. Christine Giardano, "Photographers and Filmmakers Using Drones to Reach New Heights," *New York Times*, November 13, 2015, retrieved January 2, 2017, https://nyti.ms/1OJqxNu.

25. Todd Brewster, "Push and Pull, Old and New: Notes from the Journalism Pro-fession Today" (remarks, Rutgers University, New Brunswick, NJ, March 11, 2014).

26. Michael Flaster, interview with the author, March 4, 2014.

27. Flaster interview.

28. Photogrammetry, retrieved March 28, 2017, http://www.photogrammetry.com/.

29. Nick Bilton, "Smile! A Drone Is About to Take Your Picture," *New York Times*, June 22, 2014, retrieved August 9, 2017, http://bits.blogs.nytimes.com/2014/06 /22/smile-a-drone-is-about-to-take-your-picture-2/?hpw&action=click&pg type=Homepage&version=HpHedThumbWell&module=well-region&region =bottom-well&WT.nav=bottom-well.

30. "Will TV News Helicopters Be Replaced by Drones?," CBS News, May 16, 2013, retrieved August 9, 2017, http://www.cbsnews.com/news/will-tv-news-heli copters-be-replaced-by-drones/; Diana Marszalek, "Will Drones Take Flight for TV Stations?," TVNewsCheck, August 28, 2012, retrieved August 9, 2017, http://www.tvnewscheck.com/article/61816/will-drones-take-flight-for-tv -stations/page/1.

31. "2014 Price List," Robinson Helicopter Company, retrieved August 9, 2017, http:// www.robinsonheli.com/price_lists_eocs/r44_newscopter_pricelist.pdf, page has been removed.

32. Cecilia Kang, "Drone Registration Rules Are Announced by F.A.A.," *New York Times*, December 14, 2015, retrieved March 23, 2017, https://nyti.ms/221X3ij.

33. *NBC Nightly News*, December 25, 2015; *CBS This Morning*, July 21, 2018.

34. Robert Johnson, "FAA: Look for 30,000 Drones to Fill American Skies by the End of the Decade," *Business Insider*, February 8, 2012, retrieved March 27, 2017, http://www.businessinsider.com/robert-johnson-bi-30000-drones-by-2020-2012-2.

35. Timothy Lee, "Amazon Envisions Eventually Delivering Packages in 30 Minutes via Drones," *Washington Post*, December 1, 2013, retrieved August 9, 2017, http://www.washingtonpost.com/blogs/the-switch/wp/2013/12/01/amazon-wants-to-deliver-packages-in-30-minutes-with-drones/?hpid=z3.

36. "Amazon Plans to Launch Drone Delivery Service in India," video, CBS News, August 20, 2014, retrieved August 9, 2017, http://www.cbsnews.com/videos/headlines-at-830-amazon-plans-to-launch-drone-delivery-service-in-india/.

37. John Markoff, "As Aging Population Grows, So Do Robotic Health Aides," *New York Times*, December 8, 2015, retrieved March 1, 2017, https://nyti.ms/21BbDgC.

38. Markoff.

39. Michel Foucault, *Discipline and Punish: The Birth of the Prison* (New York: Vintage, 1995).

40. Dave Eggers, *The Circle* (San Francisco, CA: McSweeney's, 2013).

41. "The Circle (2017 film)," Wikipedia, retrieved March 1, 2017, https://en.wikipedia.org/wiki/The_Circle_(2016_film).

42. "Paparazzi Drones," *CBS Evening News*, August 23, 2014.

43. "How to Make an Invisible Mask for Video Cameras," Wikihow, 2014, retrieved August 9, 2017, http://www.wikihow.com/Make-an-Invisible-Mask-for-Video-Cameras.

44. Cecilia Kangdec, "F.A.A. Drone Laws Start to Clash with Stricter Local Rules," *New York Times*, December 27, 2015, retrieved August 9, 2017, https://nyti.ms/1OtUoKm.

45. Kangdec.

46. "Welcome to a World Through Glass," Google, 2014, retrieved August 9, 2017, http://www.google.com/glass/start/what-it-does/; site has been updated and page removed.

47. "Parrot AR.Drone," video channel, YouTube, retrieved February 20, 2017, http://www.youtube.com/user/ARdrone.

48. BBC News, "'Hexacopter' Drone Flying Camera—BBC News," video, YouTube, October 29, 2013, retrieved August 9, 2017, https://youtu.be/ZTWHP8oheio.

49. BBC News.

50. *CBS Evening News*, January 31, 2016.

51. *CBS Evening News.*

52. Rachel Janik and Mitchell Armentrout, "Washington: Industry Looks to Use Drones for Commercial Purposes," *Columbus Ledger Enquirer,* April 29, 2013.

53. Professional Society of Drone Journalists, retrieved August 9, 2017, http://www .dronejournalism.org/.

54. Professional Society of Drone Journalists.

55. "Welcome to a World Through Glass."

56. Jason Koebler, "Flying a Drone with Google Glass Is 'Like Being a Bird,'" Motherboard, October 28, 2013, retrieved August 9, 2017, https://motherboard.vice.com /en_us/article/ae3wg5/its-like-being-a-bird-flying-a-drone-with-google-glass.

57. Ben Tracy, "Seattle's Space Needle Gets an Upgrade for the Digital Age," video, CBS News, December 31, 2015, retrieved March 23, 2017, http://www.cbsnews .com/news/seattle-space-needle-uses-digital-technology-to-create-new -experience-for-visitors/.

58. Corridor, "Superman with a GoPro," video, YouTube, March 12, 2014, retrieved March 23, 2017, https://youtu.be/HoIb9SwC7EI.

59. Corridor.

60. Raffaello D'Andrea, "The Astounding Athletic Power of Quadcopter," video, TED, June 2013, retrieved March 23, 2017, https://www.ted.com/talks/raffa ello_d_andrea_the_astounding_athletic_power_of_quadcopters?language=en.

61. D'Andrea.

62. Charlie Rose, "Watch: Amazing Video of Volcano Erupting in Iceland," video, CBS News, October 2, 2014, retrieved March 23, 2017, http://www.cbsnews.com /videos/watch-amazing-video-of-volcano-erupting-in-iceland/.

63. Rose.

7. ECONOMIC, REGULATORY, AND OTHER CONTEXTUAL FACTORS

1. Austen Huffard, "U.S. Stocks Drop on Media Meltdown Fears of 'Cord-Cutting' by Consumers Jolt Stocks of Traditional Media Firms," *Wall Street Journal,* August 6, 2015, http://www.wsj.com/articles/u-s-stock-futures-slightly-higher -1438863795.

2. Dan Bilefsky, "BBC to Cut 1,000 Jobs as License Revenue Falls Short," *New York Times,* July 2, 2015, retrieved March 23, 2017, https://nyti.ms/1H43Vkq.

3. Arnold Thackray, David C. Brock, and Rachel Jones, *Moore's Law: The Life of Gordon Moore, Silicon Valley's Quiet Revolutionary* (New York: Basic, 2015).

4. Josh Kosman, "Nexstar TV Increases Its Bid for Rival Media General," *New York Post,* December 8, 2015, retrieved March 23, 2017, http://nypost.com/2015/12/08 /nexstar-tv-increases-its-bid-for-rival-media-general/.

5. Andy McNamara, "Game Informer Special Issue: The Year of Virtual Reality," GameInformer, January 1, 2016, retrieved February 25, 2019, https://www .gameinformer.com/p/vr.aspx.

6. Kim Lightbody, "Meet the New Wave of Wearables: Stretchable Electronics," Fast Company, June 20, 2016, retrieved March 23, 2017, http://www .fastcompany.com/3060274/meet-the-new-wave-of-wearables-stretchable -electronics.

7. O. Lew Wood, "Pure Fluid Device," *Machine Design* (June 1964): 154–80.

8. T. Höllerer, S. Feiner, and J. V. Pavlik, "Situated Documentaries: Embedding Multimedia Presentations in the Real World" (Third International Symposium on Wearable Computers, San Francisco, CA, October 18–19, 1999), 79–86.

9. Höllerer, Feiner, and Pavlik.

10. Shree Nayar, "Omnicamera," Columbia University, 2000, retrieved March 1, 2017, http://www.columbia.edu/cu/record/23/20a/omnicamera.html.

11. Brian X. Chen, "Oculus Rift Will Cost $599," *New York Times*, January 6, 2016, retrieved March 23, 2017, http://bits.blogs.nytimes.com/2016/01/06/facebooks -oculus-says-it-will-charge-599-for-the-rift/?smprod=nytcore-iphone&smid =nytcore-iphone-share.

12. Tom Kludt, "Oculus Rift Preorders Crash Site," CNN, January 7, 2016, retrieved March 23, 2017, http://money.cnn.com/2016/01/06/media/oculus-rift-price /index.html.

13. Justin Kahn, "Oculus Rift + Touch VR Bundle Hits All-Time Low at $374 Shipped," Flipboard, August 2, 2017, retrieved August 13, 2017, https://flipboard .com/@flipboard/-oculus-rift—touch-vr-bundle-hits-all-t/f-5b535af828 %2F9to5toys.com, page has been removed.

14. Mark Gurman, "Facebook Plans to Unveil a $200 Wireless Oculus VR Headset for 2018," Bloomberg, July 13, 2017, retrieved August 9, 2017, https://www .bloomberg.com/news/articles/2017-07-13/facebook-said-to-plan-200-wireless -oculus-vr-headset-for-2018.

15. John Carey and Martin C. J. Elton, *When Media Are New: Understanding the Dynamics of New Media Adoption and Use* (Ann Arbor, MI: University of Michigan Press, 2010).

16. Bonnie Christian, "HTC Launches Vive Standalone VR Headset, No PC Required," *Wired*, July 27, 2017, retrieved August 13, 2017, http://www.wired.co .uk/article/htc-vive-standalone-vr-headset-china.

17. Laurent Giret, "Microsoft's Hololens 2 is official with launch price of $3,500," OnMSFT, February 24, 2019, retrieved February 25, 2019, https://www.onmsft .com/news/microsofts-hololens-2-is-official-with-a-launch-price-of-3500.

18. Kirk Miller, "You Can Finally Order the Much-Hyped Magic Leap AR Headset," Insidehook, August 8, 2018, retrieved February 25, 2019, https://www

.insidehook.com/nation/you-can-now-order-the-much-hyped-magic-leap
-headset-.

19. Sasa Marinkovic, "Virtual Reality Ready to Take Flight in 2016," TechCrunch, November 08, 2015, retrieved February 25, 2019, http://techcrunch.com/2015/11 /08/virtual-reality-ready-to-take-flight-in-2016/#.rcookom:4KG6.

20. "Google Announces That 10 Million Cardboard VR Viewers Have Been Shipped," GSMarena, February 28, 2017, retrieved March 1, 2017, http://m .gsmarena.com/google_announces_that_10_million_cardboard_vr_viewers _have_been_shipped-news-23707.php.

21. "Projected Virtual Reality Headsets Unit Sales Worldwide in 2016 (in Million), by Device," Statista, retrieved March 24, 2017, https://www.statista.com/statis tics/458037/virtual-reality-headsets-unit-sales-worldwide/, page has been updated.

22. Deniz Ergürel, "Worldwide VR/AR Headset Market to Hit 100 Million Devices," Haptical, March 17, 2017, https://haptic.al/worldwide-vr-ar-headset-market-to -hit-100-million-devices-bff4ad70a66f#.rhvqamui8.

23. Chuck Martin, "Augmented Reality Set to Blow by Virtual Reality," MediaPost, February 23, 2018, retrieved March 8, 2018, https://www.mediapost.com/publi cations/article/315009/augmented-reality-set-to-blow-by-virtual-reality.html.

24. David Goldman, "World's First 8K TV Costs $133,000," CNN, September 17, 2015, retrieved March 23, 2017, http://money.cnn.com/2015/09/17/technology/8k -tv/index.html.

25. Nick Pino and Jon Porter, "4K TV and UHD: Everything You Need to Know About Ultra HD," TechRadar, January 22, 2017, retrieved March 23, 2017, http:// www.techradar.com/us/news/television/ultra-hd-everything-you-need-to -know-about-4k-tv-1048954, page has been updated.

26. "Nearly 50% of US Homes Will Own a 4K TV by 2020," PR Newswire, March 4, 2015, retrieved March 23, 2017, http://www.prnewswire.com/news-releases /nearly-50-of-us-homes-will-own-a-4k-tv-by-2020-says-strategy-analytics -300044177.html.

27. Janet Morrissey, "Virtual Reality Leads Marketers Down a Tricky Path," New York Times, March 5, 2017, retrieved March 23, 2017, https://nyti.ms/2ltVuNP.

28. Marinkovic, "Virtual Reality Ready to Take Flight in 2016."

29. Dean Takahaski, "Newzoo: Games Market Expected to Hit $180.1 Billion in Rev-enues in 2021," Venture Beat, April 30, 2018, retrieved June 21, 2018, https:// venturebeat.com/2018/04/30/newzoo-global-games-expected-to-hit-180-1 -billion-in-revenues-2021/.

30. John Gaudiosi, "Oculus Expects over 100 VR Games in 2016," Fortune, March 24, 2016, retrieved March 23, 2017, http://fortune.com/2016/03/24/oculus-expects -over-100-vr-games-in-2016/.

31. Gaudiosi.

32. McNamara, "Game Informer Special Issue."

33. Michael Tisler, (comments, doctoral seminar, Rutgers University, New Brunswick, NJ, October 24, 2016).

34. Husain Sumra and Michael Sawh, "Best 360 Cameras Out and on the Way," Wareable, March 28, 2018, https://www.wareable.com/cameras/best-360-degree-cameras.

35. Sumra and Sawh.

36. Nick Statt, "Facebook's New Surround 360 Video Cameras Let You Move Around Inside Live-Action Scenes," Verge, April 19, 2017, retrieved April 19, 2017, http://www.theverge.com/2017/4/19/15345738/facebook-surround-360-video-cameras-f8-conference-2017.

37. Andrew Thomas, "Researchers Develop 4D Cameras with Extra-Wide Field of View That Could Improve Robotic Vision and Virtual Reality," Trendin Tech, July 30, 2017, retrieved August 13, 2017, http://trendintech.com/2017/07/30/researchers-develop-4d-cameras-with-extra-wide-field-of-view-that-could-improve-robotic-vision-and-virtual-reality/.

38. "MIT Researchers Turn Wi-Fi into 'X-Ray Vision' Technology," CBS News, December 9, 2015, retrieved March 23, 2017, http://www.cbsnews.com/news/mit-researchers-invent-wireless-x-ray-vision-project-emerald/.

39. Hannes Kaufmann, "Projects," TU Wien, retrieved March 1, 2017, https://www.ims.tuwien.ac.at/people/hannes-kaufmann/projects.

40. Ben C. Solomon and Leslye Davis, "Finding Hope in the Vigils of Paris: A Virtual Reality Film," *New York Times*, November 20, 2015, retrieved March 1, 2017, https://nyti.ms/1I394ry.

41. Patrick Healy, Graham Roberts, Cornelius Schmid, and Yuliya Parshina-Kottas, "Experiencing the Presidential Campaign," *New York Times*, January 29, 2016, retrieved March 23, 2017 https://nyti.ms/1SfscMC.

42. Bayeté Ross Smith, "Firsthand Account: The Assassination of Malcolm X," *New York Times*, retrieved March 23, 2017, https://www.nytimes.com/video/us/100000004817791/malcolm-x-death-new-york-assassination-360.html?smprod=nytcore-iphone&smid=nytcore-iphone-share.

43. Ricoh Theta, retrieved March 1, 2017, https://theta360.com/en/.

44. Dean Takahashi, "Giroptic's Attachment Turns Your iPhone into a 360-Degree VR Camera," Venture Beat, December 13, 2016, retrieved March 23, 2017, http://venturebeat.com/2016/12/13/giroptics-attachment-turns-your-iphone-into-a-360-degree-vr-camera/.

45. "Photo Sphere," Android Central, April 26, 2016, retrieved June 26, 2018, https://www.androidcentral.com/photo-sphere.

46. Fyuse, retrieved June 26, 2018, https://fyu.se/.

47. "The $80 Billion VR Market," *Forbes*, December 20, 2016, retrieved March 1, 2017, https://www.forbes.com/pictures/glkf45gell/alphabet/#336ccb1c836e.

48. Jonathan Vanian, "There's Now a Netflix-Like Service for Virtual Reality," *Fortune*, April 3, 2017, retrieved April 10, 2017, http://fortune.com/2017/04/03/htc -virtual-reality-subscription-service/.

49. Margaret Sullivan, "Times Reaches Online Milestone but Many Challenges Await," *New York Times*, August 15, 2015, retrieved August 9, 2017, https://nyti .ms/1IRRMjI; Sydney Ember, "New York Times Co. Subscription Revenue Surpassed $1 Billion in 2017," *New York Times*, February 8, 2018, retrieved March 5, 2018, https://nyti.ms/2Bihm5x.

50. Sullivan, "Times Reaches Online Milestone"; Jaclyn Peiser, "*New York Times* Tops 4 Million Mark in Total Subscribers." *New York Times*, November 11, 2018, retrieved February 25, 2019, https://www.nytimes.com/2018/11/01/business /media/new-york-times-earnings-subscribers.html

51. Brian Stelter, "Washington Post Digital Subscriptions Soar Past 1 Million Mark," CNN, September 26, 2017, retrieved March 8, 2018, http://money.cnn.com/2017 /09/26/media/washington-post-digital-subscriptions/index.html.

52. Marlee Baldridge, "With New Beats and Sprints, the Sacramento Bee Aims to Hit 60,000 Digital Subs," NiemanLab, June 25, 2018, retrieved June 26, 2018, http://www.niemanlab.org/2018/06/with-new-beats-and-sprints-the-sacramento -bee-aims-to-hit-60000-digital-subs/.

53. Claire Atkinson, "The Washington Post Still Plays Catch-Up, but Is Gaining on the Times," NBC News, December 28, 2017, retrieved June 22, 2018, https://www .nbcnews.com/news/us-news/washington-post-still-plays-catch-gaining -times-n833236.

54. Sydney Ember, "New York Times Co. Announces Newsroomwide Strategy Review," *New York Times*, February 5, 2016, retrieved August 9, 2017, https:// nyti.ms/23LwfE6.

55. Ember.

56. Ember.

57. Ember.

58. Max Willens, "One Year In: What the New York Times Learned from Its 360-Degree Video Project, the Daily 360," Digiday, November 14, 2017, retrieved February 27, 2018, https://digiday.com/media/one-year-new-york-times-learned -360-degree-video-project-daily-360/.

59. Chuck Martin, "VR, AR Revenue Projected to $215 Billion," MediaPost, August 7, 2017, retrieved August 8, 2017, http://flip.it/h9MlLo.

60. Nick Wingfield, "In Virtual Reality Headsets, Investors Glimpse the Future," *New York Times*, December 13, 2015, retrieved March 23, 2017, https://nyti.ms/1jXz15V.

61. "Hot New Products to Expect in 2016," video, CBS News, December 28, 2015, retrieved March 1, 2017, http://www.cbsnews.com/videos/hot-new-products-to-expect-in-2016/.

62. Jason Hahn, "Wevr Raises $25 Million in Its Quest to Become the YouTube of Virtual Reality Content," Digital Trends, February 7, 2016, retrieved March 23, 2017, http://www.digitaltrends.com/virtual-reality/wevr-raises-25-million-and-launches-transport-the-youtube-of-vr-content/.

63. "David Sarnoff," *Encyclopaedia Britannica*, retrieved March 17, 2017, http://www.britannica.com/biography/David-Sarnoff.

64. "David Sarnoff."

65. "July 2nd Fight Described by Radiophone," Egg Harbor Township, http://www.bdweb7057k.bluedomino.com/oldradio/arrl/2002-06/Dempsey.htm.

66. Wade Forrester, "July 2, 1921: Dempsey vs. Carpentier," On This Day in Sports, July 2, 2013, retrieved June 12, 2015, https://onthisdayinsports.blogspot.com/2013/07/july-2-1921-dempsey-vs-carpentier.html.

67. Forrester.

68. Amy Mitchell, "Crowdfunding Enables Diverse New Frontier for Journalism Projects," Pew Research, January 27, 2016, retrieved March 23, 2017, http://www.pewresearch.org/fact-tank/2016/01/27/crowdfunding-enables-diverse-new-frontier-for-journalism-projects/.

69. Mitchell.

70. Fritz Nelson, "The Past, Present, and Future of VR and AR: The Pioneers Speak," Tom's Hardware, April 30, 2014, retrieved March 23, 2017, http://www.tomshardware.com/reviews/ar-vr-technology-discussion,3811-5.html.

71. "Wunder360 S1: First 3D Scanning & 360 AI Camera," IndieGoGo, retrieved July 3, 2018, https://www.indiegogo.com/projects/wunder360-s1-first-3d-scanning-360-ai-camera/

72. "Annual Global Revenue," Statista, retrieved February 27, 2017, https://www.statista.com/statistics/507742/alphabet-annual-global-revenue/, page has been updated.

73. "Number of Monthly Active Facebook Users Worldwide," Statista, retrieved February 27, 2018, https://www.statista.com/statistics/264810/number-of-monthly-active-facebook-users-worldwide/, page has been updated.

74. Eli Noam, *Who Owns the World's Media?* (New York: Oxford University Press, 2015).

75. Peter Lauria, "Old Media Is Not Dead: Why Hedge Funds Have Fallen in Love with CBS," BuzzFeed News, May 22, 2013, retrieved March 23, 2017, http://www.buzzfeednews.com/peterlauria/old-media-is-not-dead-why-hedge-funds-have-fallen-in-love-wi.

76. Quentin Fottrell, "Americans Spend Most of Their Waking Hours Staring at Screens," Marketwatch, August 4, 2018, retrieved February 25, 2019, https://www.marketwatch.com/story/people-are-spending-most-of-their-waking-hours-staring-at-screens-2018-08-01/.

77. "UK Adults Spend Nearly Half Their Day on Screens," Time to Log Off, January 7, 2016, retrieved March 23, 2017, http://www.itstimetologoff.com/2016/01/07/uk-adults-half-their-day-on-screens/.

78. "Mobile Fact Sheet," Pew Research Center, January 12, 2017, retrieved March 24, 2017, http://www.pewinternet.org/fact-sheet/mobile/, page has been updated.

79. "Mobile Fact Sheet."

80. Brent Olson (The Future of Telecommunications, CITI conference, New York, October 19, 2015).

81. "State of the News Media," Pew Research Center, June 13, 2018, retrieved June 21, 2018, http://www.pewresearch.org/topics/state-of-the-news-media/.

82. Amy Mitchell, Jeffrey Gottfried, Michael Barthel, and Elisa Shearer, "The Modern News Consumer," Pew Research Center, July 7, 2016, retrieved March 23, 2017, http://www.journalism.org/2016/07/07/pathways-to-news/.

83. Adam Lella, "The State of Mobile News Audiences in 3 Charts," Comscore, July 8, 2016, retrieved June 21, 2018, https://www.comscore.com/ita/Insights/Blog/The-State-of-Mobile-News-Audiences-in-3-Charts.

84. "Local TV News Fact Sheet," Pew Research Center, July 13, 2017, retrieved June 21, 2018, http://www.journalism.org/fact-sheet/local-tv-news/.

85. Aaron Pressman, "Cord Cutting Hits Another Record, Bashing Cable and Telecom Stocks," Fortune, March 1, 2018, retrieved June 21, 2018, http://fortune.com/2018/03/01/cord-cutting-record-internet-tv/.

86. Sarah Perez, "56.6 Million U.S. Consumers to Go Without Pay-TV This Year as Cord-Cutting Accelerates," TechCrunch, September 3, 2017, retrieved March 5, 2018, https://techcrunch.com/2017/09/13/56-6-million-u-s-consumers-to-go-without-pay-tv-this-year-as-cord-cutting-accelerates/.

87. Perez.

88. Amy Mitchell and Dana Page, "State of the News Media 2015," Pew Research Center, April 29, 2015, http://assets.pewresearch.org/wp-content/uploads/sites/13/2017/05/30142603/state-of-the-news-media-report-2015-final.pdf.

89. Mike Snider, "Cutting the Cord: More Millennials Have Streaming Service than Pay-TV," USA Today, December 16, 2015, retrieved March 23, 2017, http://www.usatoday.com/story/tech/2015/12/16/cutting-cord-more-millennials-have-streaming-service-than-pay-tv/76914922/.

90. "Have You Ever Used a Smart TV?," Statista, February 2015, retrieved March 23, 2017, http://www.statista.com/statistics/262992/smart-tv-usage-worldwide/.

91. "Have You Ever Used a Smart TV?"

92. Joan E. Solsman, "Apple TV Usage Is Surging," CNET, April 4, 2015, retrieved March 1, 2017, http://www.cnet.com/news/apple-tv-usage-is-surging-at-the-expense-of-mac/.

93. Mitchell and Page, "State of the News Media 2015."

94. Bret Kinsella, "Edison Research: Internet Radio Weekly Listeners Hit 50% of U.S. Population." Edison. March 15, 2016, Retrieved February 25, 2019, https://xappmedia.com/edison-research-internet-radio-weekly-listeners-half-us-population/.

95. Kinsella.

96. Caroline Scott, "12 Media Podcasts Journalists Should Listen To in 2018," Journalism, January 3, 2018, retrieved June 21, 2018, https://www.journalism.co.uk/news/media-podcasts-journalists-should-listen-to-in-2018/s2/a715563/.

97. Mitchell and Page, "State of the News Media 2015."

98. Richard Nieva, "Facebook Launches Live Audio, Its Version of Podcasts," CNet, December 20, 2016, retrieved March 23, 2017, https://www.cnet.com/news/facebook-live-audio-podcasts-radio/.

99. Jonah Comstock, "PwC: 1 in 5 Americans Owns a Wearable, 1 in 10 Wears Them Daily," Mobi Health News, October 21, 2014, retrieved March 23, 2017, http://mobihealthnews.com/37543/pwc-1-in-5-americans-owns-a-wearable-1-in-10-wears-them-daily/.

100. Comstock.

101. Comstock.

102. Comstock.

103. Comstock.

104. "IDC Predicts 14M Apple Watch Sales in 2016 Growing to 31M in 2020," Apple Insider, March 17, 2016, retrieved March 23, 2017, http://appleinsider.com/articles/16/03/17/idc-predicts-14m-apple-watch-sales-in-2016-growing-to-31m-in-2020.

105. James Peckham, "Apple Watch 3 Sales Are Up," TechRadar, February 2, 2018, retrieved March 5, 2018, https://www.techradar.com/news/apple-watch-3-sales-are-up-on-the-last-version-could-it-be-down-to-lte, page has been removed.

106. Victor H. "Apple Selects 2015's Best Apps and Games for iPhone, iPad, Mac and Apple Watch," Phone Arena, December 11, 2015, retrieved March 23, 2017, http://www.phonearena.com/news/Apple-selects-2015s-best-apps-and-games-for-iPhone-iPad-Mac-and-Apple-Watch_id76528.

107. Nens Bolilan, "Apple Watches Can Now Control Your Go Pro: Here's How," LatinOne, December 12, 2015, retrieved March 23, 2017, http://www.latinone.com/articles/28885/20151212/apple-watches-can-now-control-your-go-pro-heres-how.htm.

108. Scott Stein, "VR's Biggest Challenge Has Nothing to Do with Technology," CNet, December 8, 2015, retrieved March 23, 2017, http://www.cnet.com/news /home-for-the-holidays-with-my-family-and-virtual-reality/.

109. Brian X. Chen, "My Virtual Life at Tech's Big Consumer Electronics Show," *New York Times*, January 8, 2016, retrieved March 23, 2017, http://bits.blogs.nytimes .com/2016/01/08/my-virtual-life-at-techs-big-consumer-electronics-show /?smprod=nytcore-iphone&smid=nytcore-iphone-share.

110. Chen.

111. Anastasia Anashkina, "This Is What You Will Be Giving if You Gift a VR Headset," video, CNN, December 4, 2015, retrieved March 23, 2017, http://money .cnn.com/video/technology/2015/12/04/tech-gift-guide-2015-virtual-reality .cnnmoney/index.html?iid=SF_video.

112. Arthur C. Clarke, *Profiles of the Future: An Inquiry into the Limits of the Possible* (New York: Popular Library, 1973).

113. Gayle King, "An Unfiltered Look at How Instagram Found Its Focus," video, CBS News, October 16, 2015, http://www.cbsnews.com/news/instagram-5-years-co -founders-kevin-systrom-mike-kreiger/.

114. Peter Laufer, *Slow News: A Manifesto for the Critical News Consumer* (Corvallis: Oregon State University Press, 2014).

115. Gordon Deal, interview with the author, November 6, 2015.

116. Edward Lee Lamoureux, Steven L. Baron, and Claire Stewart, *Intellectual Property Law and Interactive Media: Free for a Fee*, 2nd ed. (New York: Peter Lang, 2015).

117. Maria Armental, "Apple and Samsung Settle Seven-Year-Old iPhone Patent Dispute," *Wall Street Journal*, June 27, 2018, retrieved June 28, 2018, https://www .wsj.com/articles/apple-and-samsung-settle-seven-year-old-iphone-patent -dispute-1530131912.

118. "US Court Halves $500 Million Verdict in Facebook's Virtual Reality Lawsuit," CNBC, June 28, 2018, retrieved June 28, 2018, https://www.cnbc.com/2018/06 /28/us-court-halves-500-million-verdict-in-facebooks-virtual-reality-law .html?__source=twitter%7Ctech.

119. Josh Constine, "Facebook Beats in Q3 with $4.7B Profits, Record Share Price Despite Russia," TechCrunch, November 1, 2017, retrieved March 6, 2018, https:// techcrunch.com/2017/11/01/facebook-q3-2017-earnings/.

120. Mike Boland, "Who Owns Augmented Realities?" Venturebeat, June 27, 2018, retrieved June 28, 2018, https://venturebeat.com/2018/06/27/who-owns-aug mented-realities/.

121. Klint Finley, "Google's Big EU Fine Isn't Just About the Money," *Wired*, June 27, 2017, retrieved June 25, 2018, https://www.wired.com/story/google-big -eu-fine/.

122. Benjamin Compaine, "Home," BCompaine, retrieved March 17, 2017, https://sites.google.com/site/bcompaine/Home.

123. Andrea Peterson, "Here's How to See What Google's Sharing About You Publicly," *Washington Post*, November 12, 2015, retrieved March 24, 2017, https://www.washingtonpost.com/news/the-switch/wp/2015/11/12/heres-how-to-see-what-googles-sharing-about-you-publicly/.

124. Peterson.

125. Mike Snider, "How Extremist Content and Online Ads Meet," *USA Today*, March 25, 2017, retrieved March 25, 2017, http://www.usatoday.com/story/tech/news/2017/03/25/how-extremist-content-and-online-ads-meet/99590502/.

126. Adam Satariano, "U.S. News Outlets Block European Readers over New Privacy Rules," *New York Times*, May 25, 2018, retrieved May 25, 2018, https://nyti.ms/2xbNhUD.

127. Andrea Peterson, "This Smart TV Takes Tracking to a New Level," *Washington Post*, November 10, 2015, retrieved March 23, 2017, https://www.washingtonpost.com/news/the-switch/wp/2015/11/10/this-smart-tv-takes-tracking-to-a-new-level/.

128. Sapna Maheshwari, "How Smart TVs in Millions of U.S. Homes Track More Than What's on Tonight," *New York Times*, July 5, 2018, retrieved July 8, 2018, https://nyti.ms/2lYaFMV.

129. Zeynep Tufekci, "The Truth About the WikiLeaks C.I.A. Cache," *New York Times*, March 9, 2017, retrieved March 23, 2017, https://nyti.ms/2mqNH2k.

130. John V. Pavlik, "The Role of the Media in a Digital World: Technological Opportunities and Legal Challenges," in *Comunicación, Redes y Poder*, ed. Lucia Castellón and Alejandro Guillier (Santiago, Chile: RIL, 2014); Thomas Paine, "Common Sense," Independence Hall Association, retrieved March 23, 2017, http://www.ushistory.org/paine/commonsense/.

131. *NBC Nightly News*, November 16, 2015.

132. Edward Baig, "5G, Which Promises Blistering Download Speeds, Is Coming Soon," *USA Today*, March 2, 2017, retrieved March 1, 2017, http://usat.ly/2mxSKz7.

133. John V. Pavlik, "Understanding Convergence and Digital Broadcasting Technologies for the Twenty-First Century," *NHK Broadcasting Studies*, no. 4 (2005): 131–58.

134. Todd Longwell, "Imax Explores New Tech Horizons Beyond Big Screen," *Variety*, March 8, 2016, retrieved March 9, 2018, http://variety.com/2018/film/features/imax-explores-new-tech-horizons-beyond-big-screen-vr-streaming-1202721123/.

135. Sebastian Anthony, "8K UHDTV: How Do You Send a 48Gbps TV Signal over Terrestrial Airwaves?," Extreme Tech, June 4, 2012, retrieved March 1,

2017, http://www.extremetech.com/extreme/130238-8k-uhdtv-how-do-you-send
-a-48gbps-tv-signal-over-terrestrial-airwaves.

136. Anthony.

137. David Goldman, "What is 5G?," CNN, December 4, 2015, retrieved March 1,
2017, http://money.cnn.com/2015/12/04/technology/what-is-5g/index.html.

138. Tim Fisher, "How Are 4G and 5G Different?," LifeWire, May 1, 2018, retrieved
June 25, 2018, https://www.lifewire.com/5g-vs-4g-4156322.

139. "The Future's Bright—The Future's Li-Fi," Caledonian Mercury, November 29,
2013, retrieved March 1, 2017, http://caledonianmercury.com/2013/11/29/the
-futures-bright-the-futures-li-fi/0043351, site has been removed.

140. Simeon Simeonov, "Metcalfe's Law: More Misunderstood Than Wrong?," High-
Contrast, July 26, 2006, https://blog.simeonov.com/2006/07/26/metcalfes-law
-more-misunderstood-than-wrong/.

141. Simeonov.

8. AN EXPERIENTIAL NEWS PARABLE

1. "Parable," Dictionary, retrieved March 1, 2017, http://dictionary.reference.com
/browse/parable.

2. Aldous Huxley, *Brave New World* (Grandview, OH: Write Direction, 2004),
e-book, retrieved March 1, 2017, http://www.scotswolf.com/aldoushuxley
_bravenewworld.pdf.

3. Taylor Soper, "Ex-Twitter CEO Invests in $5.8M Round for VR Startup That Sim-
ulates 'Lifelike Touch' of Virtual Objects," GeekWire, December 7, 2016,
retrieved March 23, 2017, http://www.geekwire.com/2016/ex-twitter-ceo-invests
-5-8m-round-vr-startup-simulates-lifelike-touch-virtual-objects/.

4. "Tangibility Fuels Public Demand for Vinyl Record," *PBS Nightly Business
Report*, November 9, 2015.

5. Tasnim Shamma, "Emory Uses Virtual Reality to Treat Military Sexual Trauma
Survivors," WABE, December 23, 2015, http://news.wabe.org/post/emory-uses
-virtual-reality-treat-military-sexual-trauma-survivors.

6. Lindsay Schnell, "Examining the Future of Virtual Reality and the Impact It
Will Have on Football," *Sports Illustrated*, December 28, 2015, http://www.si
.com/nfl/2015/12/30/super-bowl-100-virtual-reality?xid=nl_siextra.

7. James Gaines, "How Do You Make a Young Doctor Really Understand What
It's Like Being 74? Virtual Reality," UpWorthy, May 16, 2016, retrieved March 23,
2017, http://www.upworthy.com/how-do-you-make-a-young-doctor-really
-understand-what-its-like-being-74-virtual-reality?c=huf1.

8. Carolyn Gregoire, "Virtual Reality Therapy Could Be Used to Treat Depression,"
HuffPost, February 17, 2016, retrieved March 23, 2017, http://www.huffingtonpost

.com/2016/02/17/virtual-reality-depression-study_n_9257776.html; M. R. Kandalaft, N. Didehbani, D. C. Krawczyk, T. T. Allen, and S. B. Chapman, "Virtual Reality Social Cognition Training for Young Adults with High-Functioning Autism," *Journal of Autism and Developmental Disorders* 43, no. 1 (January 2013): 34–44.

9. Neil Genzlinger, "Review: 'Dark Net' Explores the Digital Age's Toll on Us," *New York Times*, January 20, 2016, retrieved March 23, 2017, https://nyti.ms/1P6vChQ.

10. Max Taves, "VR Porn Lends a Hand," CNet, January 9, 2016, retrieved March 1, 2017, http://www.cnet.com/news/vr-porn-lends-a-hand-masturbation-will-never -be-the-same/.

11. Tasnim Shamma, "Emory Uses Virtual Reality to Treat Military Sexual Trauma Survivors," *Telegraph*, December 12, 2015, retrieved March 1, 2017, http://www .telegraph.co.uk/technology/news/12047279/How-virtual-reality-is-going-to -change-our-lives.html.

12. Jenny Stanton, "Robots Able to Read Thoughts," *Daily Mail*, January 23, 2016, retrieved March 23, 2017, http://www.dailymail.co.uk/news/article-3413693 /Robots-able-read-thoughts-generation-hackers-steal-innermost-secrets.html ?ITO=applenews.

13. FakeApp; Weihong Wang and Hany Farid, "Exposing Digital Forgeries in Video by Detecting Duplication" (Proceedings of the 9th Workshop on Multimedia & Security, Dallas, Texas, September 20–21, 2007), retrieved March 12, 2018, http://www.cs.dartmouth.edu/farid/downloads/publications/acm07.pdf.

14. "The Media Insight Project," American Press Institute, May 2, 2017, https://www .americanpressinstitute.org/publications/reports/survey-research/paying-for -news/.

15. "FDA Approves Computer Chip for Humans," NBC News, October 13, 2004, retrieved March 1, 2017, http://www.nbcnews.com/id/6237364/ns/health -health_care/t/fda-approves-computer-chip-humans/.

16. HR 4872, 11th Cong., 2nd Sess., March 17, 2010, retrieved March 1, 2017, http:// housedocs.house.gov/rules/hr4872/111_hr4872_reported.pdf.

17. "Creating Breakthrough Technologies and Capabilities for National Security," DARPA, retrieved March 17, 2017, http://www.darpa.mil/; Brian Wang, "Darpa Making Fully Implantable Devices," Next Big Future, January 22, 2016, retrieved March 1, 2017, https://www.nextbigfuture.com/2016/01/darpa-making-fully -implantable-devices.html.

18. *Dark Net*, season 1, episode 2, "Upgrade," aired January 28, 2016, on Showtime.

19. *Dark Net*.

20. "Wisconsin Employees Receive Microchip Implants," video, HuffPost, August 2, 2017, retrieved August 14, 2017, http://www.huffingtonpost.com/entry/three -square-market-microchips_us_59820e9de4b09d24e994c800.

21. Sarah Buhr, "Omega Ophthalmics Is an Eye Implant Platform with the Power of Continuous AR," Tech Crunch, August 4, 2017, retrieved August 13, 2017, https://techcrunch.com/2017/08/04/ophthalmics-is-an-eye-implant-with-the -power-of-continuous-ar/.

22. Jerry J. Shih, Dean J. Krusienski, and Jonathan R. Wolpaw, "Brain-Computer Interfaces in Medicine," *Mayo Clinic Proceedings* 87, no. 3 (March 2012): 268–79, https://dx.doi.org/10.1016/j.mayocp.2011.12.008.

23. Rolfe Winkler, "Elon Musk Launches Neuralink to Connect Brains with Computers," *Wall Street Journal*, March 27, 2017, retrieved March 27, 2017, https:// www.wsj.com/articles/elon-musk-launches-neuralink-to-connect-brains-with -computers-1490642652.

24. Neurable, retrieved March 22, 2017, http://neurable.com/.

25. Kristin Houser, "Neuroreality," Futurism, July 26, 2017, retrieved August 13, 2017, https://futurism.com/neuroreality-the-new-reality-is-coming-and-its-a -brain-computer-interface/.

26. Thomas McMullan, "This HTC Vive Prototype Lets You Play VR Games Using Brain Waves," Alphr, August 7, 2017, retrieved August 8, 2017, http://flip.it /7gk1WJ.

27. David Eagleman, retrieved March 1, 2017, http://www.eagleman.com/.

28. P. Arndt, S. Staller, J. Arcaroli, A. Hines, and K. Ebinger, "Within Subject Comparison of Advanced Coding Strategies in the Nucleus 24 Cochlear Implant" (Englewood, CO: Cochlear,1999).

29. Stephen Witt, "Is the Future of Music a Chip in Your Brain?," *Wall Street Journal*, December 7, 2015, retrieved March 23, 2017, http://www.wsj.com/articles /is-the-future-of-music-a-chip-in-your-brain-1449505111.

30. Stephen Witt, *How Music Got Free* (New York: Viking, 2015).

31. Carol Eisenberg, "New NYC Cameras Will Watch Every Move in Financial District," *Newsday*, September 7, 2007, retrieved September 9, 2007.

32. *CBS Evening News*, November 17, 2015.

33. Eisenberg, "New NYC Cameras Will Watch Every Move in Financial District."

34. "Orlando Ends Facial Recognition Program with Amazon," Reuters, June 26, 2018, retrieved June 26, 2018, https://www.reuters.com/article/us-amazon-com -facial-recognition/orlando-ends-facial-recognition-program-with-amazon -idUSKBN1JM12K.

35. Marian Stewart Bartlett, Gwen C. Littlewort, Mark G. Frank, and Kang Lee, "Automatic Decoding of Facial Movements Reveals Deceptive Pain Expressions," *Current Biology* 24, no. 7, (March 2015): 738–43.

36. John Pavlik, "OK Glass: Implications of Wearable Computers for Broadcasting and the Media" (remarks, Digital Technology and the Future of Broadcasting Research Symposium, BEA2014 Annual Convention, Las Vegas, NV, April 6, 2014).

37. Sara Malm, "A Threat for the Digital Age—an Avatar Osama bin Laden: U.S. Intelligence Warned Terrorists Could Create Virtual Jihadist to 'Preach and Issue Fatwas for Hundreds of Years,'" *Daily Mail*, January 9, 2014, http://www .dailymail.co.uk/news/article-2536440/A-threat-digital-age-avatar-Osama -bin-Laden-U-S-intelligence-warned-terrorists-create-virtual-jihadist-preach -issue-fatwas-hundreds-years.html.

38. Danny Bradbury, "Unveiling the Dark Web," *Network Security*, no. 4 (2014): 14–17, https://doi.org/10.1016/S1353-4858(14)70042-X.

39. J. Coopersmith, "The Role of the Pornography Industry in the Development of Videotape and the Internet" (Proceedings, Technology and Society International Symposium on Women and Technology: Historical, Societal, and Professional Perspectives, 1999).

40. "New Content Drives 38% Increase in Traffic to Playboy.com Site Now Features Range of Original Content," PR Newswire, July 28, 1998, retrieved March 1, 2017, http://www.prnewswire.com/news-releases/new-content-drives-38-increase -in-traffic-to-playboycom-75964402.html.

41. James Covert, "Porn Pioneer to Debut Live Virtual Reality Show," *New York Post*, December 15, 2015, retrieved March 1, 2017, http://nypost.com/2015/12/15/porn -pioneer-to-debut-live-virtual-reality-show/.

42. Catarina Cowden, "The Sex Robot of the Future Is Here and We're a Little Scared," Cinemablend, 2016, retrieved March 1, 2017, http://www.cinemablend .com/celebrity/Sex-Robot-Future-Here-We-re-Little-Scared-72454.html.

43. Simon Parkin, *Death by Video Game* (London: Serpent's Tail, 2015).

44. Robert Kubey and Mihaly Csikszentmihalyi, "Television Addiction No Mere Metaphor," *Scientific American Mind* (2003), http://www.simpletoremember .com/vitals/TVaddictionIsNoMereMetaphor.pdf.

45. B. Lang, "First Impressions of Valve's VR Head Mounted Display Prototype," Road to Virtual Reality, January 16, 2014, retrieved November 23, 2015, https:// www.roadtovr.com/valve-head-mounted-display-virtual-reality-headset -steam-dev-days/.

46. Varjo, retrieved February 25, 2019, http://www.varjo.com/.

47. Brian Chen, "Gear VR Offers a Preview of Virtual Reality in the Home," *New York Times*, November 20, 2015, retrieved March 1, 2017, https://nyti.ms /1PEeHVh.

48. Chen.

49. Chen.

50. Fiona Barry, "Inattentional Deafness: Won't Listen or Can't Listen?," *Telegraph*, June 7, 2014, retrieved March 1, 2017, http://www.telegraph.co.uk/education /educationadvice/10880108/Inattentional-deafness-wont-listen-or-cant-listen .html.

51. Ted Nelson, "XanaduSpace," Project Xanadu, retrieved February 25, 2019, Xanadu.net, https://www.youtube.com/watch?v=1yLNGUeHapA

52. Andy McNamara, "Game Informer Special Issue: The Year of Virtual Reality," Game Informer January 1, 2016, retrieved February 25, https://www.game informer.com/p/vr.aspx.

53. Ruth L. Bohan, *Looking into Walt Whitman: American Art, 1850-1920* (University Park: Pennsylvania State University Press, 2006), 26.

54. John Stauffer, Zoe Trodd, and Celeste-Marie Bernier, *Picturing Frederick Douglass: An Illustrated Biography of the Nineteenth Century's Most Photographed American* (New York: Liveright, 2015).

55. Stauffer.

56. "National Voter Turnout in Federal Elections: 1960-2014," Infoplease, retrieved March 1, 2017, http://www.infoplease.com/ipa/A0781453.html.

57. Aristotle, *Nicomachean Ethics*, trans. Drummond P. Chase (London: Everyman's Library, 1911).

58. John Dewey, *How We Think* (Boston: Heath, 1910), 9; Jean Piaget, *The Origin of Intelligence in the Child* (New York: Routledge, 1953).

59. Zhigeng Pana, Adrian David Cheokb, Hongwei Yanga, Jiejie Zhua, and Jiaoying, "Virtual Reality and Mixed Reality for Virtual Learning Environment" *Computers & Graphics* 30, no. 1 (February 2006): 20–28.

60. Juliette H. Walma van der Molen and Marlies E. Klijn, "Recall of Television Versus Print News: Retesting the Semantic Overlap Hypothesis," *Journal of Broadcast and Electronic Media* 48, no. 1 (2004): 89–107.

61. V. Bayon, J. R. Wilson, D. Stanton, and A. Boltman, "Mixed Reality Storytelling Environments," *Virtual Reality* 7, no. 1 (December 2003): 54–63, https://doi .org/10.1007/s10055-003-0109-6.

62. Sam Thielman, "Digital Media Is Now Bigger than National TV Advertising, Will Surpass Total TV by 2018," *AdWeek*, May 16, 2014, retrieved March 1, 2017, http://www.adweek.com/news/television/digital-media-now-bigger-national -tv-advertising-will-surpass-total-tv-2018-158360; Robert Hof, "Online Ad Revenues Blow Past Broadcast TV, Thanks to Mobile and Video," *Forbes*, April 10, 2014, retrieved March 1, 2017, http://www.forbes.com/sites/roberthof/2014/04 /10/online-ad-revenues-blow-past-broadcast-tv-thanks-to-mobile-and-video/.

63. Tuna Amobi (panel, Business Models and Industry at The Future of Telecommunications, CITI conference, New York, October 19, 2015) http://broadband breakfast.com/2015/10/columbia-institute-for-tele-information/.

64. Gordon Goldstein (panel, Business Models and Industry at The Future of Telecommunications, CITI conference, New York, October 19, 2015) http://broad bandbreakfast.com/2015/10/columbia-institute-for-tele-information/.

65. "The Martian (2015)," IMDB, retrieved August 9, 2017, http://www.imdb.com /title/tt3659388/.

66. Jim Axelrod, "The Martian," *CBS Evening News*, September 2, 2015.

67. LifeVR, Time Inc., retrieved March 1, 2017, http://interactives.time.com/lifevr.

68. Julian Horsey, "NASA Mars 2030 VR Experience Now Available," video, Geeky Gadgets, August 1, 2017, retrieved August 13, 2017, http://www.geeky-gadgets .com/nasa-mars-2030-vr-experience-01-08-2017/.

69. Jessi Hempel, "Zuckerberg to the UN: The Internet Belongs to Everyone," *Wired*, September 28, 2015, retrieved March 1, 2017, http://www.wired.com/2015/09 /zuckerberg-to-un-Internet-belongs-to-everyone/.

70. Edward R. Murrow, "Wires and Lights in a Box," (speech, Radio Television Digital News Association [then Radio Television News Directors Association] convention, October 15, 1958), video, RTDNA, retrieved March 1, 2017, http:// www.rtdna.org/content/edward_r_murrow_s_1958_wires_lights_in_a_box _speech#sthash.QJqBJKLH.dpuf.

71. Ben Solomon, "The Fight for Falluja," *New York Times*, August 19, 2016, retrieved June 3, 2017, https://nyti.ms/2kzwjVC.

72. Philipp Mayrhofer, "Paintings in Chauvet Cave," ARTE, June 24, 2017, retrieved June 28, 2018, https://sites.arte.tv/360/en/art-stories-360-paintings-chauvet -cave-360, page has been removed.

73. Sarah Li, Veda Shastri, and Kaitlyn Mullin, "China's Ancient Circular Walled Homes," *New York Times*, May 25, 2017, retrieved May 25, 2017, https://nyti.ms /2rY44mC.

74. Jamie Fullerton, "Saving China's Abandoned Tulou Homes," CNN, May 25, 2017, retrieved June 26, 2018, https://www.cnn.com/style/article/tulou-houses-china -fujian/index.html.

75. Trevor Snapp, Sam Wolson, Nonny de la Peña, and Jenna Pirog, "We Who Remain," *New York Times*, March 14, 2017, retrieved March 29, 2017, https://nyti .ms/2mGooGk.

Index